A Zambian journalist – in pursuit of three freedoms

Mike Daka

Gadsden Publishers

P O Box 32581, Lusaka, Zambia

Copyright © Mike Daka, 2019

All rights reserved. No part of this publication may be reproduced, stored in a retrieval system or transmitted, in any form or by an means electronic, mechanical, photocopying, recording or otherwise, without the prior permission of the publisher.

ISBN 978 9982 24 1175

Dedication

This book is dedicated to my father, Saulo Daka, my mother, Nelly Tikambenji Mwale and my children: Gerald, Dalitso, Chimfwembe and Dabwitso.

CONTENTS

Preface	1
Last Phase	
The end game – securing a farm	3
Phase One	
1. Born in a village and brought up in an African township	7
2. Off to school	14
3. Away to secondary school and a bigger world	17
4. Matero, a detribalised environment	20
5. Introduction to the wonders of books and music	24
6. Clear career choice	26
7. Reporter on the Copperbelt	30
8. Growth and early responsibilities at the Head Office	33
9. A student in India	35
10. Back home and away again and again	41
11. Recognition and promotion	42
12. Transfer to the North-Western region	47
13. Away to DDR	50
14. Return to Lusaka and to serious business	53
15. A student in the UK	57
16. The ZAMCOM project	63
17. Mann Sichalwe takes over	65
18. A new ZAMCOM is born	68
19. My transfer to ZAMCOM and back to ZANA	70
20 Leadership at ZANA	74
Phase 2	
1. Back at ZAMCOM as CEO	77
2. From government department to statutory board	78

3. Retirement from government — 81
4. ZAMCOM and FNF relations end — 84
5. Creation of an independent, self financing educational trust — 86
6. Work towards a trust continues — 93
7. ZAMCOM bill is taken to Parliament — 95
8. The Statutory Board is dissolved — 97
9. The Trust is born — 100
10 USAID Democratic Governance Project activities begin — 105
11. Mid-term review — 108
12. New broadcasting equipment arrived — 110
13. Changes at USAID, good news for ZAMCOM — 112
14. Study and marketing tour of USA and new activities — 115
15. New training and production programmes — 117
16. Complaints and accusations — 121
17. Suspension from work — 124
18. Audit findings and Board decision — 127
19. Media and donor interest — 129
20 Back at ZAMCOM — 132
21. Efforts to undermine ZAMCOM's independence — 135
22. Contract renewal — 147
23. Training at ZAMCOM thrives — 149
24. NORAD programme support — 151
25. Winding down my work at ZAMCOM — 153
26. The idea of going it alone is born — 155
27. Radio, it is — 158
28 Securing a building in Chipata — 163
29. A home at home — 167
30. Permit to construct — 168
31. Audience Survey — 171

32. Feasibility study	174
33. Rezoning the building	176

Phase Three

1. Goodbye Lusaka and ZAMCOM	179
2. Staff Recruitment	181
3. Breeze FM, "Kamphepo ya kazi kazi"	185
4. Test transmissions begin	187
5. Confirmed broadcasting licence	189
6 Breeze FM – Three types of radio	191
7. Geographical expansion	195
8. Challenges	204
9. Political cadres attack Breeze FM	206
10. Paving the way for the future	210
11. Awards	214
12. New emerging media sect	216

Selected Bibliography	219
Acknowledgements	223

PREFACE

My journey from childhood to senior citizenship was like a rollercoaster ride with a lot of exhilarating highs and many emotional lows. The different phases of my life were all quite engaging in their own ways. This book talks about the different stages of my life and the manner in which I had to constantly reinvent myself in order to achieve longevity in my professional work and in my life overall.

The first phase of my life comprised the period from my birth, through my primary and secondary school education, to the time I was introduced to journalism at the Evelyn Hone College of Applied Arts and Commerce in Lusaka, and to the time when I worked as a reporter and editor at the Zambia News Agency, ZANA. That period lasted from 1952 to 1989.

The second phase covered the period of my reinvention from practising journalist to media trainer after assuming the position of director and chief executive officer of ZAMCOM. This period lasted from 1989 to 2002. At the height of my success at ZAMCOM, I quit to set up and operate a commercial radio station in a rural part of my country.

This period lasted from 2002 to 2018. Towards the end of those sixteen years I knew that it was a good time to move on again – this time to a much calmer and quieter life – my final retirement.

The book largely explains how it was possible to achieve longevity in a profession that is so demanding but, generally, not so rewarding, especially in African countries such as Zambia.

Looking back over the forty-six years of my working life, I think that what helped me to persevere, despite all the challenges I faced, was that I was always clear about what I wanted to do. I also worked hard and gave of my best all the time. This purposefulness started in school and continued in my working life. When I was a reporter, I wanted to be a senior reporter. When I was a senior reporter, I wanted to be the news editor. Within four years, just twenty-eight years old, I was in the position I had always aspired to, that of news editor. But my ambitious spirit was still burning. I craved to be the editor-in-chief and to do so I obtained higher qualifications and was an acting editor-in-chief within two years of returning from my studies.

Still restless and wanting more flexibility in decision making I went on to become director and chief executive officer at ZAMCOM, where I spent thirteen years and during which time I transformed the organisation from a small government training department into a semi-autonomous Statutory Board and later into an independent, self-financing Educational Trust.

Yearning for total operational freedom and independence, I decided to set up my own radio station, Breeze FM, which I joyfully managed up to the end of my working life. The journey ended in very peaceful and relaxing circumstances in an area known as Kauzu Farm Block, about 30 kilometres from the village where I was born and where my journey began. After an incredible working life I had come full circle and was in a place where I felt that I truly belonged and was now living my dream.

Mike Daka,
Chipata, Zambia
2018

LAST PHASE

The End Game – Securing a farm

Although I worked for so many years as a journalist I always wanted to live on a farm of my own, perhaps because, in my teens whenever I visited my father's farm on the outskirts of Lusaka, I enjoyed the quiet atmosphere.

But efforts to get farmland in and around Lusaka, Zambia's capital city, were frustratingly unsuccessful. It was not until I relocated to the provincial capital of Eastern Province, Chipata, that I finally succeeded. Amazingly, the process of finding good farmland in a good location was quite simple. I mentioned to a number of people what I was looking for and, surprisingly, within weeks people started coming to my office with offers. I inspected two farms before I found the one I liked. This was truly beautiful and undulating land which, although degraded in some parts from the after-effects of tobacco cultivation, still had verdant areas with mature trees. After much back and forth to various government offices, with the assistance of my lawyer, I became the proud owner of one hundred acres of prime land – wooded and well-watered.

What makes this piece of land really special for me is its beautiful landscape, with two hills, Makangila and Musesa nearby and several more on the southern and western horizons and a perennial spring that becomes a small stream at the lower end of the land, feeding into a stream large enough to have a name – the Lutembwe, that marks the western border of the farm. As soon as I took possession of the farm, which I christened "The Daka Estate" for it was truly a sanctuary after all that I had been through, I approached the Soil Advisory Laboratory at the nearby Msekera Research Station to carry out a soil analysis. I wanted to have a good idea of what to grow and do at the farm. The results were useful. I was told that the farm had potential for citrus fruits and fish farming because of the reliable perennial water sources.

Shortly after the farm survey, I recruited a farm supervisor and some workers and started the initial farming activities. I took a cue from the recommendations of the Soil Advisory Laboratory and planned to utilise the farmland judiciously. Efforts to carry out reasonable farming activities were frustrated by people who were trespassing back and forth on numerous footpaths and those engaged in illegal hunting of hare and duiker. Then there was the common practice of bush burning during the dry months, from July to November. All these activities damaged crops and plants forcing me to erect a fence all around the farm.

Although I did not acquire the land and go into farming to make money, it was important that the farm pay for itself. My initial farming activities made me aware that prices of most agricultural products in Zambia are very low, so to make farming a viable business demands very high yields and I did not have the energy or desire for that. After careful consideration I decided to concentrate on what the family and the workers could eat, leaving the rest for sale. Our produce includes fruits (banana, guava, lemon, mango and orange), goats, honey, local 'village'chickens, pigeons, quail, vegetables, beans, groundnuts and maize. I, of course, also included two marvellous dogs, a german shepherd and a german shepherd-boerboel cross.

What I was most excited about was the life of peace and quiet in a natural environment. That is why I chose the site for my farmhouse very carefully in the middle of idyllic woodland.

Criss-crossing the wooded area at the back is a cobblestone pathway I laid for my morning and evening walks. In arranging the design of the house I was particular about preserving the beauty of the environment and the need to utilise – but not interfere with – the natural setting. My farmhouse was not just intended to provide a roof over my head. It was conceived and designed to give me a largely outdoor life with great views, a lot of fresh air and sunshine. It was, therefore, fairly large, covering an area of 120 metres. The concept and theme for the house was RRP, rest, relaxation and play, so it has plenty of rest areas and verandahs for relaxation. All the rooms have large windows which provide panoramic views of the surrounding forest.

I encountered many problems when building the house. It was not easy to get experienced and honest contractors or skilled workmen. The level of dishonesty was shocking. My greatest mistake was that I was too trusting, giving people money and thinking that they would use it appropriately and honestly. As it turned out they simply pocketed the money and/or purchased inferior materials. There was also a lot of overpricing and pilfering of the building materials. In the end it took four different contractors, three electricians and two plumbers to complete the house. Each subsequent contractor began by correcting the mistakes of his predecessor. In desperation I tried to work with a housing company, but it got away with my money – and that of many other developers – after failing to deliver on some of its commitments. Fortunately, the fourth contractor, who was introduced to me by no less than a Zambian of Indian origin, Ayub Patel of Liberty Transport, had proven hands-on experience and succeeded to correct and fine-tune all previous weaknesses and shortcomings. In the end the foundation, plumbing and electricals had to be redone – at a great cost, of course.

I also spent a lot of money arranging for the electricity supply to my farm and house. The cost for bringing power from the state-owned Zambia Electricity Supply Company, ZESCO, was too high. Initially, I was asked to pay K49,296.26 a figure equivalent to almost US$5,000 but after I had paid this amount I was told that the actual cost was K80,071.76 about US$8,000, later reduced to K66,555.65 (US$6,600). The cost included the supply of five poles and a transformer, which remain the property of the company. The cost was, in fact, much higher because to ensure uninterrupted power supply there was need for a solar power backup facility which cost me an additional K70,000 (US$7,000).

My favourite place on the farm is "Mphundu Square" at the western end of the residential area and dominated by two very large Mobola Plum trees, *Parinari curatellifolia*, the Sand Apple or Cork Tree. It bears pulpy, rounded, olive-green very tasty sweet fruits which when mature turn yellow-red and fall to the ground. In Zambia the fruit is known as mphundu and is always in demand in season. The "Mphundu Square" area is a very popular place for monkeys, which feast on the fruit. It is incredible now to eat the tasty fruit many years after having eaten them as a youngster.

The two Mobola Plum trees, which stand majestically opposite each other at a distance of about ten metres, must be over a hundred years old and reach high into the sky. To benefit fully from the dense shade that they create, I attached a hammock in which I lie quietly meditating for periods of one to two hours, surrounded by good fresh air and an atmosphere of natural sounds.

The only interference I sometimes have is the chattering and frolicking of the monkeys up in the branches. They do not bother me too much because with the farmland secure, and with farming activities progressing I am finally in control of my space and time and am active, healthy, peaceful and happy.

PHASE 1

1. Born in a village and brought up in an African township

My life started off very badly. The odds were totally against me because the African village is one of the roughest and toughest places to be born. Infrastructure is crudely rustic and many of the essentials for everyday living are non-existent. The situation must have been even more desperate in the early 1950s when I was born on 24th November 1952, at my mother's village, Magodi, in Chief Kapatamoyo's area, on the north-eastern outskirts of Fort Jameson (now Chipata), the provincial capital of the then North-Eastern Rhodesia.

Despite the dismal circumstances of my birth, I was, undoubtedly, of good stock. Both my parents were from the Ngoni tribe, descendants of what Derek Wilson in his book, A History of South and Central Africa, described as 'the most remarkable of Bantu emigrants from South-East Africa who (led by Zwangendaba) smashed their way for over 3,000 kilometres through East Central Africa between 1819 and 1845'. I could not have asked for a richer heritage. Their villages, Chinyaku, for my father, and Magodi, for my mother, were separated only by a footpath. I suspect that my father had not wanted to go far to look for his bride. My father's village was founded by my great grandfather, Chinyaku Daka, who had four wives. Elias, his second born child from his first wife had four children and his third born child, Saulo, was my father.

Mr. Saulo Daka and his young wife, Nelly, whose African name was Tikambenji, meaning 'What shall we say', migrated to Lusaka in 1945, in search of a better life and settled there for good. But most urban male migrants of the day sent their wives to deliver back at their villages even though there were no medical facilities, perhaps because the services in town were limited for Africans. Whatever the reason, when my mother was about to give birth to me, my father sent her to her village.

It seems that after my birth my mother and I were both very sick, most likely from poor postnatal care and accompanying illnesses, and it was thought that we were both going to die, or at least that one of us would. The seriousness of the condition was such that we were to remain in the village for two years before travelling to Lusaka to join the rest of the family. I don't remember anything from my time at the village. I was too young and, probably, too sick most of the time.

The most significant reminders of this early life struggle are my African names, Masauso or, my preferred one, Masiye. The name Masauso means 'problems' or' difficulties' while Masiye is a name normally given to orphans. My Christian name, Michael, was an imposition by the Catholic Church, which was, at that time, refusing to baptise anyone using their African name which was considered to be unchristian and unholy. My recovery at this early stage of my life, in dire and difficult circumstances in a village with no clinic or health facility nearby, might have been an early indication of my capacity for survival.

At age two, my mother and I joined my father, who had remained with my elder brother, Norman, in Lusaka. Our elder sister, Eniya, was living with our maternal grandmother, Ambuya Grace, in a nearby village. Ambuya Grace, a truly wonderful woman, was the only grandparent I had met and interacted with. Our parents occasionally visited the villages, but without us children. We had been taken there whilst very young but later only heard and knew of the names of the villages, the headmen and the chief without knowing or physically going there or meeting the many people they often talked about.

At our house in Lusaka, we regularly received visitors from the villages and were excited about the exotic foodstuffs they and our parents, when they visited the villages, brought with them, especially 'cimphonde' (peanut butter), and 'uchi' (honey). Many a time I sneaked into the kitchen to pick off, or scoop, some of these traditional delicacies when our mother was away. She always found out, of course, because there were usually telltale signs, especially droplets of honey, which led her to the culprit.

The decision by my father to migrate to the capital city, Lusaka, was extremely important for the family and its posterity. I only realised how important the decision was to me and my children fifty-seven years later when I, in turn, migrated back to my home town, Chipata. Our villages are located a mere thirty-four kilometres from Chipata and so I visited them from time to time.

When I sat outside the house of the headman of my father's village, I could see the house of the headman of my mother's village. At the time when I relocated to Chipata, the headman of my father's village was my first cousin, Somanje Daka, while the one for my mother's village, Whiteson Mashowo, was a maternal uncle. I belonged to royalty, no doubt, on both sides of the family. But I remember that when I took my family to the villages for the first time in 2001, my youngest son, Dabwitso, at age thirteen, commented to his siblings as we drove away, 'Can you imagine growing up there?' That question came into my mind each time I visited because some of the people there shared the same DNA with me and my children yet our circumstances were as different as if I and my children were from another continent. I certainly owed my father a lot for the decision he took many years ago to migrate to Lusaka because, in so doing, he gave me the opportunity to develop and broaden my mind by socialising in a multi-ethnic environment that led me to become a citizen of a much larger world.

In Lusaka, my father was working as a bricklayer in a firm run by white South Africans. The money he received from his job enabled him to rent a council house in one of Lusaka's earliest African townships, Matero. This was a planned township and its small houses were well arranged and the main roads were tarred, whereas most other roads were just graded dirt. Matero also had potable water, schools, clinics, markets and shopping areas – all in designated locations. Our house, 'Number 3155' was at the north-eastern end of the township. It had two bedrooms, a separate kitchen and a pantry which was converted into a bedroom for the children and was referred to as 'the cabin' because its extensions were mostly built with wood.

The house had no lights and no hot water. The toilet was located outside, behind the house. Bathroom and laundry facilities were communal with several households sharing one building with shower rooms for men and others for women at opposite ends and a long concrete slab for washing clothes.

The house was decent enough in those days because Matero was one of the few regular townships built for African workers by the colonial administration. The surroundings were clean and orderly and everyone talked to each other across their yards. Every morning the women called good morning to each other and throughout the day the children were loudly summoned back to their homes as they played in and around the houses.

As I grew up our parents had two more children, both of them boys, William and Friday. Our family remained quite small by the standards of families in the Matero of those days. We were six people in the house altogether, our parents and the four boys. Most families had ten or more family members. In this Lusaka environment my health picked up and I was able to get on with normal life although I remained smallish in stature while my immediate elder brother, Norman, with whom I had a two year age difference, was plump.

From the time we were all able to walk about and run, Norman and I and younger brothers, William and Friday, were responsible for looking after chickens, ducks, geese, guinea pigs, peacocks, pigeons, rabbits and several vicious dogs within the enclosure of our house. At that time, many families kept some chickens or ducks. But no one kept such a wide range of animals or birds. Many did not even know some of the animals or birds that our family had and would come to peek at them through the wire fence much to the annoyance of our father.

Keeping the birds and animals must have been both a hobby and source of income for our father; he obviously loved them. We, the children, did not because of the hard work that was demanded of us in looking after them - but we benefited from the animal protein that was never in short supply in the Daka household. We had a choice at dinnertime of having meat from any of the animals and birds kept by our father – except for the geese, guinea pigs, turkeys and, of course, the dogs. Our major responsibility was to ensure that none of these animals or birds went out of the fence – except the pigeons, of course, which flew out in the morning or during the day and flew back just before dusk. From time to time, our father took some of the geese, guinea pigs and turkeys with him when going to work and did not return with them, obviously having sold them, most probably to the white South Africans for whom he worked.

The dogs were tethered all day and were released to run around within the wire fence at night. Our father is the only one who would take them out for walks and occasionally used them to hunt for hare and duiker in the bush on the southern end of the township, which later became part of the Lusaka industrial area. Sometimes, he asked us to join him and it was both a thrilling and frightening experience.

At home, if any of the animals and birds got out of the wire fence, they did not only damage people's gardens but caused havoc and pandemonium around the nearby houses, clucking and barking and chasing neighbourhood kids and even adults. Sometimes the dogs would bite someone and all hell would break loose, with people screaming and shouting at us and some demanding monetary compensation. Strangely, there was not much interference from the local council office.

Perhaps, it was because the animals and birds did not wander about too much in the neighbourhood. However, the section officials of the political party, UNIP, which formed the first African government, regularly came to speak to our father whenever they received complaints from distressed neighbours.

In the absence of an elderly female member of the family who, traditionally, was expected to help with household chores, our mother did everything that she had to do without complaining. She also made sure that we all learned how to sweep the house, prepare meals, wash and press our clothes – especially school uniforms – and tidy our rooms. Throughout our teenage years, our mother reminded us to learn to do things on our own with the warning, 'You will not know if your wife is a good cook unless you know how to cook.' Our mother would also not tolerate anyone coming home with a toy, pencil, pen, crayon or anything that did not belong to them. You were immediately asked to take it back to wherever you got it from.

Matero was, and remained, one of the most crime-ridden townships in Lusaka. Growing up in Matero was a constantly challenging experience, full of many hard-earned lessons. Fortunately, our parents helped to keep us meaningfully occupied, upright and well behaved and as a result none of us got into any real trouble and everyone remained in school at a time when many of our friends did not complete primary school, let alone go to secondary school, college or university.

What must also have helped us, as children in the Daka household, was that our father was not a typical Matero resident spending time in the public social places such as bars or taverns. He neither smoked cigarettes nor drank alcohol. He did not even go to church with mum on weekends. His only obsession was his many animals and birds. Partly because we did our chores every day and got accustomed to the demands and rigours of the tasks but, most certainly, because of wanting, at all costs to avoid our father's wrath, we all learnt to manage things reasonably well.

Our house was located just below the hill behind which Zambia's Independence Stadium (later renamed 'Heroes Stadium') was to be built. That hill was a favourite playground for children. Whenever we could join in we ran up the hill with other kids to see who was faster and stronger and ran down again so that we could laugh at the one who came last. We also slid down on the water pipes feeding water to the houses from the tanks located on the hill. Before the construction of the stadium had begun, we used the hill and the area behind the hill, to set traps for birds or to hunt birds with catapults. We also foraged in people's fields, especially for sweet potatoes which we roasted and ate, hungrily. The construction of the stadium generated a lot of curiosity and interest among the kids and it was always fun to run up, peek at the construction site, the men, trucks and pulleys.

Over weekends or during school holidays, we helped our mother in her maize field, and later, with selling wares at her market stall. The Matero market was a crowded and competitive environment and sales were not easy because nearly everyone traded in the same items: fritters, vegetables, cooking oil and salt and, depending on the time of the year, fresh groundnuts and maize cobs. It was, no doubt, a good place to pick up basic sales skills and the first lessons about money.

Looking back, I cannot remember much conviviality in our house in the midst of all the barking, clucking and other animal noises and it may be that parents of that time did not know how to show affection to their children. Although we had food on the table, clothes on our backs and a roof over our heads there was very little family time – everyone was occupied with their own activities: our father with his work, animals and birds, our mother with household and market chores and we, the children, with school, our daily tasks around the yard and, whenever we could sneak out, frolicking and engaging in childish pranks with our friends.

I remember that there was little or no praise for work well done, but a lot of criticism and punishment for omission or wrongdoing. There was hardly any quality family time or dinner table moments because we, the children, ate together, while our mother took her meals alone, except when she had visitors and our father was usually the last one to have his meal, and mostly on his own. But we did have attention and affection, especially from our mother. We also had some meaningful stimulation and inspiration, even if it was of a very exacting type.

Generally, there was little closeness among us children. Perhaps, it was because we tended to the animals and birds separately and when free of chores each went his own way to play with friends. So we mostly only met at meal times and in the evenings when it was time to sleep. From an early age I was definitely more set in my ways and more ambitious than my two immediate brothers, Norman and William.

My attitude towards my elder brother, Norman, was ambivalent. I expected a lot more from him. It appeared, at least to me, that he seemed not to want to exert himself or to take seriously his responsibilities as the eldest male child. I felt that he never led by example or set any standards worth emulating or looking up to. With hindsight I think that in his own disinterested way my elder brother accidentally helped me to identify with myself and become independent at an early age. He was not there for me as a boy in Matero; I fought my own battles. He was still not there for me later, at school or when he started to work for the Bank of Zambia and I was in college. We were as different as brothers could be – in appearance, attitude and temperament.

My younger brother, William had a casual attitude towards life. He trained as an electrical technician and worked for Maamba Collieries, near Choma in Southern Province but later chose to settle in South Africa where he overstayed and took a long time to visit home and missed out on many important family occasions such as weddings and funerals.

And so while we children all learned a lot from our parents, we had little to share as brothers and each one followed his own way. Fortunately, there was Friday, our youngest brother who came six years after William and who, in the beginning, we all babied but much later is the one with whom I got on reasonably well, and together, we took care of our mother in her later years.

I am extremely grateful to my father and mother for passing on good values to us and for having been firm with me and my siblings. There is no doubt that the need to perform many chores under the close scrutiny of an over-bearing father, and an equally demanding mother, helped to inculcate a strong sense of discipline and hard work in all us children early in life. My only regret is that I never spent enough time with my parents in my later years. I visited them whenever I could but it was always for short periods.

Thankfully, I was able to take care of both of them in their old age and was fully responsible for putting them to rest when they died, my father in 1995 and my mother in 2012. I still remember them fondly.

2. Off to school

My mother convinced our father that I was ready for school when I was at about the age of five and started using my elder brother's crayons and pencils to scribble all sorts of things on all kinds of surfaces. Unfortunately, as a measure for school entry, the system demanded that a child be able to strech an arm across the head to touch the ear on the other side. Because I was small for my age my fingers could not reach the other ear and so I was not selected for what was then known as Sub A.

While my mother never went to school herself and had never been in a classroom and could not read or write she was determined to get me into school. And although she was what was locally referred to as a 'Dachi', a word describing a member of the Dutch Reformed Church of then apartheid South Africa, she did not hesitate to send me to a pre-school run by the Catholic Church in the nearby satellite township of Mandevu, an early informal settlement which later became one of the many sprawling 'compounds', the unplanned shanty townships that sprang up around Lusaka.

This township comprised self-built houses of African general workers who could not get houses in the formally established township of Matero. Although not from Mandevu, I and a few of my playmates were allowed to attend lessons at the pre-school there, a distance of about three kilometres. Back then the area between Matero and Mandevu was mostly bush and in the rainy season was covered with maize fields. For two years I made the walk there and back. The daily trek paid off because I was soon able to do some simple reading and writing – but only writing on the ground with a stick.

When I was seven, my mother was more than ready to have me start my formal education and on enrolment day in 1959 took me to Chingwele Primary School, a short distance from our house. Unfortunately, my fingers could still not reach my opposite ear and school authorities were reluctant to take me in despite my mother's pleas to the school authorities that, although small in stature, I had attended the nearby Catholic pre-school and already knew how to read and write. The point that she was trying to emphasise was that I was a far better candidate for school than many of the other children who were only enrolled because they had longer arms. On seeing my mother's determination, one of the teachers advised her to take me to Matero Boys Catholic Primary School run by the Catholic Church at the southern end of the township where the authorities were more receptive and after verifying that I had, indeed, been to the Mandevu Catholic Pre-School and could actually perform elementary reading and writing, they enrolled me.

My mother's persistence paid off and I enjoyed my primary school experience. It was a world far removed from the general life of kids in Matero, which was noisy and rowdy.

At primary school we only used the ground for a short time for our writing lessons before graduating to slates and finally writing in exercise books which was quite an achievement, initially writing with crayons, later with pencils and finally with fountain pens and ink. Inevitably we splashed ink all over the exercise book pages, our fingers and our uniform shirts.

School life was ordered and predictable. The day started early with all the pupils attending the 7 a.m. Mass in the Catholic Church and after the service we all lined up, according to our class levels, and marched along Nsokolo Road, crossing the busy Commonwealth Road and finally passing through the crowded shopping centre to the school. The road was tarred and traffic was limited and so we could march neatly all the way.

I was keen and engaged both in classroom and outdoor activities. With the voice of my mother always ringing in my head, saying that I could already read and write, I took seriously the need to learn how to read and write better. After school, I went straight home, took off my uniform, carefully folded my shirt and shorts and put them away. I then did my homework and helped with the household chores before going out to play. My most memorable primary school activity was participating in Zambia's Independence Day Celebrations on 24th October, 1964. The national celebrations took place at Independence Stadium, which was specifically built for the occasion. As a Standard 3 pupil I was among the many pupils from different schools who performed callisthenics and it was, indeed, an occasion of pomp and ceremony and was more fun and much more enjoyable than all the games that we had previously played on the hill and the area now taken up by the stadium.

My out-of-school time was evenly split between the church, class work and sports. Church was obligatory and I and many of my friends ended up becoming Mass servers. Some Mass ceremonies, prayers and hymns were conducted in Latin and we all memorised the prayers and responses to the priests, who were mostly European, without fully understanding what we were uttering. I was not a very good Mass server and not many priests showed much liking for me. I was, therefore, happy to discontinue with the role immediately I qualified for secondary school.

It was around this time that my mother left my father. He had returned from one of his trips to the village with a second wife, a woman younger than my mother. Polygamy was then widely practiced in our Ngoni culture, but my mother was not having any of it and chose to move out. She established a house of her own near Matero Boys Catholic Primary School. Talk about a woman being strong-willed and independent long before the idea about gender equality came into vogue! She insisted on taking the three eldest children with her and so only our youngest brother, Friday, who was not yet in school, remained with our father who, shortly after we moved out with our mother, retired from his job and left Matero to settle on a smallholding in an area called Ngwerere, north-east of Lusaka, where he had sufficient space to accommodate more animals such as goats and pigs.

A year or two later our brother, Friday was sent to Chipata to live with the family of our mother's young sister, Amai Evelesi Shupeka Jere, whose husband, Mr. Morezio Masala Zulu was a primary school headmaster and was able to arrange for a school place for him. Friday went on to study Metallurgy at the University of Zambia and later joined the mining industry where he did well for himself.

Meanwhile, when our father grew older and could not look after his birds and animals on his own, my elder brother, Norman, who then was living on a small holding in Lusaka West, moved the old man and his flocks to his farm. The splitting up of the family when I was ready to enter secondary school could have easily curtailed my education but, fortunately, it did not because I loved school and my mother was able to provide most of my school requirements.

3. *Away to secondary school and a bigger world*

In primary school I was conscientious and hard-working and always made the top three positions in class. In November, 1965, at the time when I sat for the final primary examinations, Matero township did not have a fully operational secondary school. The new school for boys, Matero Boys Secondary School, which belonged to the Catholic Marianist Religious Order of Brothers and Priests, was in the process of being built and initially its classes were being conducted at the nearby Kasamba Primary School. That wasn't good enough for me. In my mind I knew that I wanted to go to a proper secondary school, not to a school that was yet to *become* a secondary school.

My first choice was The Prince Phillip Secondary School. This was both a day and boarding school and was located in Kamwala township, one of the new African residential areas initially inhabited by low to middle level government employees, south-east of the Lusaka city centre. The Prince Phillip Secondary School had, during the colonial period, been reserved for Indian and Coloured pupils. Its gates and classrooms were only opened to African children after the attainment of political independence. The school was located a short distance from Madras, a residential area for Indian families who owned and operated shops in the Second Class Trading Area.

In January, 1966, I was in the third group of African children to go to what was truly a modern school, built and managed along the British colonial educational system. It had all the requisite facilities such as airy classrooms, a well-stocked library, science laboratories, woodwork and technical workshops, a combined assembly hall and gymnasium and sports grounds for cricket, football, hockey and rugby. I participated in hockey and basketball which I enjoyed very much and in my early years I even captained the school's junior basketball team. The school had only a few Zambian teachers and most of our teachers were from Britain, India and South Africa. The headmaster, Mr. E.G.W. Stevens, a tall stern man and the deputy headmaster, the jocular Mr. William Wade, were both British. No one knew what E.G.W. stood for but then not many pupils knew the first names of their teachers in those days. It was that kind of school; hierarchical and almost forbidding.

I had come a long way, indeed, from Matero and I knew I needed to make the most of the opportunity. My mother was sacrificing a lot to enable Norman and me to attend this prestigious school. Even though the new Zambian government had done away with school fees to allow as many African children as possible to get a decent education, we still needed to find the money for books, pens, pencils, mathematical sets and school uniforms, which included a grey blazer and a straw hat as well as sports kit.

We also had to meet the daily costs for transport from Matero to Kamwala, on the school bus which carried pupils to four schools, Gilbert Rennie Boys Secondary School (named after a former Governor and later renamed Kabulonga Boys Secondary School) initially for white boys, Jean Rennie Girls Secondary School (named after the former Governor's wife and later renamed Kabulonga Girls Secondary School) for white girls, Libala Secondary School for African boys and The Prince Phillip Secondary School for Indian and Coloured boys and girls. To cut down on transport costs, Norman was bought a bicycle and cycled to and from school while I travelled on the school bus.

Throughout the period of my secondary school education, I was more or less living in two worlds, spending the daytime at school in a post-colonial British public school environment and mixing and relating with pupils and teachers from middle and upper-middle class families and the evenings back at home in Matero with my family and friends. Each time

I disembarked from the school bus, my friends would admire or sneer at my uniform. Some would want to touch my blazer or attempt to grab and try on my straw hat. I was soon being referred to as 'the one who goes to school with Indians'.

Study time in Matero was rather limited. When I arrived home around 4 p.m. I had little time in which to study because I needed to utilise the remaining hours of daylight, which was normally less than two hours. Candlelight was helpful, but only for a short, flickering time. Candles were too expensive and my mother would not allow me finishing a whole candle in one night. A paraffin lamp was not ideal either; apart from its uneven glow, paraffin was also expensive, had irritating smoke and an offensive smell. So I needed to read as much as I could while there was natural light and only a bit after it became dark but nearly always at almost the point when I was getting serious with my studies my friends would have none of it and a sharp, shrill whistle would break my concentration. It would have been improper and unacceptable not to go outside, so the only thing to do was to stop studying, put away the books and join the gang.

On most occasions there was no real reason or purpose for calling me out. The guys just wanted company. I did not want anyone to think that I was avoiding them because I was now mixing with Indians and Coloureds at school, so we usually went to one of the beer halls or taverns. Once there those who had some coins would add them up and the tallest among us would enter the beer hall to buy a container of 'chibuku' opaque beer which we passed from one to the next until it was empty. If someone had more money, another container would be bought. Nearly always though, after the second container was emptied, someone would loudly say that they were not drunk, or that they never got drunk on opaque beer and as if on cue, someone would quickly pull out a wrap of marijuana, roll a joint, light it, puff on it a couple of times and then pass it on to the next person. And so it went round just as the beer container had done. No one forced anyone to drink the beer or smoke the joint but everyone knew that they could not decline.

One evening when I had taken some gulps and puffs with careless abandon I ended up laughing deliriously all the way home. I arrived earlier than my brothers and the effect of the marijuana made me so hungry I ate all the food set aside for our evening meal. My mother was upset because she had to prepare another meal for her other sons, while my elder brother was livid because he had to wait for an hour or so before having his dinner.

Meanwhile, I was unable to complete my homework. I was so embarrassed that I vowed never to drink chibuku or smoke marijuana again.

After that incident I joined my friends whenever I could but returned home in a fit state to complete my school work because it was clear to me that I needed to separate what was important from what was not. Going out with friends and drinking and smoking was fun but not important, while doing homework absolutely was. As a kid from a high density township, I needed to build up my confidence if I was going to survive and do well in my new environment, whether in class, the gymnasium or the sports grounds and it was obvious that the harder I worked and the better my grades became the more respect I would gain from my classmates and teachers.

My end-of-school results were good. I got a full GCE certificate. The one subject in which I had not done well was mathematics. My maths teacher, Mr. Carr, a dark Indian national, nearly always had me stand at the back of the classroom throughout his period because I had not completed my homework or not done it well enough. Mr. Carr had always tried to get me to do well in his class but in the end gave up on me and predicted that I would not achieve anything in life without mathematics. Other teachers were more appreciative of my capabilities and my form master, Mr. C. B. Kirby thought that while I was a very quiet individual I had not yet been tested to the full.

4. Matero, a detribalised environment

Matero township was divided into sections, identified by the names of the local schools while others took the names of the most popular bars. These demarcations and names had nothing to do with local authority designation but were how the people identified their territories. Each section had a street gang and anyone who strayed into a section other than his or her own, especially at night, risked being harassed; even older people were sometimes mugged. There were many individual bullies preying mostly on girls and young women. The most notorious bullies of the time included two characters known as James Tholo and Solo. No one knew their real names. Tholo (his name was derived from the English word 'tall') was well above six feet, about two metres tall. He terrified people around the areas known as Mulongoti, Shadreck Nyankhundi and Chitanda, while Solo's reign of terror spread over most of Matero. The other intimidating character was Denzi. This fellow and his brothers ruled over the areas around Saigar Daka and Kamokamo.

On the positive side of life, Matero was a melting pot of tribes from the different parts of the country. It also accommodated people from neighbouring countries such as Malawi and Zimbabwe, which were then known as Nyasaland and Southern Rhodesia. The township also hosted people from the Belgian Congo, later renamed Zaire and later still became the Democratic Republic of the Congo, a country with which Zambia shares a long, porous border.

To survive or get about from place to place in this heterogeneous environment, a person literally had to negotiate one's way. For example, when sent to the shops to buy groceries by one's parents, it took tact and diplomacy to get there with the money and it demanded even greater negotiation skills to return home with the purchased items. Any one of the bullies would grab the money, your shopping bag or tear a piece off the family loaf of bread.

Criminals came in all age groups. A lot of my childhood friends either took to drinking too much or became delinquent and were involved in brutal activities, including aggravated robbery, rape and other serious crimes. Whenever such a crime occurred, most of us knew the victim(s) or the perpetrator(s) or both because, generally, they were all residents of the same neighbourhood. Sometimes those who committed the crimes were those who we had just left behind after a drinking bout. That I always left before any serious incident occurred could not have been the result of luck, but rather providence and when I look back on that time I shudder to think how close I always was to being sucked into the consequences of the crimes, many of which were initially triggered by childish pranks.

Although many of my childhood friends got arrested, appeared in court and spent time in police cells and jail, in nearly twenty years of living in Matero no one in our family was ever charged with an offence by the police. There is no doubt that credit for that should go to our parents.

In fact, whenever I went to Matero to visit my mother in later years, I met fewer and fewer of the people I had grown up with or had been with at primary school. Many had become regular jailbirds and others had died young and violently. I remember that in the 1980s, when I was working as a reporter for ZANA in Ndola on the Copperbelt, I covered a serious aggravated robbery and murder case involving two notorious criminals, Emmanuel Phiri and Gilbert Chileshe. I had grown up with them both in Matero and they recognised me as I sat in the High Court press gallery. As they stood in the dock they smiled and boldly waved to me.

Apart from serious crimes, there were also a lot of fist fights among young people in Matero. At school fist fights always took place at the end of class with the two people who were to fight being surrounded by everyone else so that they had to fight in the middle of a circle which gave no escape to the weaker guy. So everyone had to learn to fight furiously, or be able to take a punch, because the fight only ended after one was totally beaten up or surrendered, or when a teacher or other older person came by and chased everybody away.

Since physically I was not very big, I could not use height, reach or weight to intimidate my opponents. I had to learn to duck and dive and place my punches on the nose, eyes or mouth. Fights ended quickly when an eye swelled up, or the nose or lip started bleeding, or you managed to punch the other guy in the solar plexus. I also learned who to fight or who to avoid, when to fight or withdraw or, indeed, when to run – lessons that became very useful on another level as I grew up and began to deal with office intrigue and political chicanery.

Socially, apart from the drinking places, Matero had little to offer other than the sporting activities that took place in and around the Matero Welfare Hall. The area behind the Welfare Hall, which later became fully built up, was a playground for social football. Official league games were played at Matero Stadium, home to Lusaka Tigers, a team that did well for a short period before dropping to the second tier of the national league.

Lusaka Tigers will be remembered for producing national team players such as Bizwell Phiri, Donewell Yobe, Joseph Njuka and Stanley Phiri in its heyday in the late 1970s.

The Welfare Hall itself was used to screen films, host boxing matches, weightlifting contests, table tennis tournaments and various competitions. It was also used for live music shows for popular local bands such as 'Salty Dog', whose lead guitarist Jackie Mumba, who later worked as a hospital equipment technician and drummer, Norman Muntemba, who ended up running an advertising agency, Goman Advertising, were among some of the people who remained my good friends long after our days in Matero. Salty Dog did a great rendition of 'Stairway to Heaven,' a classic song by English rock band, Led Zeppelin. My favourite Zambian band was Musi-oa-Tunya which had some of the country's greatest musicians, Rikki Ililonga on lead guitar, Derrick Moyo on bass, Brian Chengela on drums, Alex Kunda and Jasper Lungu on African drums, all people who had the talent and ability to play musical instruments well. Unfortunately, most of their music is in private collections and not available for later generations and musicians to enjoy and learn from. Fortunately on YouTube you can now find audio recordings from a number of the musicians that we enjoyed listening to back in the day. There's some great stuff on YouTube by Blackfoot, Paul Ngozi and Keith Mlevu. Also on Amazon there's a box set of four WITCH albums on CD with a great booklet about the band.

Meanwhile, watching proper, full length movies in Matero was problematic. In earlier years, a cinema van came and screened films on the outside of the wall of the hall. People gathered around to watch what was known as 'basikopo', derived from the Indonesian word 'bioskop' which filtered to Zambia via South Africa. Later, films produced by the government's Zambia Information Service were shown inside the hall.

In those early days Lusaka town had three cinema theatres, two in the city centre and one in the Kamwala residential area, near the Lusaka Central Prison. The two in the city centre, were the 20th Century for white audiencies and Carlton Cinema for Indians and Coloureds. African audiences went to the Palace Cinema in Kamwala. The 20th Century and Carlton were only opened to Africans after independence and in those early years Africans were made to sit in the front rows while whites, Indians and Coloureds sat at the back. The racial groups taunted each other with Indians and Coloureds flicking cigarette stubs towards the front, some of which landed on people's heads or on their clothes.

For quite a while my friends and I from Matero preferred to go to the Palace Cinema and on good days we were able to catch a bus to town and then walk to Kamwala. Mostly though, we walked all the way through town and during the intermissions enjoyed listening to music and eating popcorn and choc ices. As we made our way back home we retold the story of the movie. Our heroes of the time were mostly tough guys in western and war movies. They included the celebrated actors John Wayne and Burt Lancaster, American singer and cowboy actors Dean Martin and Roy Rogers and the popular villain in westerns and melodramas, Jack Palance. We happily cheered these lead actors and jeered the villains, who were mostly American Indians. One of our most popular films then was 'Cleopatra', featuring world famous film stars, Elizabeth Taylor and Richard Burton.

By the time I left Matero I had not only graduated from secondary school but I had also graduated from a way of life which had consumed many a young person. If I had escaped the temptations of the easier gang-style life, at least I came out of it streetwise. I was capable of taking care of myself at home, or on the streets and later in offices and work places. At this stage in my development, I could not have known how important this upbringing would turn out to be, especially when confronted with the many challenges that lay ahead.

5. Introduction to the wonders of books and music

One real benefit of secondary school for me was that it introduced me to what remained one of my strongest passions, reading books. My love for books was initially triggered by my mother's insistence that I could read and write when she was trying to get me enrolled into primary school. It may have been that I tried to prove the point when I finally got into school. Books exposed me to many different things and ideas and not only contributed greatly to my unending education but played a central role in moving me out of Matero and into a much larger world.

Introduction to the wonders of books and music

It started with essential reading for class work in Biology, History, Geography and Literature and quickly extended to a variety of subjects, African Writers Series, general knowledge and leisure novels. Initially, the literature books were mostly by English novelist, Charles Dickens, among them, "Oliver Twist" and Great Expectations" followed by those of English dramatist and poet, William Shakespeare. When reading Shakespeare's plays at school I had no idea that many years later I would actually visit Shakespeare's birthplace and see the house in which he was born in Stratford-upon-Avon in South Warwickshire. We had classmates such as Hector Sikaili and William Magwali who, before the teacher came in, paced around the classroom reciting passages from any book without pause. Close to examination time it was, indeed, very unsettling for many of us.

My leisure reading comprised the African Writers Series, popular novels and comics. What made it possible for me to have access to all these books and reading materials was that I found out about the Lusaka Book Exchange in what was known as the Central Arcade in the town centre. Here one paid a small amount of money to exchange an old book with any other book of one's choice. Later, as and when money was available, it was possible to buy new books from the major bookstore of the time, Kingstons Limited. By the time I was completing my secondary education I had a fairly impressive collection of books. In fact my corner of 'the cabin', the pantry at home which became the bedroom I shared with my elder brother, had a neat row of books while his end had a record player and a collection of records.

Over the years reading books remained one of my favourite pastimes. I had books in my office, and everywhere around my home as well as audio books in my car. But in time I gave up fiction, turning instead to African history, autobiographies and biographies, historical, traditional African religion, and later, leadership and self-help and motivational books. I also read many upmarket, international current affairs magazines.

Although I did not know it at that time and complained of noise whenever my brother played his music, my interest in different genres of music also began to develop at this stage. Our father had a gramophone and played mostly Zambian, Malawian and Zimbabwean 78 rpm records. I still remember one of his favourite songs, "Infa ilibe Cifundo", (Death

Has No Pity) by Enock Evans. Although I did not like most of the music that my brother listened to, I definitely appreciated some rock'n'roll and soul. Later, though, my favourite music became what is referred to as *Rumba Odemba*, popularised by the Congolese maestro, Franco Luambo Makiadi and his T. P. OK Jazz Band.

I am not very sure how it happened but in listening to the various genres of music on my brother's record player and live music at Matero Welfare Hall, Charter Hall at the Lusaka Civic Centre which was later renamed Nakatindi Hall, the popular Rockwood in Lusaka West and other places, I developed an ear for sound and learned to play the guitar. My music companion was a schoolmate and friend, Lovemore Malunga.

Then, to my own surprise, after completing secondary school, I became a rhythm guitarist in a band comprising myself and three other young Lusaka guys, Hassan Hassan, Eddie Phiri and Ned Malunga. We were young, good looking and hip. Ned, young brother to Lovemore, ended up playing full time for the Zambia Army Musical Band, 'The Rifles'. I was in Kitwe with my friends playing gigs mostly at Astra Café, a popular spot in town, when my college acceptance letter arrived and I rushed back to Lusaka to start my journalism training and career.

6. Clear career choice

I knew long before I completed secondary school that I wanted to be a journalist. Already at this early age, my English, both spoken and written, was good but, even more importantly, I think the main inspiration came from witnessing the daily goings-on in my neighbourhood. I was aware that most of what transpired was never reported on radio or in the newspapers. I strongly felt that the story of the crime-ridden and sordid conditions of life in Matero needed to be told. The choice of journalism was, therefore, not based on getting an interesting job, nor my wish or desire to have my voice heard on radio, nor to have my face appear on TV, nor to have my name seen in newspaper bylines. The choice was strongly influenced and motivated by my understanding that my career should not be simply about a job but something that would enable me to be of some wider use.

In those days, towards the end of each Form Five year institutions of higher learning and companies sent their representatives to talk to pupils about courses or jobs which they offered. And so with my mind already made up I had little problem in settling for Journalism when staff from Evelyn Hone College of Applied Arts and Commerce, one of the country's most prestigious colleges, came to speak to us. In those days Evelyn Hone College, in central Lusaka, offered the best Journalism programme in the country. The other institution with a journalism course, was the Africa Literature Centre at the Mindolo Ecumenical Foundation in Kitwe, Zambia's second largest city on the Copperbelt. The University of Zambia in Lusaka was still many years away from introducing its Mass Communication programme.

My journalism course started in January, 1971. At that time it was a one year programme, later to become a three year diploma course. On my first day at the college I was overjoyed until, while I was completing the entry formalities, I was told by the Office of the Registrar that as a Lusaka resident I was not entitled to hostel accommodation because priority was given to students from outside the capital city. To say that I was disappointed would be an understatement. I did not want to go home to Matero after class each day.

My mother was not amused, either. She had, in any case, thought my going to college was a waste of time and money and had expected me to get a job like my elder brother, Norman, had done on completing his secondary school education. She obviously wanted a return on her investment after paying so much money to get Norman, and me through secondary education at an expensive school while our young brother, William, was still at Matero Boys Secondary School. And now I was talking about needing more money for my daily transport to and from college. I had to do something and fast. Had I not grown up in Matero where anything and everything was possible? Was I not schooled in the art of deception on streets full of shady characters?

I was a day scholar for less than three weeks before I was given keys to a room which I shared with another student. I had connived with a student union leader who took me to the Office of the Registrar one morning before classes started. The story was that he had found me sleeping in the college

Assembly Hall the previous night and I was looking the part, haggard and hair uncombed. The Registrar, a warm but stern South African Coloured, Mr. Dick Snapper, would have none of it and did not want anyone to hear of it, especially in the newspapers. He asked to be given time to see what he could do and before the end of that day I was summoned back to his office where I was given a room allocation slip.

Having a room at college made it easy for me to attend lessons of the Journalism Studies class of 1971. The course was exciting and challenging, indeed. The lecturers included Professor Klansky from Czechoslovakia, who was responsible for Communication Theory, Abe Maine from South Africa, who took the Reporting and Feature Writing classes and two Zambians, Mufalo Liswaniso, Sub-Editing and Billy Nkunika, Photography and Photo Editing. The students were an eclectic bunch. The most experienced was certainly Victor Ndovi from Malawi who on his return home worked for the BBC but got into trouble with the government of Malawi's first President, Kamuzu Banda. Other natural journalists were Gilbert Mawarire of Zimbabwe, who became Prime Minister Robert Mugabe's Press Secretary at Zimbabwe's independence and Emmanuel Chayi, who served as director general of ZNBC. We also had Kaluwe Musuumba, a truly nice guy whom I had been with in secondary school and Musengwa Kayaya, an unassuming but intense individual. Then there was Fanuel Chembo, who after a false start with ZIS became the founding director of the MISA Zambia Chapter and Charles Chipanta, the slacker of the group, who spent most of his time playing around at disco houses. The head of the Journalism Studies Department was a white South African, Neville Huxham. He was smart and confident and we all admired him.

At the college my life began to come together. I now valued the hard work that I had been used to at home, the sense of responsibility and the capacity to perform many tasks with tight deadlines. The college was really good. There were enough experienced and well educated lecturers. Students had access to equipment and the library was well stocked with books for essential reading. But most importantly, the class sizes were small. At the beginning of our programme we were just sixteen students. Midway through the course two dropped out for failing to make the grade. The remaining fourteen worked hard at learning the process of communication, how to write stories and feature articles, how to edit copy and lay it out on newspaper pages, how to take photographs and lay them out in a story in a newspaper.

We also learned how to conduct interviews with and without a microphone and recorder. In our final semester we learned how to produce the student publication, "The Beacon". We also learned the art of speed writing which served me well as a journalist whilst taking down notes from long political speeches.

What made our group really special was its entrepreneurial spirit. We had the idea of setting up a video club at the college. We contributed some money from our meagre allowances to borrow videos from rental stores in town and used the department's video equipment and projector to screen the movies in the college assembly hall. We printed posters which were splashed all across the campus to announce the movies. Amazingly, the shows became so popular that they were soon the accepted regular weekly college event. Our class opened a bank account – a first for students at the college. Another innovative idea, which was strongly backed by the head of department, was that we should produce publishable stories and carry out interviews for broadcast on national radio. Our most trusting lecturer, Mr. Maine, made contacts with the English Service of Radio Zambia and the two daily newspapers, "Times of Zambia" and "Zambia Daily Mail", whose offices were within walking distance of the college. Soon enough many of the students had their work in print, sometimes with their names in bylines. Radio programmes took longer to produce and they were group and not individual efforts.

Buoyed by these successes we convinced the head of department and the lecturers that we could use our skills and contacts with the media to carry out information campaigns for companies and organisatons at rates much lower than those charged by well established public relations firms. Everyone was thrilled when we secured our biggest success, a PR campaign for the national airline, Zambia Airways. We produced feature articles and personality profiles which were published by the daily newspapers. We also produced radio programmes focusing on the airline's routes and services. The programmes carried interviews featuring the experiences of Zambian pilots, flight control staff and cabin crew. In return the airline gave us air tickets to various destinations within Zambia. In 1972, we used the tickets to fly to the provincial capital of Western Province, Mongu, to attend and cover the internationally acclaimed traditional ceremony of the Lozi people, the Kuomboka. We also used tickets to go to the Copperbelt to tour the mines and to Livingstone to see the famous Victoria Falls. No group of students had done this before and, most probably, none has done so since.

The immediate result for us students was that we all secured jobs while still at college. We were given the opportunity to apply for employment while in our final semester and were assured of being taken on as soon as we qualified. However, this created some problems in the end because no one saw the need to work on the student publication any longer. But a more serious problem was what to do with all the money that remained in the student bank account even after the various trips that we had undertaken. We suggested that it should be shared among us students because we had raised it ourselves. Our lecturers, particulary Mr. Maine, rejected this idea. In the end we agreed that it would be better spent on an end-of-course party. The party was held in the refectory after the regular dinner was finished. It was, no doubt, the biggest celebratory function held at the college by students. We had music and loads and loads of food and drinks – and girls. We invited our friends, mostly girls, and we took over the dining hall, eating, drinking, and dancing all night long as we bade farewell to our college days.

As I left the college I had no doubt, whatsoever, that my disciplined upbringing and exposure to books had contributed to my being able to outgrow the limitations of my family situation and the decadence of my childhood neighbourhood. I may not have realised at the time but I had also found my career and my calling and purpose in life.

7. Reporter on the Copperbelt

My professional life began as a junior reporter on a chilly 1st July in 1972, when I reported to the Kitwe offices of ZANA, a department under the Ministry of Information and Broadcasting Services. I was four months shy of my twentieth birthday. I was joining ZANA four years after its establishment as the major national news collection and distribution organisation. The national news agency had recruited four of us from the same class. Together with me were Emmanuel Chayi, Kaluwe Musuumba and Musengwa Kayaya. We were chosen from a larger group of applicants who had attended interviews at the ZANA offices in Lusaka.

On being selected we were given the chance to choose where we wanted to work, as ZANA had offices in all the provincial centres and main urban towns in the country. The organisation would provide housing to those who chose to work in towns other than the capital. Keen to move away from Matero, I opted to start work in Kitwe, which was home to the regional headquarters of ZANA operations covering three provinces: Copperbelt, Luapula and North-Western. The offices were located in Parklands, at the Copperbelt studios of ZBS, the forerunner to the state broadcaster ZNBC. The ZANA Kitwe office was also responsible for covering surrounding areas such as Kalulushi and Chibuluma as well as some parts of Ndola Rural District. A bonus for me was that Kitwe was where I had an aunt, my mother's immediate young sister, Amai Naomi Jere, with whom I could stay for a short period while waiting to be allocated a house.

The regional office of ZANA in Kitwe was headed by Deputy News Editor, Jimmy Chimbelu. He was slender in build, always stood upright and dealt with the staff in a very forceful manner. Chimbelu never wanted reporters to hang about in the Newsroom. He would ask, 'What are you doing here?' and shout 'Go out and get stories.' As a result what was referred to as 'township checks' were common and regular. This meant driving around the townships hoping to come across something to merit a story. On many occasions when you gave him your story to edit or check before it was sent to Lusaka, he scribbled all over it with a red pen or killed it on the 'spike' that everyone hated.

The other members of staff included Henry Chilufya, who was the most senior reporter at the station. He was very friendly and was a good writer but played hard during and after working hours. Then there were Enos Phiri, who later moved into the insurance business; Kavunda Lota, a cheery fellow who died in a road accident while on duty in a speeding convoy of a senior government official; and Felix Nkhata, with whom

I shared a house in Buyantanshi Township. I was by far the youngest member of staff in the Kitwe office and I was initially made to cover the courts, which was a good place for learning how to pay attention to detail. I later moved on to cover the trade unions, local authorities and politics. I embraced my work with energy and dedication. I wanted to be good at my work and soon enough earned the nickname 'Mike Zana'.

At that time ZBS had no reporters of its own, nor newsrooms in Kitwe or Lusaka. ZANA reporters covered the stories and prepared the news bulletins. For television news, ZANA reporters were accompanied on assignments by ZBS cameramen. The national television news bulletin was arranged in such a way that Lusaka crossed over to Kitwe to accommodate news from the Copperbelt and our deputy news editor, Jimmy Chimbelu and senior reporter, Henry Chilufya read the Copperbelt segment of the television news. It was challenging and demanding but provided a great opportunity for learning news-gathering, as well as writing and editing skills.

Although I started off as a junior reporter, I was soon operating like a fully-fledged reporter and was shortly confirmed in that position. Kitwe provided me with good practical experience. The work environment was very engaging because it brought news agency and radio and television staff to work together very closely. I also benefited in many ways from the experience and friendship of people such as Charles Mando, who for a long time was recognised as Zambia's most incisive television interviewer and Jeff Sitali, who was a Matero guy like me, and was one of the earliest journalists to embrace film production before moving into advertising.

After two years of working in Kitwe I was transferred to Ndola, the provincial capital for the Copperbelt. I did not like Ndola very much but stayed for two years. The town had achieved notoriety as a place for criminals and a lot of the stories that I wrote dealt with car thefts, house break-ins and aggravated robberies. Many serious crimes involved criminals who crossed into Zambia from nearby Zaire. Fortunately, there were some business stories, too, as Ndola was the 'hub' of the Copperbelt and home to the annual International Trade Fair. The Ndola ZANA team comprised Fred Chela, an old hand, who was the senior reporter; Felix Nkhata, my former housemate in Kitwe who had been transferred earlier to Ndola; and two old-school types, Davis Musuka and Bernard Kapekele.

I worked very well with Felix since we had bonded well whilst in Kitwe. But my closest friend was Zambia Daily Mail Bureau Chief, Fred Chita Mule, who was a creative writer and thoughtful journalist. Fred was a great guy to be around and he and I shared a love of comics, magazines, books and rumba music.

During my time in Ndola I matured as a journalist, particularly in the range of stories that I covered and the manner in which I approached them – always seeking to provide balance and adequate background. So, by 1976, when I was transferred to Head Office in Lusaka, I was sure that I was well prepared not only for new challenges but also additional responsibilities.

8. Growth and early responsibilities at the Head Office

After working in regional and district bureaux for four years, the Lusaka head office had an imposing atmosphere. Perhaps, this was because it was my first time to work in close proximity with the organisation's most senior officials. The editor-in-chief, Mr. Luxon Kaemba, was diminutive with a slight limp, but exuded a lot of authority. He was stern and distant to his staff. We occasionally met him on the staircase or saw him in the passage as he went to or from his office. His deputy editor-in-chief, Komani Kachinga, was a kind-hearted man and good journalist whose weakness was his excessive love for the bottle. He, together with the former editor-in-chief, Mr. Naphy Nyalugwe had permanent seats in the bar of the nearby Bwacha Hotel situated on Freedom Way. The seats were reserved for them because the hotel management and barmen knew that they held senior government positions and, of course, were regulars. Mr. Kachinga was at the bar most evenings and, many a time, night editorial staff had to telephone him for decisions on how to deal with complicated or sensitive news items. This happened so often that the telephone at the bar was jokingly referred to as 'Extension Zero'.

ZANA Headquarters in Lusaka occupied the entire third floor of Impala House in Chachacha Road. The southern end of the floor was reserved for the offices of the editor-in-chief, his deputy, accounts staff and the library, while the northern end was divided into three parts. The largest space was for the newsroom, which accommodated about twenty-five reporters, usually banging away on typewriters across three shifts, morning, afternoon and night.

The news editor operated in a small, poorly lit wooden compartment at the head of the newsroom. Peter John Mukanzo, 'PJ', was old, chain-smoking, forgetful but cheerful. He could never remember the name of the person he was addressing or that of the one he was looking for. He would come out of his office and say, 'Hey, what-are-you-called, where is so-and-so?' We would all laugh and he would join in.

The office of the deputy news editor was adjacent and was also poorly lit and poorly ventilated. The position was held consecutively by David Kashweka and Villie Lombanya, both of whom were later appointed to positions of senior private secretary for the prime minister, Daniel Lisulo and secretary general of the ruling UNIP party, Mr. Humphrey Mulemba. At the end of their political apppointments both Kashweka and Lombanya returned to take up senior positions in ZANA.

At the furthest end of the floor was the Sub-Editors Room. The sub-editors also worked three shifts each day but reported for work earlier than everyone else, at 5 a.m. and knocked off at midnight. The department was headed by a two-man team of chief sub-editors, Joseph Chifunda, one of the oldest members of staff and Henry Chilufya, formerly of Kitwe who had been transferred to Lusaka on promotion. The positions of news editor and chief sub-editor were initially at the third level of the ZANA hierarchy until a new position of principal editor was created as the third most senior position, to accommodate Villie Lombanya after his stint at the office of the secretary general of UNIP. The longest stretch on the northern end of the floor was the telex room, which had telex machines lined up on both sides clattering with the noise of in-coming stories from provincial offices and news agencies, and out-going stories to the newspaper offices and ZBS.

I settled down quickly, covered courts for a few months and then moved on to the government and parliament news beats. I was soon promoted to the position of senior reporter but only confirmed after passing examinations in General Orders, Public Service Commission Regulations and Financial Regulations which was a requirement of the civil service. As a senior reporter I soon became the leader of the ZANA

Parliament press corps. I had also begun to cover Presidential State House assignments including trips to some African countries, especially those in east and southern Africa, which were leading the struggle to end white rule and apartheid in Angola, Mozambique, Zimbabwe and South Africa and were known as the 'Frontline States'. Everything for me was looking up.

9. A student in India

An early break for me came a year after moving to Lusaka when an offer for a Post Graduate Diploma in Journalism course at the Indian Institute of Mass Communication of the Jawaharlal Nehru University in New Delhi was turned down by a female senior reporter who preferred to go to Europe or America. I volunteered to go in her place and in May, 1977, found myself as a student in India on a Special Commonwealth Assistance Programme scholarship. India was the furthest distance I had travelled to and for the longest stretch of time, a full academic year. I had already had some interaction with Indians whilst in high school but travelling and living in India was something else. The weather in summer was much hotter than at home and I had never seen so many people everywhere. The colours, the noises and smells were all overwhelming and even suffocating at times.

At that time the Institute campus was located in South Extension, Part II. Our group included another Zambian, Catherine Montah, from the national broadcaster, ZBS. She and I were accommodated at the JNU hostels. Other students rented rooms in houses closer to the Institute Campus in South Extension. As students from Commonwealth countries we received a good allowance, equivalent to US$500 a month, which made it possible for us to have transport and dietary options. Each day I travelled by bus to and from the IIMC campus. Buses of the Delhi Bus Company did not stop. They only slowed down to allow passengers to jump on and off. Immediately you were on the bus you pushed your way to the front, ready to jump off when the bus reached your station. There was a lot of dropping and scattering of books, especially in the early days. After falling off the bus a couple of times, I decided that during the first week of each month I would use a taxi, second and third weeks, the three-wheel rickshaw and during the fourth and final week of the month, when the money situation was tight, the bus.

I had a schedule worked out for food, too. I never got used to the hot Indian cuisine and the Institute cafeteria had a very unappealing menu, because I had arrived in India at the end of the twenty-one-month State of Emergency just after Morarji Desai, a strict vegetarian, had taken office as Prime Minister. His government was encouraging vegetarianism and the food choices in the Institute cafeteria were mostly vegetarian except for two days a week when they served mutton or fish. All the food was so hot with chilli that the cafeteria had small basins where diners cleared their throats while others were still eating. As foreign students we were badly affected by this custom.

I quickly learned some necessary Hindi phrases, such as for asking the chef to reduce the amount of chilli in the food. 'Kum mirchi dalna,' I would say. He would agree and say, 'Acha', meaning 'Okay' or 'Yes' but the food remained very hot. I suppose his minimum amount of 'mirchi' was always going to be too hot for my Zambian palate. The only saving grace was the foreign student allowance which, during the first two weeks of the month, allowed us to go to restaurants that served western food, before surrendering to the cafeteria fare for the remaining two weeks. Later when we began to know our way around the sprawling metropolis, we made more acceptable eating arrangements for the evenings. My Zambian colleague, Catherine and I bought a one-plate stove, some pots, a pan and plates and began to cook our own food.

To get a taste of our Zambian staple diet of 'nsima', a maize porridge eaten with a sauce of meat, chicken or fish, we bought 'soji', wheat meal, and it was almost like home. Murgi (chicken) and mutton were easiest to obtain. Beef needed time and special contacts.

Evenings at the JNU hostels were unpredictable. This is because Indian students were very politically conscious and active. Student union elections were serious business. The campus would be plastered with posters, campaigning would be non-stop and canvassing was carried out door-to-door. Demonstrations and strikes were also the order of the day. One time I woke up to find the university students lazing about the campus grounds.

Apparently, they were demanding the removal of the vice chancellor and the action was to take weeks. They organised what they called a 'relay strike' around the vice chancellor's residence to prevent him from going to his office. Groups of students exchanged places to ensure that the cordon around the house was maintained throughout the day and night amid shouts of "Zindabad", or "Long Live Student Power".

Another time the students commandeered most of the New Delhi buses and parked them on the campus grounds paralysing the transport system in the city. The students were complaining that the service was poor and that it needed to be improved. It took police with riot kit to storm the campus and teargas the students before the buses were retrieved and returned to the roads. With all this going on school work and general life were not easy and most times frustrating.

The students in my course were a mixed bunch from different parts of the Commonwealth combined with a core group of Indians. The Indian girls were charming and intelligent and mostly from private schools while the boys were mainly average students. One boy was supported by a government scholarship scheme for the low caste, which is how we became aware of and learned about the stratified nature of the Indian society. An unsettling problem for us was caused by the behaviour of some of the Indian students. Whenever a lecturer gave an assignment and referred to a book or a chapter in a book, if you did manage to find a copy of the book in the library, the pages of the chapter you needed would be missing. Luckily, locally published copies of most of the essential reading books were easy to get in bookstores or on street pavements around the Central Business District of Connaught Place.

The lecturers were experienced people with good professional backgrounds and there was much to learn. There is no doubt that I learned a lot, too, from the overall high standards of journalism practice in India. All India Radio provided a good service and I listened to the channel often while the quality newspapers, among them "Times of India" and "Hindustan Times" had well written and researched stories and well argued columns. For someone serious about learning, it was a good environment and I immersed myself fully in my studies. I worked hard in my class, on my assignments and in the practical work that I did as an intern at

UNI, the United News of India News Agency. At UNI I met a good senior journalist, Sunil Roy, who helped me understand further the operations of UNI, the practice of Indian journalism and, generally, the Indian way of doing things. We became close and on many occasions he invited me to his home where I ate good Indian food. Sunil made sure that the food his wife prepared for me was mild and so I totally enjoyed it.

Sunil Roy and I travelled extensively, with me in tandem on Sunil Roy's motorbike, in those days the most common means of transportation of middle level Indians. Looking back I cannot understand why I was not scared to be carried on a speeding motor bike on the notoriously congested Indian roads. There were bicycles, motor bikes, cars, buses, trucks, horse carts and cows all moving at various speeds all over the road. There was a persistent din. Most vehicles had signs written at the back saying, 'Horn Please' and horn, persistently, everyone did.

Social life was limited and the African students at IIMC and others at JNU and Delhi University tried to cheer themselves up by contributing money and buying drinks over weekends or throwing parties for any little excuse; we celebrated our own birthdays, our countries' national days and any other occasion which seemed appropriate. Buying alcohol was, of course, not easy. Government regulations designated places which sold 'take-away' drinks. There were also 'dry days' when no alcohol was sold. On weekends, which coincided with our pay days, we treated ourselves lavishly. We would go to an up-market hotel or disco house to eat, drink and dance until late. Inebriated and dancing the night away we sometimes forgot where we were until we walked outside and were greeted by the crowded scenery and beggars.

India is a sub-continent and a very large one at that. We visited many places. My most memorable visits were to Agra, Amritsar, Calcutta and Varanasi. Agra is a city in the northern state of Uttar Pradesh and is a major tourist destination because of its many splendid world heritage sites including the Taj Majal. It was good to see and walk around India's most famous monument. Amritsar, located in the state of Punjab is home to the Golden Temple, the cultural and spiritual centre of the Sikh religion. Walking barefoot into the temple was also a unique experience. In Varanasi, which is situated on the banks of the River Ganges in the state of Uttar Pradesh, we were in the grounds of the holiest Hindu place in the world. While there we witnessed the cremation of bodies on the banks of the River Ganges and watched as the ashes and remains were scattered into the river where many people were also bathing in religious rituals. The acrid smell of burning human flesh was strong as we boarded a boat and sailed along the river. Most of us did not eat any meat for weeks after this visit.

My longest journey was from Dehradun to Calcutta. Dehradun is the capital city of the state of Uttarakhand in the northern part of India. It is a popular tourist destination because of its location on the foothills of the Himalayas. Calcutta or Kolkata, as it was later renamed, where our journey ended, is the capital of the state of West Bengal and is one of the most populous cities in the world. Travelling by road from New Delhi to Dehradun, where my compatriot Catherine and I got on a train to Calcutta, was truly breathtaking as our vehicle meandered among the rolling hills. That is where the fun ended because the train ride from Dehradun to Calcutta took twenty-seven hours. It was a demanding ride because the train was overcrowded with passengers getting off and on at the many stations where the train stopped on the way. The heat was really scorching, generally in the 40s, levels not reached in most parts of Zambia. When we arrived in Calcutta, Catherine collapsed from exhaustion. The Institute authorities collaborated with the Zambian High Commission in India to get her on a flight to New Delhi where she was hospitalised. Catherine remained behind, recuperating, when I left for Zambia after our graduation ceremony. She returned in good health a few weeks later and went back to work in the ZBS Newsroom.

Overall, student life in India was very challenging. And so when there were less than a hundred days to go, we greeted each other by the number of days remaining. Instead of 'Good morning' you would say, 'Ninety-nine' or 'Seventy-four' and the mood heightened the closer we got to 'Ten' and, finally, to 'One'. But despite all the challenges, life went on and I completed my studies successfully. For my efforts in the course, I received the "Hindustan Times" Best Foreign Student award.

The course and my experience in India marked the beginning of the first critical turning point in my professional career. I was definitely ready to take on more serious responsibilities and in 1978, only a year after my return I was back in New Delhi as a member of the press team in the Zambian delegation, headed by President Kenneth Kaunda, at the 6th Non-Aligned Movement summit. It was amazing to be back in the Indian capital as a working journalist at that high level when only a few months earlier I had been a student with books in a rucksack riding a rickshaw or bus to school.

The conference was difficult to cover properly because of the many heads of government each making their long speeches. The Zambian president also had an additional schedule of bilateral meetings with presidents and prime ministers from other countries so my hours were very long. I woke up early and immediately got going and went to bed very late and very tired. Luckily, I got used to this sort of work because I was later to cover the 7th and 8th summits in Havana, Cuba, 1983, and in Harare, Zimbabwe, 1989. En route to and from Cuba I was in President Kaunda's delegation during state visits to Brazil, Grenada, Barbados and Liberia.

My next visit to India was for a brief stop-over on my way to Iraq as part of a three-man Zambian press team on a visit to that country at the invitation of the then ruling Baath Party. My colleagues were Philip Chirwa of the "Zambia Dail Mail" and Saviour Chafungwa from the "Times of Zambia".

My fourth visit was thirty-three years after my student days. I was a panellist in the Media and Advocacy Parallel Session of the 2020 International Food Policy Research Institute conference on 'Leveraging Agriculture for Improving Nutrition and Health'. The official Zambian delegation had four members, two deputy ministers from the Ministries of Agriculture and Health and two senior civil servants but none of them made a presentation at the conference. I was not a member of the Zambian delegation but had been invited to the conference to participate in a discussion in my own right as a media expert. The only other person from Zambia who spoke at the conference was Ajay Vashee, chairman of the Zambia Union of Farmers, who was also an independent delegate. Whilst at the conference, I found time to sneak out to go down memory lane and took a taxi to South Extension, Part II only to find that both the Indian

Institute of Mass Communication and the Jawarhalal Nehru University had been relocated and that the Institute was now spread over an area of about fifteen acres in the new university campus.

My participation as a speaker at the conference, attended by more than one thousand delegates from about sixty-five countries in the town where I had been a student, more than anything else, indicated the progress that I had made over the years.

Unfortunately, though, my relationship with the Indian High Commission in Zambia was not good when I returned to Zambia after my studies. The High Commission did not want to have anything to do with me after I wrote a feature article exposing the prevalence of fake medical qualifications in that country at a time when Zambia was recruiting many doctors from India. Following the publication of the story, with my byline, I was never invited, as other former students were, to any of the functions held at the Indian High Commission in Lusaka.

10. Back home and away again and again

I left India in a hurry after my study course. I had arranged my return ticket in such a way that my flight left on the evening of graduation day. Back home, I hit the ground running and was quickly working my beats, parliament, government ministries and State House. The news editor, Mr. Mukanzo, soon became quite dependent on me. My writing had greatly improved and my stint in India had given me a broad understanding of how to manage newsroom operations and different specialised desks within the Newsroom. I slowly began to make suggestions for improvements that the news editor appreciated. I was also volunteering for supervisory duties during what were regarded as 'hardship shifts' – nights, weekends, holidays. Many senior reporters and other members of staff laughed at me, wondering why I was bothering to take all the ungodly shifts when I was not being paid for the extra work.

Admittedly, the hardship shifts were horrendous. Most of the time there was little to do except be on standby for a late breaking story. Usually such stories came from official functions, particularly government and diplomatic cocktail parties. Reporters who covered these functions tended to come back to the office in a drunken state and were, therefore, slow to complete their work. I needed to be patient and tolerant to assist them to come up with reasonable copy. At times I chose to assist the sub-editor on duty to edit stories from district offices which, generally, were poorly written. Some weekends were very busy and I ended up really exhausted and unable to rest before starting a new week. Holidays, on the other hand, were what reporters mostly referred to as 'dry days'. There were few scheduled meetings or events and as desk editor my job was to try and get reporters to come up with realistic ideas for stories. All this gave me additional experience and skills which contributed further to my journalistic development.

Around this time I regularly travelled on presidential trips to foreign countries for continental and international conferences and before long I had been to most countries in East and Southern Africa, and to Sudan for the OAU Heads of State conference. Later I accompanied the president on his special UN mission to Western Sahara. During this mission he held discussions with UN Secretary General, Kurt Waldheim, in Brussels and King Hassan II of Morocco in Marrakech. He also visited Algeria and Mauritania and held discussions with their leaders, all in an effort to find a solution to the Western Sahara impasse.

11. Recognition and promotion

August 1979 was my month. On 1st August, 1979, the Government Public Service Commission, acting in the name, and on behalf, of the president, directed that I be declared an established officer under the Civil Service Pensions Act. This meant that I was now entitled to receive a pension after completing my service. Coincidentally, Zambia was hosting the Commonwealth Heads of Government Meeting (CHOGM) in Lusaka from 1st to 7th August, 1979. This was one of the most important CHOGMs for Zambia and President Kaunda, and for Southern Africa and the entire African continent.

Not only did I cover this ground-breaking conference, but at a ceremony marking the end of the conference I received the award of Best News

Agency Reporter of the Year. The award was presented to me by the prime minister of Great Britain, Margaret Thatcher, who was the guest of honour at the ceremony which was also attended by President Kenneth Kaunda of Zambia. A photograph of Prime Minister Thatcher dancing with President Kaunda featured in newspapers around the world.

As many commentators observed, the picture of a smiling President Kaunda and Prime Minister Thatcher dancing together portrayed a simplified image of the outcome of the CHOGM in Zambia. In fact, after hours of diplomacy, the heads of government issued the Lusaka Declaration of the Commonwealth on Racism and Racial Prejudice which strongly stated: 'We reject as inhuman and intolerable all policies designed to perpetuate apartheid, racial segregation or other policies based on theories that racial groups are or may be inherently superior or inferior'

The Lusaka Declaration precipitated the holding of the Lancaster House Talks in London which brought white minority rule in Rhodesia to an end, paving the way for an independent nation of Zimbabwe under the leadership of Prime Minister Robert Mugabe.

And for me, my award was in recognition of the several stories and a feature article I had written after a visit to Saurimo, capital of the diamond-rich Lunda Sul Province in Angola. In the late 1970s the area was heavily involved in the fighting between Angola's two major political factions, the MPLA and UNITA. My stories tried to explain the situation and how what was going on was having an adverse impact not only on Angola, but on neighbouring countries such as Zambia. The award spurred me to even harder work, more accomplishments and more trips to other parts of the world.

The most significant achievement, though, was my promotion to the position of news editor in 1980, two years after my return from India. I took over the position from Mr. Mukanzo who had retired at the mandatory age of fifty-five. I was only twenty-eight years old but I was competent and hard working. I headed the Southern region which comprised Lusaka, Central, Eastern, Northern, Southern and Western provinces and was based at Head Office in Lusaka. The other region, referred to as North-Western, consisted of Copperbelt, Luapula and North-Western provinces and was headed by Blake Sichone as news editor based in Kitwe.

I was in charge of head office operations and five provincial bureaus in six provinces while my colleague on the Copperbelt oversaw the operations of eight offices in three provinces.

Six of the offices were in major towns of the Copperbelt; the other two offices were in Mansa in Luapula Province and Solwezi in North-Western Province.

My promotion displeased many people in the organisation, particularly the older, long-serving members of staff. Most of them had joined the organisation much earlier than me and my promotion meant that in the civil service, which emphasised long service over merit, I had superseded them. But, I had the support of most of the younger members of staff, especially reporters, who saw my promotion as progressive and were looking forward to a new type of leadership that would encourage enterprise and hard work. The young reporters also saw me as their representative on the management team which at that time comprised people now in their forties and fifties who had joined ZANA at its establishment in 1969.

As soon as I assumed the position of news editor I experienced what in Zambia is referred to as the 'PhD (Pull Him Down) syndrome'. Apparently, several weeks after I took up office, a group of senior reporters and sub-editors met in a nearby town bar, the Lotus Inn, to plot how to frustrate my efforts and work. Two plans were mooted.

The first plan involved a senior sub-editor writing a letter to President Kaunda complaining how he had been overlooked and superseded despite his long and loyal service to the organisation and government. He pointed out that he had, in fact, earlier been my direct supervisor. (The President's office requested the office of the Secretary to the Cabinet to establish the facts of the case and report back. Since senior promotions in the civil service were essentially sanctioned by the Office of the Secretary to the Cabinet, through the Public Service Commission, the grounds for my elevation were already known and the complaint was dismissed.) Copies of the correspondence reached ZANA and I was able to come across them in due course.

The second plan was more far-fetched and nefarious. For unexplainable reasons I was thought to have originated from Zimbabwe, then Southern Rhodesia. During the 1960s and '70s many Africans from that country had migrated to Zambia to join the liberation struggle, or simply to escape the machinations of the racist settler regime. Some of these migrants ended up working as journalists in many of Zambia's media institutions, including ZANA. When Zimbabwe gained its independence in 1980 most of them left Zambia to return home. While in Zambia some of them had assumed local names and illegally obtained Zambian identity documents so that they could access the benefits offered to citizens but when they quit their jobs to return to the new Zimbabwe, their sudden departure came as quite a surprise. As a result a kind of witch-hunt followed and I was identified as one of the Zimbabweans who had remained behind. A letter was written to the Office of the Investigator General alleging that I was a non-Zambian and, therefore, could not hold what was seen as a sensitive government position.

I came to find out about this plot to have me deported when I was summoned to the Passport Office. I had submitted my old passport for renewal and instead of it being renewed I was informed that I needed to start the application process all over again. A senior passport officer told me that there was a request to establish my true origins because a report had been received suggesting that I might be from Zimbabwe.

He said that the Passport Office had also noticed that details on my Affidavit Form and those of my National Registration Card, were dissimilar. The Affidavit Form provided details of my origins, that is, the district, the chief and the village in Chipata while my National Registration Card gave Lusaka as my home area. There was some truth to this irregularity. Many people, whose parents had migrated from village to town, gave the names of the towns in which they were resident as their homes. This was to avoid the long process of having to send documents to one's home district for approval. Anyway, I was told that I needed to make a fresh application and that the documents would be sent to Chipata for verification by the authorities there. The application took several months but I finally got my new passport and the attempt to have me deported failed.

While all this was going on, I continued with my work and assisted in setting up specialist desks to deal with Business, Sports and News Features and helped to broaden the range and types of stories that ZANA was able to deliver to its subscribers.

At about this time ZANA also introduced the 'Inside Parliament' television programme which was broadcast by Television Zambia. The programme was intended to go beyond factual reporting of parliamentary business in order to bring out the mood and colour of debate and discussion in the House. These efforts paid off handsomely. The volume and quality of ZANA copy improved, resulting in the daily newspapers, radio and television carrying many of the stories.

ZANA subscribers were happy and, more importantly, those of my workmates who had been contesting and protesting against my appointment had to admit that I was doing a good job. The atmosphere and tension in the operational areas eased.

At the beginning of 1981, I spent three months on attachment to the Reuters News Agency African Regional Office in Nairobi, Kenya, where I further improved my news judgment, writing, analysis and interpretation skills. At the end of my attachment I was offered the position of Lusaka stringer for Reuters but as an employee of the government I needed to seek clearance through the Ministry of Information and Broadcasting Services. This was denied but it did not matter too much. I was, obviously, upwardly mobile at the time and quitting my job for a stringing position with an international organisation was not prudent. So I stayed, but went ahead to become the Zambian correspondent for The Financial Gazette of Zimbabwe, Radio Deutsche Welle of Germany and Afrique-Asie magazine published in Paris, France. I was also a board member of the regional feature service and training organisation, Africa Information Afrique, AIA, based in Harare, Zimbabwe.

In particular I enjoyed being the correspondent of The Financial Gazette of Zimbabwe because, due to foreign exchange restrictions in that country, my earnings could not be externalised and so I travelled to Harare regularly to get paid and have fun with my friends who had returned to that country. I would hitch-hike, mostly on a Thursday and return to Lusaka, the same way on Sunday and would be back at work on Monday morning. It was natural justice at its best because I was definitely compensated for the harassment I had endured over malicious attempts to link me with Zimbabwe.

Meanwhile, I was also up and about on presidential and other assignments and the most coveted trip that I made in the year 1981, started with President Kaunda's State Visit to Australia followed by attendance at the Commonwealth Heads of Government Conference in Melbourne.

All this travelling upset other people. Foreign trips in media organisations are seen as the highest form of benefit because of the sizable financial allowances that go with them. Everyone, therefore, expects to be included on a trip from time to time whether they are competent or not and murmurings became loud that I was travelling too much.

12. Transfer to the North-Western Region

At the beginning of 1982, I was not surprised when the new editor-in-chief, Humphrey Maunga, sent me to Kitwe to run the North-Western Region while my colleague, Blake Sichone, was brought from there to Lusaka to run the Southern Region. And so ten years after I had reported to the Kitwe office as a junior reporter, I returned as news editor and overall boss for the entire region. I was not too happy with the transfer at this particular stage of my professional career as I had just married and had to leave my wife, Catherine, and our baby son, Dalitso, in Lusaka for some three months before they could join me in Kitwe. But I took the transfer in my stride and used the time for some introspection as well as work.

My first priority was to get the district offices better organised and operating more professionally. I requested that apart from copies of news diaries that the offices were submitting to the Kitwe office, they should also send copies of the actual stories. I discussed the diary ideas with the reporters and set deadlines by which the assignments should be completed. That helped me to monitor what each station was doing and to contribute to their work by suggesting how to approach some of the more important assignments that they were undertaking. I also suggested when and how the various offices should pursue joint efforts to provide a provincial outlook or scenario on issues affecting more than one town or district.

These efforts paid off. Overall output improved as did the quality of the stories and, gradually, the image of the offices and reporters on the Copperbelt and in other areas changed for the better. The editors in Lusaka began to take the input from the region seriously, while people in the communities started paying attention to the existence and role of the ZANA reporters in their areas. Of course, this heightened level of professionalism did not please the political authorities in the region. Zambia was then under a one-party system of government that combined the structures of the ruling party and the government under what was known as 'the Party and Its Government', whose unofficial acronym was PIG. At the top of the governing structures in the three provinces in the North-Western Region were senior members of the ruling party at the level of member of central committee, generally known as MCC. Below them were provincial ministers and permanent secretaries and at district level were the party stalwarts, the district governors, DGs.

The members of central committee and the district governors were powerful officionados. What they decreed, ruled. We had few complaints from the party or government offices on the Copperbelt or Luapula Province.

There were, however, a lot of complaints from the MCC in North-Western Province, Mr. Fine Liboma. At first Mr. Liboma expressed unhappiness over the fact that the senior reporter in his province was supervised by someone based in another province. He was mostly displeased that little was being heard on national radio or television about what he and other senior party officials were saying at the meetings that they constantly held in different parts of the province.

The situation was not helped by the happy-go-lucky attitude of the senior reporter in the region, Nathaniel 'Nat' Musa, a portly, affable character who, unfortunately, liked his drink a little too much and who was one of the most inconsistent of all the reporters we had in the region. I found myself regularly summoned to the office of the MCC, 225 kilometres away, to explain one thing or other and was always told that the reporter was 'anti-party' and should be removed from the province.

The truth is that the late eighties made coverage of political leaders and their meetings extremely difficult. The declining economy and food shortages in the country made the UNIP political and government leadership unpopular. Most leaders had little of substance to say about what the government intended to do to improve the economy and only echoed or repeated President Kaunda's statements *ad infinitum*.

Transfer to the North-Western Region

Political naggings aside, work progressed steadily in the region unlike in Lusaka where things were seemingly not going too well, because by the end of my first year in the North-Western Region, the senior editors in Lusaka realised the folly of their decision to transfer me to Kitwe.

Performance at the Head Office had begun to slacken. Radio and television news bulletins were being delayed while the number of ZANA stories appearing in the daily newspapers was declining. At first the senior editors tried to ignore what was happening but later were forced to admit that they had made a mistake.

By the end of my second year a decision was taken by the new editor-in-chief, David Kashweka, a ZANA old hand, to strengthen the Lusaka office by having *both* news editors there. The leadership at the Kitwe office was to revert to the lower level of deputy news editor. However, it took another two years before the housing authorities allocated me a house and I was able to return to Lusaka.

In the interim I had time to think about my career thus far and what I wanted for my future. Although I had no clear idea how best to plan for my future or how to set goals, I definitely knew that I was discontented with my *status quo* and also knew that I could do much better. I realised that the management structure at ZANA did not favour someone like me. Among the four editors who were at the fourth management level, two news editors and two chief sub-editors, I was the youngest and most junior in terms of years of service. For me to rise to the position of principal editor, deputy editor-in-chief or even editor-in-chief it would be necessary that the other three editors at my level move up, go elsewhere, or die.

There was also the option of my looking for a job elsewhere. The most attractive jobs at the time were those in public relations because, among other perks, they seemed to provide good salaries and personal-to-holder cars. I was not particularly keen on a PR job because I thought that a job demanding one to run errands for a chief executive of an organisation suggested that one did not want to be – or think that one could rise to – the top position.

Of course, I knew that I had previously superseded many others in ZANA to get to the position of news editor. To repeat that act I needed to do something really significant. The most sensible thing to do was, obviously, to attain a higher qualification. I could never have imagined then, not even in my wildest dreams, what the impact of these thoughts on my personal advancement would be or how my progression would unravel. I simply began to think about opportunities for further education. It was extremely difficult to get any useful information about universities in Europe or America from my base in Kitwe and the Council Library had only outdated periodicals and magazines. So with my goal in mind and waiting for an opportune time before making further arrangements, I immersed myself in professional networking activities.

I assisted in the creation of the Kitwe Press Club of which I became the founding chairman. In the 1980s the Kitwe Press Club was one of the country's most active press groups. Its membership was broad because of the presence of a large number of lecturers and students of the pan-African journalism school, the Africa Literature Centre, which was located at the Mindolo Ecumenical Foundation. My committee opened up membership to non-journalists, too, and many faculty members and students of the Copperbelt University joined up. The club meetings were held at the Hotel Edinburgh and were always well attended because we always had prominent guests drawn from various sectors, including visiting dignitaries from Lusaka.

My transfer to Kitwe had not been made in good faith. I could have reacted badly to it by quitting my job or working to rule whilst there. Instead I utilised the time well and benefited from the experience of running a regional operation, spearheading the development of an effective media club and developing useful contacts and long-term associates outside the media fraternity.

13. Away to DDR, the Deutsche Demokratische Republik

While I was waiting to return to Lusaka, I was offered the opportunity to attend a six month Advanced Journalism course at the International Institute of Journalism, IIJB, in East Berlin, East Germany from January to June, 1985. I found communist East Germany an interesting place, although the general atmosphere was drab and greyish most of the time.

A colleague in Lusaka, who had just been to the country, had given me introductory letters to Zambian students and young officials of the African National Congress of South Africa who had been based at the ANC office in Lusaka. The two groups were in DDR for training in various disciplines. The Zambian group comprised men only while the ANC 'cadres' included men and women. Members of the two groups kept me fully engaged at parties most weekends and there was much fun to be had.

Apparently, the Zambian students had a lot of money to splash around because they were doing roaring business crossing to West Berlin and buying rare goods such as designer jeans and music systems to sell on the eastern side where these items were not available. Many locals and foreign students in East Berlin wanted goods which they saw on the West German television channels which were being received in the East.

I enjoyed my class sessions and work and I was a top student and well regarded by my colleagues and faculty members. The lecturers were experienced, mature people open to discussion. I particularly liked the Scientific Socialism classes because they helped me to understand this completely different world view. Things were made a lot clearer for me by a classmate, Kandi Nehova, a senior official from the Lusaka office of SWAPO, the South West African People's Organisation of Namibia, whom in return I assisted with explaining western media concepts.

I travelled a lot in East Germany because the Institute gave us seasonal train tickets throughout our stay. It was quite dangerous to travel alone, especially on the trains where drunken East German workmen tended to be hostile and aggressive towards Africans. It was said that they resented their government spending a lot of their tax money on bringing Africans over and giving them higher education which as locals they were not able to obtain. One Namibian journalism student, Charles Mubita, was assaulted and badly injured on a train one evening. There were also cases in which African students were thrown out of moving trains just before the trains moved off. Fortunately, my Zambian and South African friends had warned me about the need to get out of train coaches which appeared to be filling up with such workmen and I was, therefore, able to travel safely all the time.

I visited Dresden, Leipzig, Potsdam and in Berlin, the Brandenburg gate and Checkpoint Charlie, the best known Berlin Wall crossing point between East Berlin and West Berlin during the Cold War. A totally unique place which I visited was Spreewald, a landscape shaped in the Ice Age, which was designated by UNESCO as a biosphere reserve in 1991. It is an irrigation system consisting of more than 200 channels through which people move from place to place in canoes; motorised transport was not allowed. Moving through the canals to the restaurants dotted alongside the waterways was a refreshing experience. No usual noises of human or motorised traffic of any kind, just the swishing and lapping of boats gliding on water and birds chirping.

I also spent several weeks in Cottbus where editors at a newspaper, at which some classmates and I were posted for practical work, had arranged a field trip to an open-pit coal mine. They were disappointed when I was not impressed. They did not, of course, know that I was from Zambia, which is home to Nchanga Open Pit, one of the world's largest open pit mines. A tour of a former concentration camp, Sachsenhausen, in Oranienburg was emotionally challenging. Sachsenhausen-Oranienburg was a Nazi concentration camp used primarily for political prisoners from 1936 to the end of the German Third Reich in May, 1945. The remaining buildings and grounds were later opened to the public as a museum. Although we were visiting forty years later, the atmosphere was still chilling and every one of us was quiet and thinking to themselves about what had taken place in the camp.

My main attachment programme in the DDR was with the Allgemeiner Deutscher Nachrichtendienst, the country's sole news agency. ADN had a news exchange arrangement with my organisation, ZANA, and I was hoping to use the time to understand their approach and policy for international news. Unfortunately, no one was available to explain anything in any reasonable detail and my time there was spent mostly looking at incoming international news. I never witnessed the selection process, nor saw the edited version which was channelled to the local newspapers or international news agencies such as ZANA. Nearly everyone who worked there appeared sullen and tight-lipped and I was unable to establish any relationships. I was, therefore, happy when my attachment was over.

Fortunately, at the Institute and within Berlin, we did have German friends although, as an African student, it was dangerous to walk around with German girls. Police stopped you to ask for IDs from the girls just in case they were under age. We were told that the penalty for being found with an under-age girl was severe. As had been the case with India, East Germany was not regarded by many as an attractive place to go to. I went there and I am happy that I did. It gave me a unique insight into life in Socialist Eastern Europe.

14. Return to Lusaka and to serious business

It was not long after I returned home that, towards the end of 1986, my family and I finally moved back to Lusaka, where I was appointed to oversee the operations of the Head Office and the Southern region while my colleague, Blake Sichone, took over responsibility for offices in the Copperbelt, Luapula and North-Western provinces. I did not take long to settle down. The transfer was more disruptive for my wife, Catherine and our two kids. It took a while for her to get a placement at the Head Office of ZCCM in Lusaka, while finding a good and well located nursery school for the children was not easy. As a place to live and work for a young family, Kitwe, had been convenient. My office was less than two kilometres from our house in the Riverside residential area and our older child, Dalitso, started going to a nursery school located behind our house. My wife's work place was much further away, near the town centre.

Not so in Lusaka. The distances were much longer, my work load heavier, the hours more demanding and official transport had to be shared with other people. But I absolutely enjoyed my work as news editor. I was to stay in that position for ten years, one of the longest serving news editors in the organisation. I was resourceful and strong-willed – two essential qualities of a news editor of that era; perhaps a little heavy-handed from what many people were to say later. I wanted things to be done properly and on time. Each reporter had to submit three diary ideas before 9 a.m. Stories for the national radio lunch hour news bulletin had to be in the basket on my desk by midday and so on. As this was a time before cellphones, reporters covering important assignments away from the office had to find the nearest telephone and dictate a few paragraphs before coming back to the office to write a more detailed story.

As news editor I had invitations to many cocktail parties and dinners from diplomats at their embassies in the Embassy Park, or residences in the upmarket Kabulonga residential area. Most invitations for large and intimate occasions were from the British, American, Norwegian and Danish ambassadors and their senior staff. At all the functions I behaved well and appropriately and I built some lasting relationships.

A few months after I arrived back in Lusaka, I attended my first management training course, which helped me to properly understand my role as a supervisor and manager. The course, which was attended by managers in the departments of the Ministry of Information and Broadcasting Services was organised by the National Institute of Public Administration, NIPA. I learned a lot about what a manager was and the role of a manager which helped me in my work where, generally, there was no admission of wrong-doing by most members of staff. It was always 'I don't know', or blaming someone else. In situations in which there was overwhelming evidence, subordinates tended to plead for forgiveness, pity or sympathy. When you sought an explanation about why someone had not done what he or she was supposed to do, you usually got a convoluted and long-winded story. Hardly ever did someone admit their mistake, or apologise, and so mistakes recurred and the blame game continued. Anyhow, I was tough, especially about meeting deadlines, but I balanced this by also being fair, I hope.

I continued to travel and, in 1987, I was in the press corps accompanying President Kaunda to New York for the United Nations General Assembly. It was exciting to be in the city known as the Big Apple and to cover the UN General Assembly. While in the United States the president visited Washington where he held talks with President Ronald Reagan at the White House. I remember President Reagan commenting on how well dressed the Zambian journalists were. (We were all in new suits, of course.)

Two incidents in New York remain vivid in my mind about the impersonality of people there. Between covering the UN General Assembly and going to one of President Kaunda's meetings with another head of state, we had some time off to do a little shopping. I went into a children's clothing shop and after finding what I thought would be a nice pair of jeans for my son, Dalitso, I asked a shop assistant whether the trousers would fit a four-year-old boy. 'I don't know. You should know, you are the father!' he retorted. In another incident, I was trying to get a taxi to go to the offices of "Newsweek" magazine where the president had gone for an interview. My colleagues in the presidential press team had gone ahead because I had been held up in the communication room where I was filing my stories to Lusaka. At the taxi rank near the UN buildings, I asked someone whether he knew the location of the "Newsweek" magazine building. 'Call Information,' he responded. Do people talk to each other here? I wondered.

There were more trips to come: to Canada, China and North Korea, as well as Italy and the Vatican. I also accompanied President Kaunda to the funeral and burial of Yugoslav President, Josip Broz Tito. They were all very engaging and inspirational.

I have never felt so proud to be a Zambian as I did when I travelled the world with President Kenneth Kaunda. He stood tall, was calm and confident while emphatically and insistently presenting his ideas and Zambia's and Africa's position, especially on the need to end racism in Southern Africa. Everyone who met him, fellow leaders, other politicians and government officials, diplomats and ordinary citizens welcomed him warmly and with much respect and those of us in his delegations felt - and were immersed in - the grandeur of each occasion.

After long trips abroad, I was always quickly jolted back to the reality of Zambia. The disparity in the levels of development, starting with the infrastructure from the airport, the uncaring mini bus drivers and the uncooperative attitude of workmates all confirmed that I was, indeed, back home, so after my visits to the USA and Canada, I decided to follow up on my plans to go for further education.

Fortunately, in Lusaka information about courses and scholarship opportunities was readily available and I spent some time at the British Council library and the United States Information Service library gathering information before selecting what appeared to be suitable programmes. I made several applications to universities in both Britain and the United States of America and early in 1988 I received positive responses from a couple of them. My choice was the University of Wales in Cardiff, United Kingdom, which offered a one-year Master of Arts course in Journalism Studies.

Armed with an acceptance letter, I inquired for scholarships from my contacts at the British High Commission and the British Council. As it turned out the British Council was at that very time asking for applications for scholarships under the British and Foreign Office Post Graduate Scholarship Programme. The scholarship programme, later renamed the Chevening Scholarship Programme, was regarded as the most prestigious awards scheme available to international students for study in the United Kingdom and was for mid-career professionals. The scholarships covered the full cost of study in the UK and targetted candidates who were seen as future leaders who could benefit their countries on their return home.

I applied for the FCO scholarship and a few months later received my award letter. I was exultant as I was one of the first journalists in Zambia to be awarded this scholarship. My excitement was toned down a great deal during the months leading to my departure because there was a lot of negotiation to do at work. I needed to inform my senior editors about the scholarship and apply and get approval for paid study leave. Although my scholarship was supposed to meet the full costs of my stay in the UK, paid study leave was crucial because it would ensure that I received my salary, which the family at home would use for their upkeep while I was away. We had three children, two boys, Dalitso and Dabwitso, and a girl who was between the two boys, Chimfwembe.

Gerald, who was born much earlier, when I was studying in India spent his early years with his maternal grandparents. He joined the family in 1988 while I was studying in the UK.

Credit should go to my wife, Catherine, for playing a major role in looking after the children in the early years when I was constantly away from home. Catherine was also responsible for the children's early education through her employers, ZCCM, who managed one of Lusaka's best primary schools, Nkhwazi Primary School, where all the three younger children spent their early school years.

My wife's contribution towards the children's development at this stage was critical because, as a middle-level civil servant under ZANA, I was unable to afford the school fees. So with everything in place, in October, 1988, I left for Cardiff to undertake my MA in Journalism Studies at the University of Wales.

15. A student in the UK

I arrived in Cardiff, the capital of Wales, in mid-October, 1988, as the weather in the UK was beginning to get nippy. I found the city rather laid back and quite agreeable for someone prepared to get on with some serious studies. The University of Wales is recognised as one of Britain's major teaching and research universities. It is located close to the town's civic centre and student residential accommodation is within easy walking distance of lecture theatres, libraries, the student union shops, restaurant and bar, the main shopping centre, as well as surrounding pubs. Most of the student residences were self-catering flats with single study bedrooms. My accommodation, in a privately-owned four-bedroomed house, was very close to the sprawling university campus. It took me two minutes to walk to my school at 69 Park Place, three minutes to the bus stop and one minute to the Barclays Bank University Branch and the ATM machine. It was really convenient.

Students in Cardiff were known to enjoy some of the lowest rents in the UK and with everything within walking distance, we saved time and money, although the latter was always never enough. I shared the house with three other students, a Kenyan, a Tanzanian and an Indonesian, each in their self-contained room with common living room and kitchen. We were all pursuing different postgraduate degree programmes and only saw each other in the morning just before going off to our schools, or in the evening when preparing or eating dinner. The other three had arrived in the UK earlier than me. The British Council had a scheme for bringing students with little travel experience a month early so that they could acclimatise to the British way of life by living with local families before the universities opened.

By the time I arrived, the three had settled in with the Kenyan and Tanzanian contributing money for food and eating together as a cost-saving measure. I was asked to join the arrangement since the Zambian maize meal-based staple diet of 'nsima' and the East African 'ugali' were not dissimilar. I pulled out of the arrangement as soon as I realised the Tanzanian guy didn't have the slightest idea how to cook and the Kenyan was only slightly better. In any case, our eating times were awkward because we were in different schools and our study hours and habits were also different. That said, I settled down in Cardiff quickly and was soon able to find my way around the city, to the supermarkets, markets, pubs and many other places. I also made new friends and spent most weekends and free evenings with a Ghanaian who happened to be a very good cook.

I was very clear in my mind about why I was in Cardiff. I was thirty-six years old, had held the position of news editor for eight years and was ready to upgrade my professional knowledge and credentials and seriously go up the promotion ladder. So pub time (and there were many interesting pubs in the neighbourhood) had to be limited, as were the meaningless trips and tours organised by the university and student groups.

I made my own trips whenever I needed a break from student life and the Welsh environment and mostly went to London to meet with my good friend, Mann Sichalwe, who was completing his MA studies in Leicester. Mann was director of ZAMCOM, the training department of the Ministry of Information and Broadcasting Services and had, like me, decided to further his education. Whenever we met in London we would go on a pub crawl with London-based Zambian students.

It was during our meetings in London that Mann and I started talking about our plans for when we returned home. We were both frustrated with the general lack of professionalism in our media institutions and among most staff members. However, while we knew that there was need for improvement, we were not sure how to bring this about. Each time I returned to Cardiff I felt refreshed, hangover notwithstanding.

My course group was small. We were only twelve in our class. I was the only one from Zambia alongside a Tanzanian, a Nigerian and two Zimbabweans. We also had one Chinese, two from Brunei, a Turk, two South Koreans and one student from Yemen. If I had worked hard in my previous training programmes, I committed myself fully and worked even more vigorously in Cardiff. The Head of Journalism Department was a respected British journalism personality, Don Rowlands. My favourite lecturer was Geoff Mungeon, who co-authored the book, "The Fog of War" on how the British government managed news about the Falklands conflict. I embraced everything totally and the year passed quickly as I worked through tutorials and assignments, essays and library research, workshops and the dissertation. I clearly remember my university library visits. Every time I went to the library most of the chairs and other sitting spaces were taken up by undergraduate students. Many of them would be in pairs, boys and girls and would be kissing or cuddling. I never could understand how they completed their assignments or course work. They disturbed me a lot and I could never spend meaningful time in the library, always ending by taking books back to my room. It was awful in winter because of the cold and the high heating charges.

As someone from a news agency I chose a practical subject for my dissertation: "African News by Africans: An Assessment of PANA News in African Newspapers". African leaders, through the auspices of the Organisation of African Unity, OAU had supported the establishment of the Pan-African News Agency, PANA. This continental agency was tasked to collect and disseminate information on and about Africa, arguing that information distributed by world news agencies such as the AFP, AP, Reuters and UPI was both inadequate and consistently negative. PANA was, therefore, to change the distorted image of Africa by promoting the collection and distribution of news on the continent.

Six years after PANA began its operations, I felt that the question which needed asking was, 'How was the organisation fairing in its main task of collecting and disseminating news and information on Africa and how much of this news and information was being published in African newspapers?' The leadership of PANA was convinced that the agency had gone some way towards making the dream if its founders a reality.

With its headquarters in Dakar, Senegal, PANA had organised the network of national news agencies into five regional pools with their centres in Lagos, Khartoum, Kinshasa, Lusaka and Tripoli. National news agencies sent their news items through their regional pools and were also free to send their copy direct to Dakar. Journalists based at PANA headquarters and at two bureaux located in Addis Ababa and Harare, and international organisations dealing with news of interest to Africa, comprised the other major sources of PANA news.

In highlighting what it saw as its successes PANA pointed out that when operations began in 1983, the Agency received news from six African national news agencies and transmitted less than seven thousand words each day, while six years later it regularly received news and features from about twenty news agencies and transmitted an average of twenty thousand words each day. PANA also claimed that its success could be measured by the forty or so national news agencies that had contributed to the service since it started operating and that forty-two out of fifty member states of the founding body, the OAU, had already signed the PANA Convention and were ready to join up. The agency was also convinced that there had been an increase not only in the quantity of news about Africa carried by newspapers and radio stations across the continent but also in the amount originating from African news agencies and PANA.

My study sought to help establish the extent to which PANA news items were used over a period of five months in Zambia's leading newspaper group of that time, the "Times of Zambia", which published a daily and a Sunday edition. I utilised content analysis as the major research methodology and the assumption that I made was that the selection of the newspapers and the period for study were appropriate enough to yield a representative result. A further assumption I made was that the data concerning PANA and other news agencies was analysed in an objective way to allow for effective conclusions to be drawn. My dissertation supervisor was Dr. Bogdan Szajkowski, a Polish immigrant to the UK. Because the number of students was small and we had a lot of time with our supervisors, Bogdan and I got on very well. He was supportive of my efforts in many ways. He was always available when I needed to meet him and he was open and direct with advice and suggestions.

Bogdan was also considerate when I needed a recommendation to the British Council Accounts Office for my numerous visits to the British Newspaper Library in Colindale, North London, where I carried out most of my research work. He always – with a smile and a wink – included a couple more days for my stay in London. Fortunately, the newspaper library was not too far from the Colindale Station which was on the Edgware branch of the underground Northern Line. The library was open Monday to Saturday from 10 a.m. to 5 p.m. and I arrived early so that I could have enough time to identify, order and read the newspapers and items I was looking for. The British Newspaper Library in Colindale provided access to major collections of British and foreign newspapers as well as popular magazines, trade papers and comics.

I registered for a Reader's Pass which gave me admission to the Library Reading Rooms, which were spacious and imposing and, of course, very quiet, so different from that of the University Library in Cardiff. Most items in the library collection were kept in closed stores and had to be ordered to the Reading Rooms. The "Times of Zambia" newspapers, whose foreign pages I analysed, were available only on microfilm and by the time I was finished my eyes were aching from the strain of looking through hazy projected images for hours on end.

My study showed that statistics on PANA's operations were very modest when compared with those of western news agencies. For example, while PANA transmitted 20,000 words a day, AFP transmitted 600,000 and Reuters 800,000 words a day. I was very pleased to observe that from August to December 1986, ZANA, my news agency, was the third highest contributor to PANA. The leader was the Zimbabwe Inter-Africa News Agency while the Agence Zairoise Presse was second.

I also found out that PANA had not accurately quantified the extent to which its services were used in Africa because no scientific study had been carried out. My own study established that African newspapers were using PANA news items but also that the newspapers continued to use a large number of news items originating from AFP and Reuters, as well as several other smaller western news organisations. AFP and Reuters, with their vast resources, were able to collect news and information from many more places than PANA, which mostly relied on the national news agencies whose operations were almost entirely limited to the major African cities.

The conclusions drawn from the study were that PANA was indeed operational, its news items were being used by African newspapers, but that the organisation and its supporting national news agencies needed improved telecommunication facilities, increased funding and more and better trained staff to be able to facilitate the efficient and effective flow of information on and in Africa.

A Zimbabwean colleague, William Bango, and I completed and handed over our dissertations in early July, 1989, but not all the students completed their dissertations on time. A female student from Yemen was unable to submit her dissertation while a male student from China 'mysteriously lost' his work. 'Mysterious' in that the period of submission coincided with the student Tiananmen Square democratic reform demonstration in his home country. We left him behind at the conclusion of the course and we all thought that the incident in his home country may have contributed to the loss of his dissertation, thus giving him time to stay in the UK while the situation in China calmed down.

With three months to go before the end of the course, I applied for a fully funded summer course on 'Britain Today' organised by the English Speaking Union at Jesus College, Oxford University. My time there was equally productive. I was away from Cardiff, my university, familiar faces and in a complete different environment, very peaceful and quiet, with lush green grounds and I was learning new things quite unrelated to my course but useful to my career. I returned to Cardiff at the beginning of August and had a couple of weeks before returning home. Back in Zambia, I received my MA degree certificate by mail, because I could not raise the money to return for the graduation ceremony. Now I had both practical experience and a solid academic qualification and was truly ready for more and higher responsibilities.

At about the time just before I returned home my school authorities asked me whether I wanted to enrol for the PhD programme. I declined because I wanted to get back into active journalism and not enter academia. I never thought the world of teaching or research, which a PhD at that time would have led me to do, was for me. And when I visited the Zambian High Commission offices in London to bid farewell to a friend, General Mike Lisita, who was the Military Attache, most of the staff were surprised that I was returning home.

The economy in Zambia was in a mess, salaries had lost their value, the cost of living had gone up and there were shortages of basic commodities. Many of those, like me, who had the opportunity to study abroad tended to want to stay in those countries after completing their studies. That thought never crossed my mind, then or later, and I was certain that I was unsuited for living abroad, especially in the UK. It was enough to benefit from a superior education system and to enjoy myself while doing so. I also did not like the cold weather or the dampness and I particularly detested wearing many layers of clothing to keep warm.

I had held the position of News Editor for nine years. I had a small wonderful family and was sure that I was now ready to move up the ladder and did not think or feel that remaining in the UK gave me or my family better options or prospects. While I enjoyed my visits to various countries in Africa, Asia, Australia, Europe, Canada or the United States of America and had visited more than 60 countries, some of them more than once, the thought of living abroad was never an option for me. I never felt or wanted to remain or live in any of the places that I went to and spent some time in. For me there was no place like home and home is where I wanted to be and where I wanted to make my contribution.

16. The ZAMCOM project

I spent thirteen years at ZAMCOM - unaware at the time of what that number would mean for me.

The Zambia Institute of Mass Communication became one of the most important media training institutions in Zambia and the Southern African region in the 1990s. The idea for setting it up was born out of a general agreement signed between the government of the Republic of Zambia and the Federal Republic of Germany in June, 1977, during a state visit to that country by Zambia's founding president, Dr. Kenneth Kaunda. During the visit, Germany's foreign minister, Hans-Dietrich Genscher, indicated that cooperation in the field of mass communication training with Zambia would be possible through the FNF, the Friedrich Naumann Foundation, an organ of the Liberal Party. Follow up discussions were held in Lusaka between representatives of the Foundation and those of Zambia's Ministry of National Guidance, Information and Broadcasting Services (as it was then known) leading to the signing of an agreement between the two sides on 7th March, 1980, with Zambia and FNF cooperating in the development and utilisation of Communications media for the benefit of the people of Zambia.

The result of all this was the establishment of ZAMCOM as a government department under the Ministry of National Guidance, Information and

Broadcasting Services. Other departments falling under the jurisdiction of the Ministry were the Zambia News Agency (ZANA), the Zambia Broadcasting Services (ZBS), the Zambia Information Services (ZIS) and the Department of National Guidance. ZANA and ZIS were in 2005 merged into the Zambia News and Information Service (ZANIS) as the sole government information and public relations department.

ZAMCOM was a fledgling department with no premises of its own. It operated from a house in the Rhodespark residential area of Lusaka where the FNF initially secured its own office accommodation. It was almost a briefcase organisation conducting courses, workshops and seminars as need arose in different places hired for the purpose.

A major boost to the plans of developing ZAMCOM came in 1982, when ZBS vacated the old broadcasting house, situated between Independence Avenue and Government Road, premises that had been home to radio and television in Zambia since the late 1950s. When ZBS relocated to the new Mass Media Complex in Alick Nkhata Road, the old structures, which had housed the radio and television studios, were allocated to ZAMCOM, while the administration office block became the headquarters of the Ministry of National Guidance, Information and Broadcasting Services. The Government also offered ZAMCOM an old house on Church Road, within walking distance of the ZAMCOM premises, for conversion into a student hostel, which proved to be a valuable asset.

The old broadcasting premises were not immediately ready for occupation. Apart from the structure being fairly old, when evacuating the premises ZBS employees were rather careless. They pulled out whatever they thought they needed to take along with them without caring about the damage they caused to the building or equipment that they did not want. There was, therefore, need to assess the usefulness of what was left behind. There was also need to renovate and redesign the building to create classrooms and new studio facilities.

The renovations included turning the former ZBS radio studios into an audio and video studio training facility, transforming the old television studios into classrooms and creating an administration area. Work on these renovations was completed in 1988 and the newly-refurbished ZAMCOM was now ready to undertake its training functions. In order to guarantee the smooth running of the Institute, FNF was allocated offices on the ZAMCOM campus. FNF was manned by a project manager, Dr. Rolf Freier, who was the resident representative of the Foundation, a technical advisor, Gert Wurmbach, who supervised the renovation work and later coordinated broadcasting training activities and an integrated expert, Dr. Jaroslav Novotny, whose area of specialisation was photography and development support communication.

The Ministry of National Guidance, Information and Broadcasting Services contributed to the development of the Institute by creating five lecturer positions and providing administrative support staff headed by a director. Initially three lecturer positions were filled but two of the lecturers resigned quite soon over grievances concerning poor conditions of service. The position of director was, over a period of time, held by several individuals seconded from the ministry or its departments. Most of the people who held the position were administrators and were either unsuited for the position or disinterested in the work of the training department. Most training activities during this period were, therefore, carried out with the help of lecturers or media experts from Germany and local trainers from the Department for Continuing Education of the University of Zambia.

17. Mann Sichalwe takes over

The weak staffing position at ZAMCOM persisted until 1985, when Mann Sichalwe, undoubtedly one of Zambia's most talented and proficient broadcasters, took up the directorship of the Institute. Mann had just returned from undertaking a Bachelor of Arts degree programme in the United States (one of the very few people with that level of qualification at the time) and his bosses at ZBS did not know what to do with him or how to utilize his new qualification or knowledge. After presenting news on radio and television for several months the position of director at ZAMCOM fell vacant and he asked to take it up on a departmental transfer.

Obviously, as a way of getting rid of what his bosses regarded as an over-qualified and over-confident member of staff, ZBS management supported his application and the ministry approved the move.

At ZAMCOM, Mann was to pair up with an equally enthusiastic FNF representative, Dr. Rolf Freier, and together they set out to build the new department. However, in trying to develop and establish a true identity for ZAMCOM, Mann and Rolf encountered numerous difficulties. The most serious problem related to the status of the Institute. As early as 1986, Mann began to request for autonomy or what he described in letters to the Ministry as 'an independent body for ZAMCOM'.

The main problem with ZAMCOM operating as a government department was that it was subject to the terms and conditions of the Civil Service. This meant that salaries for the Zambian staff were low while other conditions of service were either poor or non-existent. It was, therefore, difficult to recruit or maintain staff of high calibre. As a result, ZAMCOM was used as a dumping ground for incompetent or troublesome officers from other departments or the ministry headquarters. This situation made it difficult to establish proper institutional structures, policy guidelines, operational procedures or management processes.

There were also problems with defining ZAMCOM's future orientation. Management was not sure whether to concentrate on in-service training or to conduct long-term training such as certificate or diploma programmes. In addition, operating as a government department meant that ZAMCOM was affected by government bureaucratic procedures. A course or workshop could not be conducted without first seeking the approval of the permanent secretary in the parent ministry. It was, therefore, not rare for approval to be given after a course had been completed. There were also many instances in which FNF would advance money for organising a course or workshop, which had to be paid back to FNF when the cheque finally arrived from the ministry.

Despite all these problems, renovation work continued and in early 1987, the FNF representative, Dr. Freier, reported that a sum of 1,509,500 Deutsche Marks had been spent on the project between 1980 and 1986. The money had been used to buy equipment and to pay for courses, seminars, workshops, publications and to meet the fees for local and foreign guest lecturers. Dr. Freier listed the facilities in place at the time as a complete two-colour camera u-matic video studio with editing control and audio insert facilities and portable u-matic and video 8 reporting units. There was a complete two-channel audio studio, two complete mono audio studios and different types of portable audio equipment – all state-of-the art equipment of that time.

There was also a maintenance workshop with mechanical and electronic tools and measuring apparatus, a still photographic darkroom with assorted enlarger units and an automatic processing unit and eight 35mm cameras. There were teaching aids such as sound, slide and overhead projectors, portable typewriters, whiteboards and flipcharts. The library contained about 2,000 titles.

In September, 1987, Dr. Freier again took up with the ministry the problems facing the Institute. This time he was more specific about the type of status required for a new ZAMCOM. In addressing the issue of autonomy, Dr. Freier said: '...It is our opinion that the Institute would immensely benefit if in future it is reconstituted as a statutory body making it meet the requirements of its mission and mandate.' At this stage the issue of autonomy for ZAMCOM still seemed to be far-fetched because the ministry did not appear to be fully committed to the development of the institution.

The direction towards assuming the core function of providing in-service practical training for working journalists was recommended by the Management Services Board (MSB), a training and consulting department operating under Cabinet Office. This followed extensive discussions between Mann Sichalwe and Chief Consultant, Mr. J.E. Kariuki which led to an agreement that the board should assist ZAMCOM in translating the Institute's 'outputs into more systematically organised short and long-term action programmes'. The board advised ZAMCOM to take into account the education and training being provided by other media institutions such as the University of Zambia and the Evelyn Hone College, both in Lusaka and the Africa Literature Centre in Kitwe before deciding how to develop its own training programme. At that time the University of Zambia, through its newly established Department of Mass Communication, was offering a four-year undergraduate programme in Mass Communication, the Evelyn Hone College was providing a three-year diploma course in Journalism, while the Africa Literature Centre offered a one-year diploma course in Journalism.

MSB counsel was: 'Your main thrust, however, will be in the organising of practical training and development opportunities to officers working in the media departments of the Ministry of National Guidance, Information and Broadcasting Services as well as other staff in ministries and organisations involved in adult education, public relations and other activities which have to make use of mass media in their effective operations.' Board Deputy Director, J.P. Msimuko recommended further that: 'You will also be involved in organising various conferences, seminars and meetings to facilitate the exchange of information and knowledge in new media technology and in the provision of consulting services to your clients.'

According to MSB the new ZAMCOM needed to have a legally established governing body and a professional advisory committee. MSB was confident that in the long term ZAMCOM should develop into a financially self-sustaining institution.

18. A new ZAMCOM is born

As preparations for the commissioning of the Institute premises progressed, management was insistent that unless ZAMCOM was given more autonomy, it would not operate effectively and the investment that had been made in refurbishing the campus and purchasing modern equipment would go to waste.

All efforts by Mann Sichalwe and Dr. Freier to bring the matter to the attention of the authorities yielded no positive results. But a unique opportunity to take the issue to the highest authority emerged when confirmation was given that President Kaunda would officiate at the commissioning ceremony of the Institute premises on 25th October, 1989, as part of Zambia's silver jubilee independence celebrations. This was not an opportunity to be missed and Mann Sichalwe took full advantage of the practice prevalent in the Civil Service of asking organisations which were to be honoured with the presence of the president, or any senior government official for that matter, to prepare a draft speech. Even though he hated speech writing, Mann prepared a comprehensive draft outlining the origins and developments of the Institute. He emphasised the substantial investment that had been made by the FNF and the uniqueness of the facilities and institution that had been created. He noted that if ZAMCOM continued to operate as a government department, its operations would grind to a halt when the assistance from FNF was stopped. He was bold enough to suggest a complete transformation for ZAMCOM.

Mann's draft speech went through the hands of bureaucrats at the ministry and finally the president's office at State House without any meaningful alterations being made, either to the basic content or the literary presentation. And so it was that at 10 a.m. on 25th October, 1989, when the President commissioned the new ZAMCOM campus on Government Road, his speech was both in content and substance just as Mann had written it. The most significant part of the speech came midway through the delivery. President Kaunda said, 'Comrade Chairman, I would, therefore, like to be assured that as I commission these buildings, I am launching a new era in the life of ZAMCOM. This era must witness the termination of the project and the transformation of the department into a statutory body...The new ZAMCOM could operate along the lines of the...Management Services Board or the University of Zambia as the case may be by appropriate legislative enactment.' With these words the transformation of ZAMCOM was, indeed, set in motion.

It is important to appreciate that during this period Zambia was a one-party state and that this simple statement by President Kaunda bore the full authority of a presidential decree. That very week the Ministry went into action. A committee was set up to prepare for the transformation of ZAMCOM into a Statutory Board. The committee was divided into several sub-committees, to examine specific issues related to Role and Philosophy, Assets and Liabilities and Finance and Curricula. In my position as news editor at ZANA, I was appointed to serve as a member of the Role and Philosophy Sub-Committee and I participated wholeheartedly in its work.

The main recommendations of the committee formed the basis for a cabinet memorandum prepared in June, 1990, which sought government approval for the establishment of ZAMCOM as a Statutory Board. This approval was given in January, 1991, and a bill was presented to parliament culminating in the enactment of the Zambia Institute of Mass

Communication Act of 1991. The Act, whose date of assent was 28th August, 1992, established ZAMCOM as a Statutory Board.

The amazing thing was that the bill was enacted by one government and assented to by another.

This was because President Kenneth Kaunda and his United National Independence Party which had governed Zambia since it gained political independence in 1964 lost the multiparty presidential and parlimentary elections of 31st October 1992. The Movement for Multiparty Democracy candidate, Frederick Chiluba convincingly won the presidential election with 76 per cent of the votes cast and also won 125 of the 150 seats in Parliament.

19. My transfer to ZAMCOM and back to ZANA

During my stay in the United Kingdom in 1989, I had made up my mind that I would not continue to work for ZANA. I remember vividly how reluctant I felt going to the office of Editor-in-Chief, David Kashweka, and reporting that I had completed my studies and was now ready to return to work. The work atmosphere at ZANA had always been punctuated with an air of hostility. This worsened when I returned from my studies, now better qualified than most other members of staff. It made my work really difficult. I returned recharged, with a lot of good ideas and was eager to discuss them with the editor-in-chief and the editorial board but it could not happen. Everything that I said was vigorously challenged. Nothing that I did seemed right.

I sought an audience with my boss and told him that I did not feel welcome or part of the team. He said I was being over-sensitive and that I would settle down after some time.

I did not settle down at all but, surprisingly, my plans to advance in my profession began to manifest at a remarkable speed. It was much, much later that I came to understand the power of the mind that I had apparently unleashed with my thoughts and plans to further my education and professional prospects. But even when I came to understand how things turned out the way they did, I was still shocked with the speed at which things had surged forward. After all, I was working in a bureaucratic civil service system, where elevation – if it happens at all – happens at a snail's pace. But not for me.

It all started with my friend Mann Sichalwe providing the initial ladder. This was before the directive by President Kaunda to have ZAMCOM turned into a statutory board. Mann Sichalwe's former organisation, ZBS, had just been turned into a corporation, ZNBC, and had offered him the position of director of programmes. He was ready to move and that meant that his position as director at ZAMCOM was going to fall vacant. He suggested that I consider replacing him. I accepted immediately because of the difficulties that I was having at ZANA. However, before Mann could move, President Kaunda's directive at the commissioning of ZAMCOM precipitated significant transformational changes at the Institute. Mann decided to stay on because he preferred to head his own Statutory Board than be subordinate to someone else at ZNBC.

The choice for me was to remain at ZANA as news editor or move to ZAMCOM to take up the vacant position of deputy director. Without hesitation I opted to take up the ZAMCOM post.

I had done all I could have done as a reporter and editor at ZANA and the work was no longer inspiring or exciting. Apart from the hostility of older workmates with whom I worked, journalism practice in Zambia during the one-party state was very challenging because institutional leadership was authoritarian, while political and government leaders were autocratic. All stories were, therefore, carefully selected and edited and largely focused on presenting a good image of the ruling party, UNIP, and its government. On many occasion, as news editor I was required to go the the office of Member of Central Committee in charge of Information and Publicity, Mr. Bob Litana, to explain why certain stories had been written and passed on to the newspapers and ZNBC. The stories which tended to upset the authorities were mainly those about shortages of commodities, and citizens scrambling for basic food items such as bread, cooking oil, mealie meal and sugar whenever and wherever they appeared. Other stories which provoked the wrath of senior party and government officials were about lack of social services in the sprouting shanty townships on the outskirts of cities and towns, or demands for salary increases made by trade union leaders on behalf of their members.

The opportunity to move to the training department even at the level of deputy director was most welcome and as soon as Mann and I agreed what to do, we approached the permanent secretary at the Ministry of Information and Broadcasting Services, Mr. Basil Kawele, and told him about our plans. He liked the idea and suggested that I apply for a departmental transfer through my head of department, the editor-in-chief. I discussed the matter with Mr. Kashweka without giving away too many details and he, somewhat reluctantly, agreed to support my move. My promotion and transfer to ZAMCOM were approved by the Public Service Commission several weeks later. The decision was communicated to me in a letter signed by the new permanent secretary, Mr. Gulfteen Kaira. The effective date of my promotion was 22nd November, 1989, just a month after my return from my studies in the UK.

During the period that I was deputy director at ZAMCOM, Mann and I made a really good team.

We were both committed to proving ourselves and saw ZAMCOM as providing us with the opportunity to do so. We planned enthusiastically and were idealistic about how to develop the Institute into a key media training centre. The planning discussions happened anywhere at any time. Sometimes we discussed ideas in Mann's office upstairs. At other times, we played around with ideas in my office downstairs. We toyed around with different scenarios while walking around the classrooms, or when strolling along the corridors, or outside in the grounds. We were both eager and passionate and never ran out of ideas. Mann's strengths lay in broadcasting and mine in print journalism and so we developed a training programme covering both areas of specialisation and everything was looking up.

Things seemed to be going really well especially when, just after some weeks into my new job, I was sent to the National Institute of Public Administration (NIPA) to attend a Senior Management Development Programme organised by the Government Planning and Management Improvement Project. The course was directed by Brendan Glynn and Brendan O'Driscoll from the Institute of Public Administration of Ireland (IPA). Special presentations were delivered by senior government personnel and other specialists.

The course was attended by district executive secretaries, deputy directors, assistant secretaries and other technical staff at similar levels. Subjects covered included management and administration, models of public service management, environmental analysis, organisational theory and structure, leadership and team building. I could not have asked for better preparation as I took up my new position and responsibilities at ZAMCOM.

Unfortunately, I was only able to use ideas from the course for a period of one year because on 26th December, 1990, I received a letter from the new permanent secretary, Bridget Mwanakaoma, transferring me back to ZANA as deputy editor-in-chief, effective 17th December, 1990, as part of a government media reorganisation exercise. Editor-in-Chief, David Kashweka, had been transferred to the Ministry of Education as deputy permanent secretary and his deputy, Simon Sikalele, was made to act in the position of editor-in-chief. My new position of deputy editor-in-chief was at the rank of assistant secretary in the civil service and at the same level with that of director at ZAMCOM.

Mann was not amused by this decision. After all the planning that we had carried out together there was need to move ahead and he needed my support and involvement, particularly in overseeing the training programme, while he continued to lobby government to see through the process of realising ZAMCOM's autonomy. But, being the good friend that he was, he understood that my transfer was important for my career development and so I returned to ZANA with his good wishes.

Sadly, the process of transforming ZAMCOM into a statutory board was marred by tragedy; Mann Sichalwe, the man who had worked tirelessly and ingeniously to bring about the remarkable transformation of ZAMCOM, was not there to witness this momentuous occasion. While the Zambia Institute of Mass Communication Act of 1991, which established ZAMCOM as a statutory board, was assented to by the new president of Zambia, Frederick Chiluba, on 28th August 1991, Mann had tragically died in a road traffic accident outside Kafue, south of Lusaka a year earlier, on 29th August, 1990. He was returning from Livingstone, where he had been conducting a ZAMCOM workshop, when his vehicle overturned, robbing the Institute and Zambia of one of its most illustrious broadcasters.

Mann Sichalwe had been a personal friend for many years. His untimely death affected me greatly. Apart from having been a very close friend, Mann had been so talented and had had so much to live for and had deserved much more from life. He was one of those people who were truly talented. He was what in broadcasting terms is referred to as 'a broadcasters' broadcaster'. He had a rich, deep, resonant voice and a sincere, warm personality. News of his death left me – and the nation – stunned.

20. Leadership at ZANA

My return to ZANA sent shock waves through the senior staff ranks. Amazingly, I had risen above the three editors who had previously been at the same rank with me: News Editor, Blake Sichone, Chief Sub-Editor, Henry Chilufya and Principal Editor, Jameson Chifunda. I ignored their sulky faces and got on with my work. At least the reporters and other junior employees were excited about my return.

I spent some time helping to build the confidence of the staff and encouraging closer coordination between the departments. Within six months ZANA's acting editor-in-chief, Simon Sikalele retired from government service and I took over from him. Less than two years after returning from Cardiff, I had attained the highest position in the organisation.

I remember the day I moved into the editor-in-chief's office. It was just over seventeen years after I had walked into ZANA's Kitwe office to start work as a junior reporter. And now, at age thirty-eight I was in charge, albeit briefly, of the national news agency, which at that time was the major news and information collection and distributing organisation in Zambia. My first act, when I sat in the editor-in-chief's chair, was to look around the office wondering what it was that made most of the previous occupants of the office behave as if they were omnipotent and that nobody else mattered. From the time that I started going for meetings with previous editors-in-chief, I knew that I did not particularly like the office.

Even the furniture was unwelcoming. But what always displeased me most was the atmosphere and conduct of editorial meetings, which took place around the boardroom table. Editorial meetings were like funeral wakes. There were so many grey heads among the elderly editors who sat around at the beginning of the work day and late afternoon, ostensibly to plan and review the performance of the organisation. The most senior editor for each desk reported on what his or her desk was doing or had done as if by rote.

In the mornings, the news editor would give the number of stories covered by the reporters the previous day, then some generalised ideas about the stories that the reporters were following up. In the afternoons he would report on how the stories were developing or had been dealt with. I remember how one day I took everyone by surprise when I asked what the impact of ZANA stories was in the columns of that morning's newspapers. I wanted to know how many of the stories transmitted to the subscribers had ended up in print. The news editor had no idea and there was silence around the table. It was exactly the same with the chief sub-editor, who was responsible for foreign news. He would give to the meeting the number of foreign stories that had been sent to the national broadcasting station and newspapers each day but gave no indication of how many of these stories were used in radio or television news bulletins or by the newspapers. Nobody seemed to care.

I changed all that when I became editor-in-chief. I changed the approach to the editorial meetings so that each editor did not only report about work done but also about how much of the news copy sent out had actually seen its way into news bulletins and newspaper columns. The editors did not like what they saw as additional work but it helped us to have not only a quantitative but qualitative analysis of the work of the news agency. This also meant that editors became much more careful with the type of stories covered by reporters and sent to the subscribers. This was a simple, but very important step in improving the workplace attitude as well as the nature and content of the ZANA news service.

At about this time, I got a breather from the daily drudge of ZANA when the USIS office in Lusaka offered me an opportunity to visit the USA for a month on a US Visitors Programme.

The visit, which included editors from various African countries, took us to media-related institutions in seven states: California, Illinois, Michigan, Minnesota, Tennessee, Washington DC and Washington State. Group visits are all the same. They are characterised by endless walkabouts and generalised speeches. But, what was memorable for me was living with the Mormon family of Mr. and Mrs. Yuan Martial in Sacramento, the state capital of California. There was also the jazz music in Chicago and on Beale Street in Memphis, Tennessee, the melting pot of delta blues, jazz, rock 'n' roll, R&B and gospel music. In Chicago the skyline was dizzying while in Memphis, I was saddened when I saw *the* second-floor balcony at the Lorraine Motel *where Martin Luther King* was shot *dead* on 4th April, 1968.

Upon my return home I tried hard to get things better organised but my stint in the editor-in-chief's office, like that of my predecessor, Simon Sikalele, was short-lived. One incident remains fresh in my mind from my stint in the office of editor-in-chief of ZANA. It was a visit by a senior diplomat of a major Asian country. After the usual courtesies, he said to me, 'Whenever you need anything do not hesitate to ask for help. We assisted your friends in many ways.'

I was shocked but tried not to show it. I knew that I was being offered the possibility of accepting bribes. I never got back to the diplomat although we met a couple of times and exchanged pleasantries at some diplomatic functions.

As I carried on with the work of editor-in-chief I reflected on the fact that I had joined ZANA as an inexperienced twenty-year-old and was now part of the top leadership of media in Zambia. I also noted that the most important lesson that I learned was that one could work with people who he or she did not like at all. What was important was to focus on the work that one needed to perform and to respect everyone for their contribution to the overall output.

PHASE 2

1. Back at ZAMCOM as CEO

The next stage of my life came suddenly. While I was still trying to settle down in the ZANA high office a strange, but not entirely surprising, decision was made by the government. While I was still acting as editor-in-chief of ZANA, the ministry appointed me to act as director of ZAMCOM as well. The thinking was that, with the death of Mann Sichalwe, I was the only senior employee in the ministry who knew what had been going on at the Institute. I accepted the appointment but chose to work from my office at ZANA. The two offices were separated by a distance of about five kilometres. Neither the registrar nor book-keeper at ZAMCOM could make decisions without consulting me, so documents, papers and letters were brought to the ZANA offices for me to approve and sign. In other words I ran two government departments from one office.

In truth, I could not get myself to visit ZAMCOM; I was still in shock over Mann's death. But move to ZAMCOM I had to, because three months later I was appointed as the substantive director. My appointment, on secondment, was formalised by the Public Service Commission and was effective from 1st April, 1992. The secondment was for an initial period of two years and was part of another reshuffle of heads of government media. A former work mate, Villie Lombanya, who had been director of ZIS was appointed editor-in-chief of ZANA. Lombanya had earlier worked at ZANA and had held the position of deputy news editor before he was appointed senior private secretary to the secretary general of the ruling party, UNIP, Humphrey Mulemba. Several years later he returned to ZANA and was given the position of principal editor before he was appointed director of ZIS. His position at ZIS was taken over by Benson Sianga, who had been assistant secretary at the ministry headquarters.

My stint at the helm of ZANA was too short for me to have made any real meaningful contribution. I had merely started making the initial efforts that were intended to address the organisational structural issues and strengthen editorial functions. Perhaps, it was just as well that I did not stay long. I doubt very much if the hostile and negative atmosphere would have changed or improved. Confirmation that most of the senior people at ZANA were happy to see me go came from the fact that no traditional farewell function or party was organised for me after working there for seventeen years. Regardless, I was happy to know that I was out of ZANA for good this time and willingly left for ZAMCOM, for the second time.

I remember feeling quite queasy about showing up there, but when I did, I took time to meet the employees and staff of ZAMCOM and FNF in their offices. Eventually, of course, I had to go to Mann's office – my new office. I remembered it well because I had spent so much time there while working as deputy director or visiting him. I walked in slowly but could not get myself to sit down at 'his' desk on that first day. Over the following days and weeks, the situation improved, albeit, slowly. For a long time, though, Mann's presence remained very pervasive. I felt his presence everywhere I went, both inside and around the Institute premises. Everywhere where we had been together walking and talking, planning for ZAMCOM's future.

My attitude and conviction greatly improved when it struck me that if there was anyone Mann would have wanted to take over from him, it was definitely me.

2. From government department to statutory board, the initial steps

I moved to ZAMCOM as director a few days before my thirty-ninth birthday and as soon as I had settled down I immersed myself fully in work aimed at finalising arrangements for the transformation of the Institute from a government department to a statutory board. The major advantages of operating as a statutory board would be that while receiving an annual grant from the government, through the ministry, ZAMCOM would now be able to charge fees and retain the money for its own use.

In spite of the excitement generated by the passing by parliament of the Zambia Institute of Mass Communication Act of 1991, the transformation from government department to statutory board was rather slow; the process took eight months. The Act was passed and assented to in August, 1991, but it was not until April, 1992, that the Statutory Board formally came into existence. As soon as the bill was passed in parliament arrangements began for selecting members of the board or Governing Council as it was referred to in the Act.

The Governing Council of the new ZAMCOM comprised mostly people who were heads of media or media-related institutions. They were appointed by the Ministry of Information and Broadcasting Services in February 1992 and were drawn from the print and broadcast media, a publishing house, a journalism training institution and included a private businessman and the permanent secretary of the Ministry of Information and Broadcasting Services. The first council comprised of Permanent Secretary, Josephine Mapoma, who was the chairperson, Head of Department of Mass Communications at the University of Zambia, Professor Francis Kasoma, Acting Director General of ZNBC, Emmanuel Chayi. Others were Acting Executive Director of Multimedia Zambia, Jumbe Ngoma, Acting Managing Editor of the Mining Mirror Newspaper, Hammington Lintini and Resident Representative of Friedrich Naumann Foundation, Hartmut Giering. (Giering took over from Rolf Freier who had been reassigned to the FNF office in South Africa) and Lusaka businessman, Colonel Brightwell Banda, rtd. Ms Mapoma was later replaced by Laurah Harrison, Hammington Lintini by John Musukuma and Emmanuel Chayi by Duncan Mbazima.

The decision to draw members from media and media-related institutions was made deliberately to avoid getting government stooges or political acolytes on the board. But while the thinking behind the idea was good there were issues of conflict of interest that arose as soon as the council began to carry out its work. The first problem that arose related to council members seemingly unwilling to pay ZAMCOM workers higher salaries than those paid to their own employees. As one member bluntly put it, 'Why should ZAMCOM employees get more money than their counterparts on the newspapers or ZNBC?' Discussions over conditions of service became protracted and in the end meetings were held at the Ministry of Information and Broadcasting Services from which I, as director, and my management accountant were excluded while an accountant from the Zambia Daily Mail newspaper was brought in to work on the salary figures.

The resulting salaries and conditions of service had nothing to do with what ZAMCOM was about or the intended purpose for transforming the organisation. The truth was that the salaries and conditions were not attractive enough to attract staff of high calibre. For instance the Governing Council could also not agree on what type of car should be bought for the director. The matter took so long to resolve that I ended up buying my own vehicle, a Toyota Cressida, which I used for both my personal and business activities. I accepted the not-so-good conditions of service for me and my staff in order to get on with work but asked for a review in a year's time when, I assured members of the Governing Council, the financial situation at ZAMCOM would be much, much better. With that said work commenced and the first meeting formalised my appointment as director from 1st March 1992. The council also approved a new organisational structure and appointed Thewo and Company, a leading Zambian auditing firm, as institute auditors.

That I kept my promise of generating sufficient income for the Institute was evidenced by the fact that my conditions of service later provided me with a new vehicle, payment of my children's school fees at one of Zambia's best secondary schools, Chengelo Boarding School, a two-week fully paid annual family holiday and other conditions of service similar to those of chief executives in the ZIMCO group of parastatal companies. Meanwhile, the introduction of a new organisational chart and revised conditions of service meant that a decision had to be made about which employees would be retained by the new ZAMCOM. Those whose services were not required were either sent back to the ministry or declared redundant. Senior employees, numbering seven, were seconded to the Statutory Board for an initial period of two years. This group included myself and the German non-pensionable expatriate officer, Jerry Novotny. Those who were surrendered to the ministry, together with their posts, included a library officer, stenographer and a clerical officer. Eight daily classified employees, comprising cleaners and office orderlies, were declared redundant.

Of course, this decision created disharmony between myself and some ministry staff and the animosity continued through the various phases of ZAMCOM's development. The feelings of hostility were heightened when

I took the decision to physically separate the ZAMCOM premises from the building which housed the ministry headquarters. Since the ministry offices and ZAMCOM campus had all previously belonged to the broadcasting station, ZBS; they were on one plot together with EBS, the Educational Broadcasting Service. In order to begin the process of creating a separate identity for ZAMCOM, I felt that it was important that its premises be separated from those of the Ministry and EBS. So I arranged for a fence to be erected to create an independent ZAMCOM campus.

As I began to settle down at ZAMCOM a great opportunity to learn about radio and media training came through Radio Production and Training of Trainers courses offered by the BBC Radio Training Centre at Grafton House in London in November, 1992, and I enjoyed both thoroughly. The Radio Production Course truly introduced me to radio – very good radio. There was a lot of practical work involving sound recording, interviews and live broadcasts. Particularly fascinating for me was the way sound was used in programmes. The most exciting exercise was a practical live broadcast that took place outside Buckingham Palace during the changing of the guard ceremony.

The Training of Trainers Course was very challenging. Each of the participants had two practical training sessions. Our trainer, Anne Spalding, said in her report, 'Mike has a very polished training style which ensures he comes across as an authoritative professional. His two practical training sessions were well-prepared and well-structured with clear training objectives.' She added, 'Mike's enthusiasm and knowledge of his subject area were very evident in his sessions and I believe that whenever he has the opportunity to take some training events, he will be accepted as an expert and someone from whom his students can learn a great deal.' As I had hoped, the BBC training helped me with the process of converting from an active journalist to a media trainer.

3. Retirement from government

Because my secondment to the new ZAMCOM was for a period of two years only, I needed to choose between returning to ZANA and the

Civil Service or take early retirement and continue to work at the Institute. My choice was clear. I was not scared of retirement, nor deluded by the false sense of security that is generally, but erroneously, associated with Civil Service jobs. I was also strongly against returning either to ZANA and its culture of conflict or to the politically overburdened Ministry of Information and Broadcasting Services.

I had a taste for working in a less constricting environment but, more importantly, was confident in my capacity to grow the Institute and create stability for myself and the staff. Although my secondment to ZAMCOM continued to 1st April, 1994, I wrote to the ministry on 2nd July, 1993, requesting early retirement from the Civil Service with effect from 1st October, 1993. I did not see the point of waiting for the secondment period to run the full length before making up my mind about what I needed to do. In those days civil servants could request for early retirement after a period of unbroken service of twenty years and I had served the government for twenty-one years, seventeen of these in various positions at ZANA and the other four at ZAMCOM.

But a letter from Permanent Secretary, Josephine Mapoma on what should happen at ZAMCOM after my retirement indicated that some council members had other ideas. She wrote, 'Since your secondment to ZAMCOM and subsequent appointment to the position of Director remains in effect until 1st April 1994, I suggest that we use this time to review the recruitment procedures pertaining to the posts of Director and Deputy Director.' She added, 'Kindly, therefore, furnish my office with a report on how you propose the two posts should be filled upon the expiration of your contract next year.' Ms Mapoma concluded with, 'Please note that in line with declared government policy on statutory bodies, the Council may in future wish to advertise the two posts, to which you will be perfectly entitled to respond.' I responded the next day, reminding her that the Council had interviewed me and appointed me director of the new ZAMCOM on 2nd June, 1992, and that following my retirement I wished to continue serving as director but on contract terms.

On 12th January, 1994, I received a letter from the permanent secretary in which she informed me that the Public Service Commission had directed that, 'you be deemed to have been permitted to retire from the

Civil Service with effect from 31st December 1993'.

I was asked to submit pension papers as soon as possible so that arrangements could be made for the calculation of my retirement benefits.

'May I on behalf of this Ministry and, indeed, on my own behalf take this opportunity to thank you most sincerely for the able manner in which you rendered your services to the Government during the last twenty one (21) years unbroken service and wish you well for the future.' Ms Mapoma wrote. The letter was copied to the permanent secretary, Establishment Division, permanent secretary, Ministry of Finance, the auditor general and the secretary, Civil Service (Local Conditions) Pensions Fund.

With those words and at just forty-one years old, my work for the government and career in the Civil Service came to an end on 31st December, 1993. It was, without doubt, the most important decision I had taken up to that stage of my working life. My pension from twenty-one years of government service was the princely sum of K15,975,796.82 (about US$23,700) and I received it on 13th May, 1994, five months after my retirement. I did not publicise the news about my retirement from the government or the fact that I had been paid my pension and most people, including my staff, did not know that I had retired from the civil service to work at ZAMCOM on contract. I was still young, had a good job and a nice sum of money. I could have gone crazy, as many retirees in Zambia tend to do. I could have bought a car or splashed the money around to impress my friends and women or girls. I did not do any of those things. I actually benefitted from an unplanned outcome of the training that was taking place at ZAMCOM. Many outstanding financial and business experts were explaining to the journalists the policies and economic measures that the new government had introduced in the country. I listened intently and did what most journalists do not do – instead of focusing on how to write the news stories and produce programmes from what was being told to the journalists, I decided to try out some of the government's promising ideas and measures. For example, through my bank, I made arrangements to invest nearly all of my pension money in Bank of Zambia Treasury Bills. Apparently the price decontrol measures put in place by the new MMD government, as part of the 1992-93 economic reforms, had raised the Treasury Bill interest rate to over 100 per cent.

Flush with the gains that I made I proceeded to build a house in Chalala residential area. I was among the first people to start building houses in this newly established neighbourhood on the south-east side of Lusaka. The construction of the house was a very exacting exercise because there were no access roads, nor water despite the high service charges imposed by the Lusaka City Council on developers of this new residential area. Through toil and hardship I managed to get the house to reach roof level whereupon I sold it to an employee of the Bank of Zambia for K60 million (an increase in value of over 300 per cent from my pension amount within a period of about five years).

I later proceeded to make investments in Chilanga Cement (later renamed Lafarge Cement Zambia), Standard Chartered Bank and Zambian Breweries Limited through the Lusaka Stock Exchange. I also opened a dollar account to safeguard the value of my money against the depreciation of the Zambian Kwacha.

With my money and financial future thus nicely secured, I carried on with my work at ZAMCOM in the same position but now on contract – as of 13th January, 1994. I was ready to start taking some tough decisions and I did so without shirking my responsibilities but – as always seemed to be the case – at the risk of upsetting some people and attracting animosity.

4. ZAMCOM and FNF relations end

One of my earliest tasks was to sort out the relationship between ZAMCOM and FNF. Cooperation between the new ZAMCOM and FNF continued until 1994, when it was mutually agreed to terminate the agreement. ZAMCOM was no longer a project and FNF's role was becoming superfluous. In the beginning the role of FNF was very clear, helping to reconstruct the buildings, purchase equipment for the studios and provide teaching aids. FNF also made most of the arrangements for organising courses and workshops and hired the trainers. Costing and budgeting for courses and workshops was carried out by FNF staff and ZAMCOM management and staff were not privy to this process. Initially this arrangement had worked well because ZAMCOM staff handled very

ZAMCOM and FNF relations end

little money apart from their own salaries which they received individually through the government system. The little money that was earned by ZAMCOM through fees was handed over to the ministry to be remitted to the Ministry of Finance as government revenue.

The situation changed dramatically with the establishment of ZAMCOM as a statutory board. ZAMCOM had to prepare its own budget and so I enquired of FNF what their contribution to the budget was going to be. This upset the new FNF Director, Hartmut Giering. He preferred that his organisation continue to directly meet the costs of hosting the workshops that it was responsible for. He informed me that FNF could not contribute cash to the ZAMCOM budget and neither could it pay for using the facilities it had helped to refurbish, or had bought.

My position was that you cannot give birth to a baby and then undermine its growth and development, so I suggested that we discontinue the relationship and seek other ways to cooperate. I convinced the permanent secretary and the other board members that this was the most realistic way of ensuring ZAMCOM's future development. Giering grudgingly accepted this situation and in June, 1994, reluctantly wrote to the permanent secretary giving six months notice for terminating the Agreement. The notice was in accordance with Article VII of the Agreement which stated that '...the Agreement may be terminated on 30th June or 31st December of any calendar year by either party giving six months prior notice...'

Following the termination of the Agreement Giering wanted FNF to continue operating from the ZAMCOM premises. I felt this was not a good idea because I wanted ZAMCOM to create a new independent image, not least because many people attributed everything at the Institute, including the training that was taking place and even the clean surroundings, to the presence of FNF, the Germans. I was convinced that ZAMCOM needed to develop other partnerships if it was to expand its training programme and broaden its activities so I gave FNF four months in which to find alternative accommodation. At the end of that time they moved their office but they were in operation for only one year after leaving the ZAMCOM campus.

As part of its reorganisation FNF closed all its offices in Southern Africa except for the one in Johannesburg, South Africa. Dr. Freier, former

Resident Representative in Zambia, became the Regional Representative and was able to oversee the closure of the Zambian office at the end of 1995. Impressed with developments that had taken place at the Institute since it became a statutory board, he directed that most of the equipment belonging to the FNF office in Zambia be donated to ZAMCOM. This included a microbus, BMW car and computers.

I remember how uncomfortable I felt when I drove around in the BMW. In Lusaka, in those days, BMWs were mostly associated with people who were thought to be drug dealers. I soon convinced the board that it would be best to sell the car and we did.

5. Creation of an independent, self-financing educational trust

When enacting the Zambia Institute of Mass Communication Act of 1991, members of parliament had cautioned against dependence on donors, but the transformation of ZAMCOM from a statutory board into an independent self-financing educational trust, could not have been possible had it not been for the support received from USAID. That ZAMCOM became a major recipient of USAID support was accidental. It happened that the Institute gained its partial autonomy by becoming a statutory board about the same time that the country was holding its 1991 multiparty elections. The nature and results of the elections, as well as the smooth transfer of power from Dr. Kenneth Kaunda and UNIP to Mr. Frederick Chiluba and MMD, attracted international attention to Zambia which translated into development support programmes, one of which was USAID's Democratic Governance Project.

The US$4.5 million Zambia Democratic Governance Project was one of the first major USAID democratic governance initiatives in Africa. According to USAID, in 1992 the agency's strategy and capacity for this kind of work was formative and the programme was designed as a flexible 'learning process approach tailored to the pioneering nature of the initiative'. The project was a five-year programme and had five components, Civic Education, Constitutional Reform, Legislative Performance, Media

Independence and Policy Coordination.

The Civic Education component provided institutional support to FODEP in carrying out a nationwide civic education campaign. Under the component a Civic Action Fund was established which gave small grants to NGOs. The component also supported the preparation of a new civics education curriculum and text books for government secondary schools.

The Constitutional Reform component supported the work of the Constitutional Review Commission which was appointed by President Chiluba in October, 1993. Under this component the project provided funds for the inaugural meeting of the commission, the establishment of the commission secretariat and the costs of printing and disseminating the constitution.

Legislative Performance was intended to enhance the effectiveness of the National Assembly. In the first phase, a Legislative Performance Studies Group within parliament was to prepare recommendations for institutional reform for adoption by the Office of the Speaker. If these reforms were accepted, a second phase was to provide support for National Assembly staffing, library and publications and for a legal drafting fund. However, this component did not happen because the speaker of the National Assembly, Mr. Robinson Nabulyato, was said to have been dissatisfied with the project objectives.

The Policy Coordination component facilitated the creation of a Policy Analysis and Coordination Division at Cabinet Office by providing short-term technical assistance, training workshops, study tours and computer equipment. The purpose of the division was to improve the analytical quality of cabinet memoranda and minutes and to monitor the implementation of cabinet decisions in line ministries.

The Media Independence component supported independent and professional journalism by funding policy studies, short- and long-term training for media specialists. Although ZAMCOM became a major beneficiary under this component, the Institute was not targeted at the outset. Research officials who carried out the initial survey to identify possible project partners had thought of collaborating with PAZA. However, after discussions with various organisations and after visiting

ZAMCOM, the researchers decided to locate most of the component activities at the Institute and the Department of Mass Communcation at the University of Zambia.

The overall project was given legal status through a broad Project Grant Agreement signed between the governments of the Republic of Zambia and the United States of America on 28th September, 1992. Deputy Minister of Planning and Development Cooperation, Dean Mung'omba signed on behalf of the Zambian Government and USAID Zambia Mission Director, Fred Winch signed for the US Government. Separate memoranda of understanding were also signed to pave the way for the implementation of activities of the various components.

The media component MoU was signed on 7th May, 1993, by Minister of Information and Broadcasting Services, Dr. Remmy Mushota and USAID Director, Mr. Fred Winch and the objective of the component was 'to promote freedom of the press and the development of a free and independent media in Zambia'. USAID, however, made a proviso referred to as 'condition precedent'. This read as follows: 'Upon presentation of evidence, satisfactory to AID, that applicable legislation, regulations and provisions, have been changed, altered or amended so as to afford the Zambia Institute of Mass Communication (ZAMCOM) the level of independence and autonomy from government control necessary to successfully achieve the objectives of the Media Independence Project Component, an MoU with ZAMCOM will be executed...'.

I felt that the Media Component of the Democratic Governance Project was God sent because operating ZAMCOM as a statutory board under the Ministry of Information and Broadcasting Services was frustrated by the constant need to explain things to senior officials such as the minister or deputy minister, the permanent secretary and all sorts of other middle level officials.

I was also frustrated by the declining amounts of money grants received from the government each year despite all the convincing reasons that I and my officials gave to justify the money to be allocated annually for ZAMCOM's training programme. In 1992, the government grant to ZAMCOM was K31.4 million (US$340,000). Over the next two years it was K68.5 million (US$185,000) and K102.9 million (US$159,000)

Creation of an independent, self-financing educational trust

respectively. The decline was not evident in terms of the amount allocated in the Zambian currency, but with the depreciation of the value of the Kwacha these amounts had much less value against the US currency. In 1995, the allocation dropped to K72.9 million (US$105,000) and by 1996, when ZAMCOM was becoming an independent Educational Trust, it was K66.5 million (US$67,000). Under the system of Cash Budget introduced by the new MMD government this meant a monthly allocation of less than K6 million (US$6,000). Not a lot of money but welcome, nonetheless, as a contribution towards meeting the bill for the increased salaries and other operational costs.

Much more income was being raised internally from course fees and production activities in the radio and television studios. In 1995, the government grant was twenty per cent of the Institute's income while by June, 1996, when ZAMCOM was preparing for transformation into a self-financing educational trust, the government grant was a mere eight per cent of the Institute's total income. That the Institute was now in a position to raise more money than it received from the government gave me the confidence to believe that ZAMCOM could go it alone.

I was aware that my quest for complete autonomy was supported by government policy and action in its early years in office. After winning the 1991 multiparty elections, MMD had declared its intention to make the media sector more independent of government. This was in line with the government's commitment, at that time, to greater democracy and more open government. The need to restructure government media was also in conformity with the programme of privatisation of state or parastatal companies.

I was also aware that in March, 1992, the Zambia Privatisation Agency had commissioned a study on the Privatisation and Commercialisation of State-Owned Media and Printing Companies. Coopers and Lybrand, who carried out the study in July 1993, recommended that the state should, through the Ministry of Finance and the Ministry of Information and Broadcasting Services retain control of ZNBC, Zambia Daily Mail and the web offset printing press of the Zambia Printing Company. Coopers and Lybrand further recommended that the government should privatise the Times of Zambia and its printing company, Printpak. Other recommendations were that ZANA should be wound up and reconstituted as a much smaller organisation which would be jointly owned by all media organisations. It was recommended also that ZIS should remain a department of the Ministry but that ZAMCOM should become a public trust.

This thrust towards privatisation and commercialisation of the government-owned media was driven by then Minister of Information and Broadcasting Services, Dipak Patel. However, shortly after the report was presented to the Ministry of Information and Broadcasting Services, Patel was reassigned to another ministry. His replacement was Dr. Remmy Mushota with whom I took up the recommendation to turn ZAMCOM into a trust and proceeded with efforts to gain complete autonomy.

After obtaining the approval of ZAMCOM's Governing Council in March 1992, I initiated communication with the Ministry of Information and Broadcasting Services and the Ministry of Finance. The first positive response from the government came through a letter dated 29th March, 1993. It was signed by Acting Permanent Secretary in the Ministry of Information, Mr. Martin Luo, who confirmed that the ministry had accepted plans to hive off the Institute which had hitherto been functioning as a statutory board under the ministry so that it could be turned into an independent body. He said the minister was soon scheduled to make this recommendation to the Cabinet Committee on Information and Broadcasting Services for a decision.

To facilitate the process, I was asked to provide a write-up on the future vision of ZAMCOM as an independent body. I was asked to provide information on how much funding the trust would require from the outset, opportunities for other sources of income, employment levels and the financial status of ZAMCOM. I provided the information promptly.

Five days later I received another letter asking for additional information on procedures to be followed in the delinkage process and creation of the new entity. I was also asked to provide more information on employees still in government service and the estimated total redundancy package needed to retire them. Again I provided the information as quickly as I could.

In July, the Ministry of Finance appointed a full Board of Survey to value all the assets. The Board of Survey completed its work in February, 1994, and put the value of the Institute moveable assets at K303.7

Creation of an independent, self-financing educational trust

million (US$471,000) and that of land and buildings at K229.7 million (US$356,000), giving a total value of K533.4 million (US$827,000). After the valuation of the assets, a decision was needed to determine under what conditions the assets were going to be transferred from the government to ZAMCOM. The Ministry of Finance, in a letter signed by Mr. M.L. Sabhlok, posed this question to the Ministry of Information and Broadcasting Services. The permanent secretary in the Ministry of Information and Broadcasting Services asked me to explain how the assets should be transferred to the Institute. My explanation pointed out that since ZAMCOM was to be turned into a non-profit making educational trust, the only reasonable option was to transfer the assets to the Governing Council as a grant. I explained that although the assets would be transferred to the Institute, the Governing Council was going to hold them in trust for the public. I said it would be the responsibility of the Governing Council to ensure that the assets were utilised in the public interest and for the purposes they were intended. I reminded the permanent secretary that government assets had been transferred under similar arrangements from ZIMCO to ZAMIM and from ZSIC to the Zambia Insurance Business College. ZAMIM and the Zambia Insurance Business College were both operating as educational trusts.

Shortly after, the ministry accepted the idea of transferring the assets as a grant and proceeded to prepare a draft 'Cabinet Memorandum for the Delinkage of ZAMCOM from the Government'. I was asked to provide information towards the preparation of the memorandum highlighting financial and political implications of the delinkage as well as benefits to other government ministries.

In my explanation I gave a breakdown of the annual operational grants that ZAMCOM had received from the government since it became a statutory board. The total amount was K275.7 million (US$789,000). I pointed out that as an educational trust, ZAMCOM would no longer receive any grants from the government. I said ZAMCOM's training and broadcasting equipment was more than ten years old and required replacing. I reminded the ministry that the government was at that time upgrading equipment for ZNBC and ZIS, the Institute's biggest clients. This, I went on to argue, would render ZAMCOM's equipment obsolete.

'If the Institute is not turned into an Education Trust, the Government would need to invest in new equipment which would cost in excess of K1 billion ($1,452,000),' I wrote. I explained that other ministries would benefit from the new ZAMCOM in several ways, among them, training, implementation and evaluation of information campaigns and use of conference and broadcasting facilities at reasonable cost. I also addressed the issue of political implications for the delinkage of ZAMCOM. I declared that delinking ZAMCOM from the government would have very positive political implications, particularly at a time when the subject of press freedom was under active debate in the country. 'By delinking ZAMCOM, the government will underline its commitment to the programme of media privatisation,' I stressed.

On 1st June, 1995, the permanent secretary indicated in a letter that '… The Ministry is willing to delink ZAMCOM from the Government and is working on technicalities to that effect.'

Two weeks later I received a letter from the Ministry of Information and Broadcasting Services which said that following initial consultations with Cabinet Office, the ministry had been directed that ZAMCOM prepares a survival plan to accompany the cabinet memorandum.

The plan was to state clearly how the organisation would operate after delinkage, if donor support was withheld, withdrawn or not forthcoming. This was done promptly.

In November, the Ministry of Finance reconvened the Board of Survey to revalue the assets of the Institute. The Board of Survey report indicated that the values of the assets had all risen slightly. The value of moveable assets was put at K362.5 million (US$382,000), that of Institute buildings at K360 million (US$380,000), the hostel at K70 million (US$74,000) giving a total of K792.5 million (US$836,000). After presentation of the report, the Ministry of Finance authorised the transfer of the assets to the Institute. The Handing and Taking Over documents were signed the very next day. I signed on behalf of ZAMCOM while Acting Permanent Secretary, Mr. Milton Chalimbana signed for the Ministry of Information and Broadcasting Services.

The transfer of assets to the new ZAMCOM as a grant was a fillip to the educational trust that was to be established. However, I would have appreciated if the Institute liabilities were also offset. I had mentioned this, in passing, to Minister of Finance, Ronald Penza, who frankly told me that pursuing the matter of liabilities would simply delay or frustrate the whole question of delinkage. So I ignored the question of liabilities although I knew that the new educational trust would start operations weighed down by outstanding commitments of the statutory board and the government department.

6. Work towards creating a trust continues

On 20th November, 1995, a letter from the permanent secretary, which I had been waiting for, arrived on my desk. It said that cabinet considered a recommendation by the minister of Information and Broadcasting Services on the delinkage of ZAMCOM from government. It added that cabinet had accepted the recommendation that ZAMCOM be delinked from the government and turned into an educational trust. The letter explained that government's assets would be transferred to ZAMCOM as a grant and that the Zambia Institute of Mass Communication Act, No. 9 of 1991 be amended to incorporate the creation of a trust. The permanent secretary's letter concluded, 'You are, therefore, hereby directed to implement this Cabinet decision and report progress on the matter in due course. I am also making legal consultations with the Ministry of Legal Affairs on the same.' I scribbled "Great News!" on the letter before sending it to my secretary, Ms. Bridget Nkonde, for filing.

Despite this progress, legal consultations between the Ministry of Information and Broadcasting Services and the Ministry of Legal Affairs were not going as quickly as I had hoped. There was confusion about what role government was to play in the two tasks that needed to be carried out. The first task was to wind up the Statutory Board by amending the Zambia Institute of Mass Communication Act of 1991.

The second task was to set up the educational trust. ZAMCOM engaged the services of Lusaka lawyer, Mrs. Josephine Nyirongo of Aquar Chambers to assist with these legal tasks. Mrs. Nyirongo immediately took up the matter with the Ministry of Legal Affairs by having an audience with the draughtsman responsible for drawing up the repeal bill, Mr. Aven Muvwende.

I too met with Mr. Muvwende, as well as with Chief Draughtsman, Mrs. Eva Jhala and Attorney General, Mr. George Chilupe to clarify the procedures to be followed. I was told that the Cabinet Legislation Committee comprising about eight ministers needed to approve the draft bill before it was tabled before a full cabinet meeting. I was also told that the minister of Legal Affairs was the only person who could include the ZAMCOM draft bill on the agenda of the next meeting which was due to be held in a week's time. The minister of Legal Affairs was Dr. Remmy Mushota, whom I had dealt with when he was minister for Information and Broadcasting Services. So I had no problem telephoning him and explaining my predicament. He was most understanding, especially as he had known about the plans for transforming ZAMCOM while he was still at the Ministry of Information and Broadcasting Services. True to his word, Dr. Mushota ensured that the Zambia Institute of Mass Communication Draft Repeal Bill was included on the agenda for the Cabinet Legislation Committee December meeting. The Ministry of Information and Broadcasting Services was taken unawares by this development but the minister, Hon. Amusaa Mwanamwambwa, a real gentleman and perhaps not quite your typical Zambian politician, did not question or raise an issue about how the draft bill had found itself on the meeting's agenda but merely asked me to accompany him to the meeting. In the chair was Dr. Mushota. Those in attendance included Attorney General, George Chilupe and several ministers: Newstead Zimba, Community Development; William Harrington, Environment and Natural Resources; Kabunda Kayongo, Science, Technology and Vocational Training; Chitalu Sampa, Defence; Simon Zukas, Works and Supply and Hon. Mwanamwambwa. There were no issues of concern to the Cabinet Legislative Committee and the draft bill was approved without much ado.

Later that year at the Institute's Annual General Meeting, Minister Mwanamwambwa pointed out that the AGM marked the end of the life of ZAMCOM as it had been constituted over the previous five years. He said the AGM also paved the way for the establishment of a new ZAMCOM which would operate as an independent educational trust. He noted that over the past five years ZAMCOM had steadily registered growth in terms of activities, income as well as assets. 'ZAMCOM's success is most remarkable when you consider the fact that, in only five years, the Institute has developed from a small government department to a recognised regional media training institution.' Hon. Mwanamwambwa explained. He said that as the minister, who had been overseeing the transformation of ZAMCOM, he was convinced that the Institute had met all the conditions for attaining autonomy.

Hon Mwanamwabwa proceeded to dissolve ZAMCOM's Governing Council in readiness for the creation of the Educational Trust. He said he would proceed to formally wind up the affairs of the old ZAMCOM through an appropriate statutory instrument. In view of the fact that the new Board of Trustees could not be appointed until the old ZAMCOM had been legally wound up, the minister arranged for a ninety day interim period during which the outgoing Governing Council would oversee the operations of the Institute in a caretaker capacity.

7. ZAMCOM bill is taken to Parliament

The euphoric mood that had arisen over the progress that was being made at ZAMCOM was short-lived because there was the urgent task of getting the bill to parliament. I had hoped that this would be possible during the January, 1996 session. However, although the bill was ready it was set aside in view of the urgency of the Constitutional Amendment Bill which took up most of the time of that session of parliament. I was informed that the ZAMCOM Bill would now come up during the April session. I worked really hard to make this happen. I talked to several key people at the Ministry of Legal Affairs, Cabinet Office, parliament and Government Printers to ensure that the bill would be ready. As part of the preparation the Ministry of Information and Broadcasting Services asked me to write a draft excerpt to be included in the minister's speech which I did, gladly. I made sure it was simple and to the point, emphasising what the new independent status of ZAMCOM was all about.

The big day finally came and the Zambia Institute of Mass Communication (Repeal) Bill was tabled before the Fifth Session of the Seventh National Assembly. It appeared on the Order Paper for First

Reading on Wednesday, 15th May, 1996. A pleasant surprise awaited us when we found that it was the first bill to be considered that day. The Order Paper said the bill was intended 'to provide for the repeal of the Zambia Institute of Mass Communication Act, 1991.'

The session started at 10 a.m. and Speaker, Robinson Nabulyato, was in the chair. After the traditional parliamentary prayer, business began. The first item was Presentation of Bills, First Reading. The Clerk read out 'The Zambia Institute of Mass Communication (Repeal) Bill, 1996.' Then the Minister of Information and Broadcasting Services, Honourable Mwanamwambwa said, 'Mr Speaker, I beg to move that a bill entitled the Zambia Institute of Mass Communication...' When that was done, the clerk informed the house that the second reading would be on Thursday, 16th May, 1996.

On Thursday, 16th May, 1996, the bill came up for Second Reading. Presenting it, Minister Mwanamwamba said, 'This bill, which I am presenting, seeks to repeal the Zambia Institute of Mass Communication Act No. 9 of 1991 and establish an Education Trust under the Land (Perpetual Succession) Act Cap. 228 of the Laws of Zambia.' The minister went on to give details about how the Institute had evolved and enumerated its functions and responsibilities.

Hon. Mwanamwambwa then said, 'Mr. Speaker, in line with government's policy to liberalise or commercialise some media organisations, the Government has decided that ZAMCOM be turned into an Education Trust, and that all its assets be held by the Trust.' He gave the value of the assets and explained that the decision to delink ZAMCOM from the government was a result of a diligent viability analysis which determined that it was capable of operating as a commercially viable organisation. He told the House that ZAMCOM's proposed status would also enable it to become a truly SADC centre, specialising in training working journalists in the region, thus earning Zambia 'the much needed' hard currency. He said other advantages for delinking ZAMCOM from his ministry included the fact that the government would phase out providing annual cash grants to the Institute which would largely be self-financing.

The minister then presented his carrot by saying, 'As proposed in Clause 7 of the Bill, I assure the House that every effort shall be made to ensure that all the workers are transferred to the new Trust and that no job will be lost.' He concluded by declaring that 'This Bill is a straight forward one, and I implore the Honourable House to support it unanimously. Mr. Speaker, I beg to move.'

The whole house, government and opposition members of parliament received the presentation with their traditional accolade of 'Hear, Hear!' and the debate that followed was mostly uninformed and perfunctory. Seven MPs spoke, all in support of the bill which was then committed to the committee of the whole house. The committee considered the bill on Friday, 17th May, 1996. The session was chaired by Chairman of Committees, Deputy Speaker Simon Mwila. Thereafter, with the bill going through the second and third readings without alteration, the process of winding up the Zambia Institute of Mass Communication Statutory Board and the establishment of the Educational Trust was completed.

The Zambia Institute of Mass Communication (Repeal) Act No.19 of 1996 was assented to by President Frederick Chiluba on 18th June, 1996, exactly one month after the bill was passed by parliament. The Act, among other things, provided procedures for the winding up of the affairs of the Statutory Board. Article 3 (1) said, 'The Minister shall, before commencement of this Act, ensure that a proper record of the Institute's assets and liabilities is published in the Government Gazette for the information of the public.' And Article 3 (2) read; 'When the Minister is satisfied that all necessary agreements and arrangements have been made for the winding up of the affairs of the Institute, he shall, by Statutory Instrument, order that the Institute be dissolved on such date as may be appointed in the Statutory Instrument.'

After all the work that had gone into preparing for the transformation of ZAMCOM from a statutory board to an educational trust, we were almost there.

8. The Statutory Board is dissolved

My next task was to impress upon the ministry the need to speed up this process of winding up the affairs of the Statutory Board. At the end of May, the Ministry of Information and Broadcasting Services requested the Ministry of Legal Affairs to prepare a Statutory Instrument to enable Minister Mwanamwambwa to order that the Zambia Institute of Mass Communication, as established under the Act of 1991, be dissolved. The Governing Council at its meeting resolved that all employees be paid their benefits before winding up the Institute. This was done at the end of September, 1996, using funds from the final government grant.

This payment was made possible because the new permanent secretary, Ms. Laurah Harrison, agreed to release the remainder of the grant for the year in a lump sum. Meanwhile, other crucial work carried out included a major organisational analysis which, among other things, involved the review and evaluation of job descriptions and the drawing up of a performance appraisal system. The Management Services Board was engaged to undertake the assignment and concluded the work in October, 1996.

The formal dissolution process of the Statutory Board began with the publication of Government Gazette Notice 507 on 18th October, 1996. The notice listed all the assets that were supposed to be transferred to the Institute and was signed by the permanent secretary. The publication of the Gazette Notice was followed by Statutory Instrument No. 182 (Vesting of Assets and Transfer of Staff) Order, 1996 which provided for the transfer of assets and staff on the coming into force of the Instrument. The assets and their values were listed along with names, National Registration Card numbers and engagement dates of all the employees. The Instrument was signed by Minister Mwanamwambwa.

The next task was for the minister to 'dis-appoint' members of the Governing Council and appoint trustees of the Educational Trust. There was also need to issue the order to dissolve the old ZAMCOM. The letters for the Zambia Institute of Mass Communication (Dissolution) Order and for terminating the appointments of the members of the Governing Council were signed by the minister while he was in his constituency, Liuwa, in Kalabo district, campaigning for re-election.

How my people managed to find their way to the remote village, on the border with Angola, to get the minister to sign the order was a reflection of our determination. The ZAMCOM mission to Kalabo in Western Province was made possible because of the support that we again received from Permanent Secretary Harrison, who agreed that our team could accompany the ministry mechanic, Mr. Chalwe, who was being sent to Kalabo to repair the minister's vehicle, which had broken down. ZAMCOM staff members, Emmanuel Bwalya, book-keeper and Ned Chivube, radio studio operator were entrusted with the assignment. My briefing was that whatever happened they had to get the minister to sign the documents.

My fear was that we could not be sure about the outcome of the forthcoming 1996 general elections. The worst thing that could happen was for Hon. Mwanamwambwa to lose the parliamentary election, or his portfolio, when a new cabinet was appointed. This could result in serious delays because of the need to brief a new minister about ZAMCOM and the delinkage process.

A considerable part of the journey was carried out on foot, over the sandy plains of Western Province. Emmanuel Bwalya talked about how agonising this was and how he wanted so much to rest but for being warned that if anyone stopped, it would not be possible to continue with the journey.

To say that the minister was surprised to see them would be making a gross understatement.

Hon. Mwanamwambwa, without any fuss, signed the documents. I wonder how many people holding that high position would have signed those papers in similar circumstances? Emmanuel Bwalya and Ned Chivube returned to Lusaka with their feet badly blistered but, nonetheless, having accomplished their mission.

At the end of the year party they were each presented with the 'Worker of the Year' award and a new pair of shoes for their determination and perseverance. The mission to Kalabo most certainly underlined my determination to complete the work to transform ZAMCOM. I – and ZAMCOM, obviously – owed a lot to Hon. Mwanamwambwa for helping us accomplish the task.

Very soon afterwards, the Zambia Institute of Mass Communication (Dissolution) Order, 1996 was published as a supplement to the Government Gazette dated 25th October 1996. The order read, '...Whereas I am satisfied that all necessary agreements and arrangements have been made for the winding up of the affairs of the Institute, I hereby order that the Institute shall stand dissolved as from 31st October 1996.'

Thereafter I asked Mrs. Nyirongo of Aquar Chambers to write to the Minister of Lands and apply for the incorporation of ZAMCOM as an educational trust under the Land (Perpetual Succession) Act Cap 288. The Certificate of Incorporation was issued by Minister of Lands, Dawson Lawson Lupunga on 24th January, 1997. The transformation process had been long, bureaucratic and tedious but I had remained steadfast and focused on the end result which was finally accomplished.

9. The Trust is born

After successfully completing the transformation of ZAMCOM, I proceeded to initiate work on the preparation of the Constitution and Trust Deed of the Educational Trust. This task was given to the ZAMCOM lawyers, Aquar Chambers, and as this work was going on I also began to put together the composition of a new board of trustees. Aquar Chambers, and particularly Mrs. Nyirongo, should be credited with assisting me in coming up with a trust deed that legally gave real autonomy to ZAMCOM. It is important to emphasize one cardinal point here. What we planned for and put in place was that if anything was to happen later to threaten, or take away, ZAMCOM's autonomy, it would not be because of a weak or unsuitable legal framework.

The Trust Deed was designed in such a way that authority was taken away from the Ministry of Information and Broadcasting Services and vested fully in the Board of Trustees. The minister of Information and Broadcasting Services was given power to appoint the members of the first Board of Trustees after which a self-perpetuation mechanism took over responsibility for the appointment of subsequent trustees. The Trust Deed also entrenched the provision that made the director of the Institute a fully fledged trustee unlike in the past when he was an ex-officio member of the Governing Council. My argument was that the director was the only person on the board with real understanding, concern and responsibility over the operations of the Trust.

The Trust is born

Towards the end of October, 1996, I submitted copies of the draft constitution and trust deed to the Ministry of Information and Broadcasting Services. In the accompanying letter I explained why the board would comprise individuals who would be carefully selected from key professions. I enclosed copies of their *curricula vitae* as I had been directed to do and as expected, the ministry attempted to impose two additional people on the board, a senior official from the Loans and Investment Department at the Ministry of Finance and a representative of the ruling MMD.

It was not easy to thwart this attempt to infiltrate and emasculate the new Board of Trustees. Luckily, the uncertainty and confusion arising from the preparations for the 1996 general elections helped to forestall these machinations.

In setting out to put together the new board I also had the benefit of hindsight from my previous experience with the old Governing Council. Trustees on the board of the Educational Trust needed to be selected very carefully to ensure that the new board would be independent and strong if ZAMCOM was to be not only autonomous but work towards becoming self-financing. To that end I contacted various professional associations for nominations of representatives to the board. These included the Bankers Association of Zambia, Law Association of Zambia, the Zambia Institute of Chartered Accountants, the Zambia Association of Chambers of Commerce and Industry and the Media Institute of Southern Africa, Zambian Chapter.

The new team comprised a legal practitioner, Mr. Constantine Chimuka; an accountant, Mrs. Anne Mwale; a human resources specialist, Mr. Maxwell Sichula; a print journalist, Mr. David Simpson and a medical doctor with broadcasting experience, Dr. Manasseh Phiri. The only government official on the board was the permanent secretary, Ministry of Information and Broadcasting Services, Ms. Laurah Harrison. As ZAMCOM Director, I was also now a substantive trustee. These first trustees were appointed by Minister Mwanamwambwa for varying periods from one to four years to ensure that at any given time there would be trustees on the board who had served long enough to have institutional knowledge and memory. This was important to ensure effectiveness and continuity.

The composition of the Board of Trustees was both at face value and from the point of view of experience and knowledge, very impressive. The human resources specialist, Maxwell Sichula, was director of the Zambia Chamber of Small and Medium Business Associations, funded by the USAID Mission in Zambia. He had had a distinguished career in ZCCM where he reached the level of Director for Human Resources. He was well respected in the community and a popular figure, particularly because of his involvement in lawn tennis as a player and administrator. He had a warm and engaging personality and a friendly countenance and demeanour. The lawyer, Constantine Chimuka, was a partner in the legal firm, Ellis and Company. He had a fine, dapper appearance. The journalist, David Simpson, was editor of the respected "Profit" magazine, the country's leading business publication. He was also a representative of MISA, the Media Institute of Southern Africa, Zambian Chapter. The accountant, Anne Mwale, had a brilliant mind while the medical doctor, Dr. Mannasseh Phiri, a well-known personality on both radio and television, was simply himself, humble and unpretentious.

The First Meeting of the Board of Trustees was held on 23rd December, 1996. The meeting opened with me giving the trustees a brief history of the Institute before taking them on a tour of the premises. After the meeting reconvened Mr. Maxwell Sichula was elected chairperson with Dr. Mannasseh Phiri as vice chairperson. Ms. Harrison, who had been chairperson of the previous board, became an ordinary member. She did not attend meetings, sending a subordinate at the ministry to represent her. The board established two committees, the Staff Sub-Committee and the Planning and Finance Sub-Committee. The Staff Sub-Committee was chaired by Mr. Chimuka and members were Dr. Phiri and Mr. Sichula.

The Planning and Finance Sub-Committee was headed by Mrs. Mwale and its members were Mr. Simpson and the ministry representative. The director was made a member of both sub-committees.

The sub-committees co-opted people from outside with special expertise to help with specific matters when need arose. Thewo and Company were retained as auditors for the trust. The meeting went on to consider the 1997 budget and then resolved that all employees be paid their terminal benefits up to 30th September, 1997, for their service to the old Statutory Board. The terminal benefits were paid and everyone was happy.

The Trust is born

However, the celebrations over this bounty did not last long. This is because the board had also resolved that those wishing to secure employment with the trust would have to reapply for their positions. It was explained that there was no guarantee that all those who reapplied would get their positions back. As recommended by the board, all the employees were temporarily re-engaged for a period of three months during which time their suitability was reviewed. The conditions of their engagement were clearly spelt out. At the expiration of the three months management begun to retrench and replace some employees with others better experienced and qualified. In all ten employees were retrenched. These included staff in the Accounting Department who were laid off in order to reorganise and strengthen the department as recommended by the auditors. The Zambia Institute of Chartered Accountants, ZICA, was approached to assist the new ZAMCOM to establish a small but competent and effective Accounting Department. A few months later the broadcasting manager was dismissed from his position on disciplinary grounds.

Obviously, retrenchments and dismissals did not go well with some people and Permanent Secretary Harrison, officially enquired of me on what was going on and why. I explained that the choice for ZAMCOM was simply to adapt or collapse and that ZAMCOM needed to transform itself quickly from being an amorphous and lethargic grant-aided institution to a lean and dynamic customer/service oriented organization. I assured her that management was committed to ZAMCOM's survival as a self-financing institution and reminded her that the environment in which the Institute was operating was unsupportive because the core clients, comprising public and private media institutions, were unable to afford – or were unwilling to pay – course fees. 'The survival and success of ZAMCOM will not be possible unless the process of reviewing staffing and operational arrangements and management systems becomes an on-going exercise dependent on institutional needs and employee performance,' I stressed. The matter appeared to have been closed but it resurfaced virulently, later on.

Meanwhile, another pressing matter which I dealt with was the securing of Certificates of Title for the Institute properties. Apparently, there were no records of the original Certificate of Title for the Institute campus which was issued to the broadcasting authorities that occupied the premises during the colonial period and for a short while after Zambia attained political independence. The process of securing the Certificate of Title was, as anticipated, long and cumbersome. The boundary marked by the wire fence, which had been erected after ZAMCOM became a statutory board, facilitated the sub-division work that was carried out by the office of the Commissioner of Lands. During the third week of May, 1996, the ministry assisted me in writing to the Commissioner of Lands requesting the sub-division of Stand No. 3529, Ridgeway, Lusaka. The letter signed by Acting Assistant Secretary (Administration), Kenneth Lesoetsa, requested the surveying and re-numbering of the plot 'so that ZAMCOM could acquire Title Deeds...'

The original Certificate of Title was issued to the Federal Broadcasting Corporation of Rhodesia and Nyasaland on 1st February, 1958, and the Zambia Broadcasting Corporation was a tenant or lessee for the unexpired residue of the original term of 99 years from 29th December, 1965. The proposed sub-division was for approximately 6,800 square metres.

The Lusaka City Council at its meeting in November, 1996, approved the application for sub-division. Director of City Planning, Mr. D.K. Abrampah confirmed this to the Commissioner of Lands in a letter dated 10th December, 1996, and requested the Commissioner to allot new numbers to the sub-division. The matter lapsed for several months because the two people who were following up with the Ministry of Lands and the Lusaka City Council were among those who were retrenched when the Trust came into being. I followed up the matter from where they left off and in mid-March, 1998, ZAMCOM paid the survey fees and property rent to the Ministry of Lands. The property was demarcated and the Ministry of Lands gave ZAMCOM a letter of offer followed by a Certificate of Title for stand number LUS/3529/A.

Similar efforts were made to secure the Certificate of Title for Plot No. 4614/2, Andrew Mwenya Road where the hostel was located. After prolonged efforts that Certificate of Title was also secured. I believe that ZAMCOM was one of the very few former government institutions in Zambia to hold title to their properties.

10. USAID Democractic Governance Project activities begin

With the 'condition precedent' for ZAMCOM's independence and autonomy secured things speeded up with the USAID Democractic Governance Project. Firstly, what was known as the Democratic Governance Project Administration Unit was opened on Mutende Road in the Woodlands residential area. The LSUDG-PAU was headed by Dr. Georgia Bowser, a no-nonsense African-American woman who, like me, wanted to get things done – and on time.

Immediately after the signing of the MoU, Dr. Bowser arranged for a Training Needs Assessment of both media practitioners and educators, the results of which showed that a lot of training work needed to be done within the media sector, with both print and broadcasting showing signs of positive expansion. In addition, the TNA determined the exact technical assistance needs required to develop the new curriculum and course materials and the extent to which new equipment resources were required at both ZAMCOM and UNZA. The TNA also provided for the upgrading of the Department of Mass Communications at UNZA and the retraining and reorientation of working journalists through ZAMCOM.

At ZAMCOM the project helped to improve the policy analysis capability of working journalists by sponsoring well-targeted short-term training courses in specialised areas such as economic and political reporting, investigative journalism and news analysis. The training programme helped to upgrade journalistic skills and improve professional standards of media practitioners while also helping to create a core of professional local media trainers.

The project also supported efforts to strengthen financial and productive performance within ZAMCOM and helped to introduce the concept of TQM, Total Quality Management, through Dr. Alex Moore, an African-American consultant of Atlanta, Georgia. Dr. Moore was tall and well-built. He was a true showman and a glib talker. He was also very convincing on his feet as he preferred to move around as he talked, whether in a classroom situation, in conversations with groups or in one-on-one situations. His task was to assist ZAMCOM define a clear philosophy and mission, business objectives and to draw up departmental and institutional strategic plans.

ZAMCOM had five departments: the Training Department was headed by an accomplished media trainer, Edem Djokotoe; the Broadcasting Department was headed by former ZNBC employee, Chibamba Kanyama; the Computer Department's head was Yese Bwalya; the Research Department's operations were overseen by Mrs. Given Daka. The fifth department was the student hostel.

My plans were to have each department operating as an autonomous entity. Edem was doing a good job already but needed help knowing how to build the business side of media training. Chibamba Kanyama had his work cut out for him in the Broadcasting Department because the government had just liberalised the airwaves and there was a lot of training needed by the new radio stations, while the syndication of high quality radio and television programmes was an option worth exploiting. The establishment of the Computer Department was also timely because most media organisations were beginning to computerise their operations and there was great need to train their staff. The expansion in both the number of institutions and the manner in which they were carrying out their work created the need for ZAMCOM to understand the trends and the impact of existing training arrangements and the Research Department was geared to undertake this important role. The Hostel was mostly acccommodating course and workshop participants and needed to be redeveloped and run on commercial basis outside the Institute's training activities.

So Dr. Moore came to ZAMCOM at the right time and conducted himself impressively in plenary sessions. He did a lot to bring my staff out of the shells of their departments and get them thinking seriously about developing their departments whilst still working as a team. He helped to introduce the concept of TQM. He coached, if not, cajoled the managers for improved performance and how to provide customer-based services. He definitely emphasised and re-emphasised the need for self-managed team work in a quality environment.

In the end a TQM Management Committee was established with Research and Development Manager, Given Daka as coordinator. Departmental mission statements were revisited and strategic business plans revised. At UNZA the project also assisted in the Staff Development Programme by sponsoring Masters' degree training in the USA for two faculty members. The project also provided desktop publishing equipment to enhance the department's publishing activities. Visiting resource persons contracted for ZAMCOM training assisted with conducting seminars for UNZA faculty during their stay in Zambia and in order to broaden journalists' perspectives, the project sponsored two journalists and one media manager from the independent media to undertake internships with US media organisations for a period of six weeks each year.

Another consultant concurrent with Dr. Moore at ZAMCOM was Felton Square, a media engineer from the Journalism Department of Southern University. Felton was young but more reserved. He, too, was African-American but with a demeanour more endearing than Dr. Moore's flamboyance. The purpose of his consultancy was fourfold: to review the communication/computer equipment used by ZAMCOM's potential customers; to assess the extent to which ZAMCOM's equipment could be used with the potential purchase of new equipment; to identify for purchase by the project the most cost-effective equipment that would meet the needs of ZAMCOM; and to develop a cost scheme for the equipment.

Felton's findings were that ZAMCOM's equipment was woefully inadequate and recommended new equipment for radio, television and computer training of a total value a little over US$1,000,000.

USAID Governance Adviser, Jim Polhemus, hit the roof and Felton reworked the requirements significantly. The result was not completely satisfactory to Jim Polhemus, or USAID, but provided a working framework. It was at this time that USAID Zambia Mission Director, Joseph Stepanek, visited ZAMCOM. He agreed that ZAMCOM was a good facility which needed to be supported but stressed the issue of limited funds and the need for us to cut back.

Meanwhile, although Dr. Bowser was at the time in Lafayetteville, North Carolina, she and I communicated continuously by e-mail and fax, liaising about scaling down on equipment, sorting out arrangements for preparing the computer room and acquisition of the computers.

The scaling down on equipment was carried out for two reasons; firstly, the budgetry issue and secondly because some other media organisations argued that it would be unethical to provide ZAMCOM with a competitive edge in the private media market place. I agreed with Dr. Bowser that we needed to focus strictly on equipment that would enhance ZAMCOM's training activities. The emphasis on training was vindicated by the conclusions made by the various consultants, as well as comments from workshop evaluations, on ZAMCOM's potential as a regional training centre.

11. Mid-Term review

The Zambia Democratic Governance Project Agreement between the Zambian Government and USAID provided for midterm and final reviews of progress on the project activities. And so, after thirty-six months, the midterm review was carried out from 22nd May-15th June, 1995, with USAID requesting Michigan State University to carry out the task under an ongoing cooperative agreement for monitoring and evaluating the Zambia Democratic Governance Project.

MSU assembled a team of five, each with specific assignments, led by Prof. Michael Bratton from MSU's Department of Political Science. Apart from leading the team, Professor Bratton looked at the political overview and the legislative performance areas of the project. Other team members were John Rigby (Project Management/Civic Education), Dr. John Makumbe, a political scientist with the University of Zimbabwe (Policy Coordination), Dr. Folu Ogundimu, a lecturer in the Journalism Department of MSU (Media Independence) and Dr. John Harbeson (Constitutional Reform).

The terms of reference for the review were to assess progress towards project goals and purposes, to consider whether the original project rationale still held and to propose corrections to project design, if these proved necessary. The media independence consultant, Folu Ogundimu, a Nigerian national, was professional, very demanding and thorough in his search for detail. I spent a lot of time with him talking about aspects of the Project. He had a lot of questions, such as 'Was the initial project design appropriate? Did the design team correctly identify priority opportunities for consolidating democratic governance? Did it choose and design the right project interventions? Did it propose suitable institutional arrangements for project management?'

The report was ready in July, 1995, and the review established that in spite of initial delays, the Media Independence component was finally on track. It reported progress at ZAMCOM where eight two-week courses had been held attended by 105 participants drawn from various print and broadcast organisations and the internships of two journalists at a newspaper in the USA. Progress was also reported at the Department of Mass Communication of the University of Zambia with the staff development programme as well as the provision of desktop publishing equipment. I felt that one main recommendation emerged from the review regarding the Media Independence component. The review team requested USAID to streamline the procurement procedures so as to speed up the implementation of activities in the component.

As soon as the the midterm review was concluded, I presented a request to Dr. Bowser for the acquisition of computer equipment to support, mostly, print journalism training activities because, apart from a few computers, ZAMCOM had a dozen odd manual portable typewriters. This was, indeed, a serious problem because ZAMCOM's programmes were intended to upgrade writing and technical skills of the journalists who attended its courses and workshops. The Institute could not do this while confining participants to using manual typewriters; the irony being that some of the young journalists who attended ZAMCOM training programmes had never used, nor, in some cases, even seen typewriters.

Some time was lost while trying to determine local availability, cost of equipment, delivery time and service back-up. Most local suppliers offered the equipment at more than twice the amount USAID had budgeted for, prompting USAID to obtain a quotation from a US supplier who not only offered superior models to those suggested by local suppliers but with a saving of over US$12,000 on the total price.

The computer training laboratory was located in an annex building previously used by ZIS. The contractor moved on site on 20th September and completed its work within two months and the equipment arrived a few weeks later. When all the work was done and the new Computer Training Laboratory was ready ZAMCOM had a fine, well-equipped computer training facility. Computer training activities and production work started immediately and our trainers and participants were happy.

12. New broadcasting equipment arrives

After it was agreed to scale down the cost of broadcasting equipment, Stedman Howard, USIS Director, sent an emphatic message to USAID Chief, Joseph Stepanek, making the case for USAID to purchase the equipment. In his message dated 28th March, 1996, Howard stated 'I appreciate the opportunity to provide some thoughts and comments on the Media Component of USAID's Democracy and Governance Project and specifically on ZAMCOM.' He noted that the Project's initial objectives were to support the emergence of independent media to improve the quality and standards of journalism among the existing cadre of working journalists.

'The decision to work with ZAMCOM was a good one...It is important that ZAMCOM be acknowledged to be the place to go for state-of-the-art training,' Mr. Howard stressed, pointing out that client organisations were upgrading their equipment and that for ZAMCOM to establish its position as the trainer of choice, it needed to upgrade its own training studios to meet the technical standards of its clients.

Mr. Howard explained that ZAMCOM had winnowed down its requirements to essential hardware which could be acquired with a maximum expenditure of US$700,000. In conclusion he said 'I am comfortable with the conclusion that the equipment is necessary and that this figure represents the basic inventory sufficient to enable ZAMCOM to meet the training needs of its clients. It is my recommendation that USAID proceed to fund the acquisition of this equipment.'

After this most engaging justification, the mood within USAID improved, somewhat, and I was asked to get at least two new quotations. However, before we could get new quotations, there was a bombshell from USAID Director, Stepanek. On 16th July, 1996, he issued a press statement announcing that the US Government had cut US$2.5 million from four projects in Zambia, saying that the cut was the result of the initial review of US-Zambian bilateral and multilateral relations announced by the State Department on 31st May, 1996. He cited US Government concerns that the constitutional amendments, adopted in the pre-election period, limited the right of the Zambian people to choose their president freely and seriously threatened the integrity and credibility of the electoral process.

Apparently, the amendment which raised the most concern was the one that included a provision limiting those seeking the presidency to first generation Zambians thereby prohibiting first Republican President, Dr. Kenneth Kaunda, from contesting the presidential elections. The USAID Director said, 'The amendments are seen to reverse the commitment to the open, multiparty democratic political system included in the agreement signed by the Government of Zambia at the outset of the Democracy and Governance Project in 1992.'

He explained that the initial cuts, within USAID's Democracy and Governance Project, included the project to assist Cabinet Office in streamlining its internal processes and procedures, a project to upgrade training equipment at ZAMCOM and support to the American non-governmental organisation, NDI, for its work in the elections. The three components were in addition to an earlier decision to suspend the project to assist parliament in improving its internal processes and procedures. These projects represented a total amount of US$1 million in bilateral assistance.

Dr. Stepanek announced that USAID would also reduce the bilateral aid programme from the level of US$19,024,000 to US$17,500,000, an additional cut of US$1.5 million. Taken together, these cuts amounted to approximately US$2.5 million. He warned that in light of the US Government's concern about Zambia's democratic development, USAID's assistance programme in Zambia would remain under continuous review and additional cuts were possible.

This news was devastating, particularly because the USAID decision came after the Zambian government had given the approval to delink ZAMCOM, thus meeting the 'condition precedent'. The cutback by half meant that now there was only US$500,000 for all the equipment inclusive of the procurement and other expenses already made in setting up the ZAMCOM computer laboratory.

Shocking as the news was, I recovered quickly and agreed with Dr. Bowser to forestall further setbacks by taking measures to safeguard the remaining funds. On 22nd July, 1996, Dr. Bowser sent a message to USAID Botswana seeking approval for the amount of US$500,000. She stressed that the total procurement, including that made for the computer equipment, would not exceed the budget allocation. In cutting back we did away completely with equipment for the television studio and reduced on the radio studio facilities.

In early September Dr. Bowser asked her home office to confirm the amount already spent on ZAMCOM equipment. The home office confirmed a figure of US$183,588 leaving a balance of US$316,412. She then pushed for approval for spending the remainder on procuring broadcasting equipment. The approval was given and the order placed on 6th March, 1997. The equipment arrived in Lusaka six weeks later. Installation works started immediately and was completed by 16th May, 1997. Although not the complete configuration, ZAMCOM had earnestly begun to upgrade its digital audio and video equipment, and was getting ready to provide high level training and high quality production services. Meanwhile Dr. Bowser was preparing to close her office and return to the USA. The Southern University Democratic Governance Project office in Lusaka shut down on 30th September, 1997.

13. Changes at USAID, good news for ZAMCOM

The other good news of that period actually came a year earlier on 16th October, 1996, in a one paragraph letter from Curt Wolters, Program Officer at the USAID Mission in Zambia. 'The USAID Mission to Zambia takes this opportunity to inform you that its Director, Dr. Joseph Stepanek, has completed his tour of duty in Lusaka. His replacement, Walter North, assumed his new duties on 9th October, 1996,' Wolters wrote. 'Thank God! May we have more sense and reason,' I wrote on the letter before sending it for filing.

Indeed, Walter North turned out to be an unassuming, friendly and engaging man who sought to work closely with USAID collaborators. He certainly managed to turn things from the hostile relationship that Stepanek had created to a much more easy-going but serious partnership. For example, when USAID began to plan for a new programme for Zambia, for the period 1998-2002, Mr. North distributed for review and comment a short summation of his initial thoughts. USAID anticipated including five areas in its new strategy.

Family

My first wife Catherine and our two sons, Dalitso and Dabwitso and daugther, Chimfwembe in Perth, Australia. December, 2007

With 2nd wife Baanga Kwa Zulu Natal, 2014

With children on holiday at Lake Malawi, 2003

Foreign Assignments with ZANA

Presidential briefing at Non Aligned Heads of State summit in New Delhi, India, 1978

President Kaunda arrives in a Western Sahara refugee camp, April, 1988

Presidential Press Corps in China, 1988

In Kim Il Sung's palace, North Korea, 1988

ZAMCOM

At the US Embassy with Jesse Jackson and Lucy Sichone, 1997

BHC letter suspending cooperation

British High Commission
Lusaka

Independence Avenue
P.O. Box 50050
15 101 Ridgeway
Lusaka

Telephone: 251125
Telex: 41150 (a/b UKREP ZA 41150)
Facsimile: 253798

8 August 1997

Mr Maxwell Sichula
Chairman
ZAMCON Board
PO Box 50386
LUSAKA

Dear Mr. Sichula,

This mission has been preparing with Mr Mike Daka a project to improve the quality of training available to journalists at the Zambia Institute of Mass Communication. In view of Mr Daka's absence it has been decided to put this project on hold until further notice.

Yours sincerely,

Barrie S Jones
Deputy High Commissioner

cc: Ms Laurah Harrison
    PS/Ministry of Information & Broadcasting

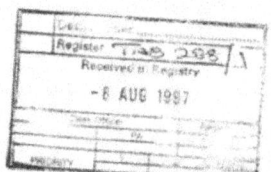

Group photo with trainers, Prof. Francis Kasoma and Cedric Pulford, 1992

ZAMCOM course ending ceremony, 2001

Breeze FM

The Lima Bank building turned into Breeze FM radio station premises after renovations

The Breeze FM new digital studio

Politics and Breeze

Escorting then opposition leader, Michael Sata out of the Breeze FM building after an interview, 2010

PF party cadres attack Breeze FM radio station, November, 2015

Breeze FM Training

Presenting a certificate to Annie Kamala of Nkhota Kota Community Radio, Malawi, 2009

Training Ugandan Parliamentarians as a USAID consultant, 2003

Training Kasempa Community Radio managers, 2003

Awards

Vice President, Guy Scott presenting me with the Bright Mwape/Lucy Sichone Award, 2012

Eastern Province Permanent Secretary, Dr. Chileshe Mulenga pinning the First Ever Special Single Class Golden Jubilee Medal for distinguished service on my left lapel, October, 2014

International Activities

As VC of Media Institute of Southern Africa (MISA) presenting Press Freedom award to Hon Aleke Banda of Nation Newspaper, Blantyre, Malawi, 2007

Panelist at a conference in Beirut, Lebanon, 2016

Addressing a media conference in Johannesburg, South Africa, 2000

Other Trips & holidays

On holiday at the Gold Beach Hotel in Flic en Flac, Mauritius, October, 2013

On the banks of River Jordan in Amman, Jordan, November, 2006

Retirement on the Farm

The farm house

Loading for market the 2017 maize harvest

Preparing to mount bee hives

Relaxing on the farm grounds

These were private sector development, agriculture/rural enterprise development, integrated health services, democracy and governance and basic primary education.

During this early period, I raised the matter of USAID's cutback of support to ZAMCOM despite our having fulfilled the DG Project 'condition precedent' by attaining complete autonomy. I had the support of Dr. Bowser and Jim Polhemus, who were, at that time, both soon to leave Zambia. The USAID Director promised to revisit the aid cutback with Washington. A message drafted by North and sent to the Secretary of State, Washington, DC, through the American embassy in Lusaka on 30th April, 1997 read; 'Subject: Incremental Funding of Southern University – USAID is obligating its final commitment of funding to Southern University, a sum of US$1.1 million. Most of these funds will be used to complete obligations under existing commitments to Southern University so that they can wind down their activities.

After a scrubbing of the Southern University budget, it appears that out of the US$1.1 million obligation, USAID may be able to free up resources to provide some support for bridging activities in the media area. The Mission believes it makes sense to take advantage of this opportunity and to use it to provide bridging support to ZAMCOM for the procurement of equipment to assist with ongoing and planned training activities.

ZAMCOM has been identified as a well managed, privately run institution by USAID's recent DG evaluation and by other observers. ... Moreover from a management point of view, USAID's ability to work through the existing Southern University procurement mechanism, before it expires, is attractive.' Shortly after, a curt reply came back. 'Africa Bureau supports Mission decision ...to provide bridging support for ZAMCOM,' it read. Dr. Bowser sent me a quick note, 'Mike, we desperately need the equipment costs,' she said. I sent two quick messages for quotations for equipment dropped from the earlier purchase, mostly for the television studio and lighting.

The new USAID Democratic Governance Advisor, Miles Toder, arrived in the country during this time. He called on me at the Institute on the morning of Monday, 8th August, 1997. I had just resumed work after being on two weeks forced leave. (Details on this matter are discussed later.) Toder did not hide wanting to know what my plans were. He said he wanted to know whether 'ZAMCOM was Mike Daka and Mike Daka was ZAMCOM' and whether or not the Institute could survive without me. He was honest about the direction he felt the project should take which was to focus on government and civil society activities. He said support to institutions like ZAMCOM would continue and wanted my confirmation over the need for additional equipment. I emphasised that the equipment would help strengthen ZAMCOM's capacity for providing improved training and acquiring self-sustenance. He said he would consult further before deciding whether to support the procurement of additional equipment.

Toder also asked questions about ZAMCOM, its previous operations and whether it was possible to achieve self-sustainability in the future. At the end of our meeting I took a liking to Miles Toder. I thought he was direct and honest and not in any way patronising. I hoped he would decide in favour of buying the equipment. However, for quite some time, I heard nothing from him and, during the third week of October, I decided to call. He did not respond until after my third attempt. He apologised for not returning my calls and assured me that the project was still on course.

He explained that since the Southern University Democratic Governance Project office in Lusaka had shut down, his office would now undertake the acquisition of ZAMCOM's additional equipment after finding out how much money was left for the project and then ensuring that proper purchasing procedures were followed. I emphasised that it was in ZAMCOM's interest that the supplier finally selected was able to offer equipment which was compatible with that already in place at ZAMCOM and its major clients and that the supplier should also be able to provide adequate after sales service.

In November, 1997, Miles Toder requested a 'physical inventory of non-expendable property provided by Southern University under the Democracy and Governance Project.' He said 'your completion of the report will enable USAID to resolve questions of title and ownership of previously purchased equipment and to move ahead with our next planned procurement.' The reaction from Georgia Bowser, when I mentioned this request, was that the last thing she did before leaving Zambia was to give USAID a copy of the inventory.

She said neither Southern University, nor her office, put bar codes on the broadcasting equipment. 'Miles is really flexing his muscles,' she added. Mr. Toder was, indeed, flexing his muscles. However, we were able to prepare the inventory and presented it to him without much delay.

Towards the end of the year, I telephoned Toder as he was about to depart on Christmas leave for two weeks. He asked that I provide two more quotations in accordance with USAID regulations and that in his absence I should liaise with Acting Executive Officer, Mwansa Shitima. Before the Christmas break, Mwansa and I were able to secure the additional quotations and in February, 1998, Miles Toder confirmed that the order for the additional equipment had been made and a week later I had a visit from the London suppliers.

The equipment finally arrived in Zambia a few months later and was handed over to ZAMCOM on 11th June 1998. The installation completed the programme of upgrading training and production equipment at ZAMCOM. It also marked the end of the Media Independence Component activities of the USAID Democratic Governance Project. ZAMCOM had complete digital audio and video equipment, making its studios some of the most modern and advanced in the region. The possibilities and potential for the utilisation of these facilities were only limited by the ideas as well as the capacity – or lack of it – of the training staff and course participants.

I was glad that it was all over! It had taken seven long years to get ZAMCOM to this level of institutional development. The period was extremely challenging but also very enriching for me. I had grown professionally and had sharpened my negotiation and interpersonal skills. I had certainly also developed my practical management knowledge and skills. I was totally indebted to Dr. Bowser and USAID for their unwavering support to the ZAMCOM project.

14. Study and marketing tour of USA and new activities

In her last act before departing for the USA, Dr. Bowser organised a study visit for me to help me plan for ZAMCOM's continuity and sustainability. The trip lasted for three weeks and took me to Washington

DC, where I visited API, EDI, ICJ, Foreign Press Center, Freedom Forum, NPR, USIA and VOA. I also travelled to four states: Michigan, Florida, Louisiana and California where I visited several universities and other media institutions.

In Michigan I visited and held talks with senior staff of the Michigan State University, East Lansing Campus.

My visit to Florida was in two parts, in the capital, Tallahassee, I went to the School of Journalism, Media and Graphic Arts at the Florida Agricultural and Mechanical University and in St. Petersburg I visited the famous Poynter Institute of Media Studies and the St. Petersburg Times newspaper.

In Baton Rouge, Louisiana's capital, I met the director of the Center for International Development Programs of the Southern University System, Dr. Gloria Braxton, who was head of the DGP and had literally paid for my trip to the USA. I also visited the Department of Mass Communications in the College of Arts and Humanities at Southern University, the largest historically black university in the United States and I also visited Louisiana State University.

My visit also took me to WBRH 90.3FM, a non-commercial jazz radio station, operated by students of Magnet High School and the production and administrative offices of Louisiana Public Broadcasting, a state network of six non-commercial television stations licensed to the Louisiana Educational Television Authority.

I also visited the offices of the 'Advocate' newspaper which had provided six-week attachments for Zambian journalists and editors selected after their participation in workshops run by ZAMCOM under the DGP. The climax of my visit to Baton Rouge was a special luncheon at which I was presented with three awards: 'Distinguished Service to the Zambia Democratic Governance Project', 'Honorary Council Member of the City of Baton Rouge' and 'Freedom of the City' honour. In New Orleans I made a call on Xavier University and the 'Times Picayune' newspaper while in Los Angeles, California, my first two stops were to Masai Films, Inc, a private video production company and the Department of Design in the School of Arts and Architecture at the University of California, Los Angeles.

My programme included a round-table discussion moderated by Don Mizell, a lawyer with wide experience in corporate management and marketing, especially in the music industry, broadcasting, new media and intellectual property rights. The discussion was held during a brunch sponsored by Susan and Sidney Miller of BRE magazine at the Miller residence. Participants included California State Senator, Diane Watson. During the discussion, there was general appreciation about the importance of an institution such as ZAMCOM and several recommendations were made for helping it become self-supporting.

Among the ideas and funding approaches discussed were the need to establish an endowment fund for both operational and capital expenses and the setting up of radio syndication service and exchange programmes with black radio outlets in the US.

I then took part in an early morning programme at KJLH-FM radio station, LA's number one black-owned and operated radio station – owned, in fact, by celebrated blind music genius, Stevie Wonder. I completed my visit to Los Angeles with visits and discussions at the Anneberg School of Communication at the University of Southern California; Bailey Broadcasting Services, a multifaceted broadcast organisation dedicated to radio excellence and Black Radio Exclusive Magazine, BRE, America's black entertainment premier magazine for twenty-one years. I got a real feel of BRE's clout and stature when publisher, Sidney Miller, invited me to a live performance of Grammy winning multi-platinum music icon, Prince.

During my visit to the USA I obtained first-hand information that would be beneficial to ZAMCOM, about the running of a media training institution which meets the needs of journalists and ideas about state-of-the-art short, practical workshops and the methodologies for them. I also observed strategies taken by developed media institutions for planning and executing their work and established relationships through which United States-based institutions and ZAMCOM were to exchange training materials, manuals and/or staff, and maintain ongoing cooperation.

15. New training and production programmes

When I returned home from the USA, I was full of ideas about how to reorganise and strengthen ZAMCOM but the most immediate task was making its existing clients pay the new course fees. Although ZAMCOM's core business was media training, most media organisations, newspapers and radio stations were not in a position to, or supportive of, meeting the costs of training their staff. This reality became clear during the first year of operating as a statutory board when ZAMCOM introduced course fees for the first time. At the close of that year most media organisations had failed to pay the fees for their participation in ZAMCOM courses and workshops.

Finally, a decision had to be taken to write off most of this as bad debts. Fortunately, the USAID Democratic Governance Project had provided a great scholarship scheme under its training component through which media organisations were able to send their staff to ZAMCOM courses without bearing their own costs. In fact, provision was even made for participants to receive a 'per diem', intended to help them meet transport and other costs. Undoubtedly, this 'per diem' was a tremendous incentive for course participants, but there were always complaints related to the amount paid and when it was paid, or not paid. There were also complaints about the size of the lunch portions but hardly ever complaints about the quality of training received.

It was obvious to me and my staff that donor-supported training was only a temporary solution because in the end ZAMCOM needed *clients* who could pay. We were always conscious of the danger of moving from dependence on government to dependence on donors. My thinking in those early days was to use donor support to build capacity and to generate our own income through the services and facilities that we would be in a position to provide. As an effort towards making the media organisations appreciate that staff training was important and that training carried a cost, we introduced a 'participation fee' to be borne by those who sent staff to the courses and workshops. This arrangement worked, but for a short time only. Soon the Institute had built up a fairly large debtors' list and again the participation fees owed by the various media organisations had to be written off.

So when the USAID Democratic Project was coming to an end, I had begun looking for other agencies from whom we could get support for our training programme. There were several agencies with whom we ran *ad hoc* courses and workshops, including the Swedish Embassy, NORAD and the British Council. These workshops allowed us to carry on with media training activities. However, the difficulty presented by *ad hoc* workshops was that you could not come up with an annual training programme. You could not be definite about course or workshop dates. You were not even certain about expected income and it was not possible to budget properly. A temporarily respite was provided through support from the European Commission who funded a project called 'Media Training in Areas Relevant to Democratic Governance'.

The general objectives of the project were to build the technical and professional capacity of journalists in both the government and privately-owned media to work more effectively and more efficiently in an emergent democracy and to strengthen the media's public service role. The project ran from January to December, 1998. Each month ZAMCOM organised a two-week course. The intention was to help journalists objectively cover areas such as parliament and the judicial process and religion. We also hoped journalists would be able to report economic and financial issues with greater depth and more understanding, produce more informative radio documentaries and television magazine programmes to raise the civic consciousness of the public and galvanise them to participate more effectively in the political process.

In all ZAMCOM trained 144 journalists and media practitioners, which was a good number, with capacity and potential to help improve operations in their media institutions. A more comprehensive capacity building programme, supported by the British government, helped to strengthen ZAMCOM. The project initially provided assistance to ZAMCOM in carrying out market research as a lead-in to project activities by investigating the potential regional market for ZAMCOM courses and identifying clients and competitors in the region.

The exercise was carried out with assistance from Critical Skills Development of Sheffield, England and I travelled with officials from CSD to Botswana, Lesotho, Swaziland and South Africa where we held discusssions with media executives and government officials. The project's main aim was to help make ZAMCOM financially viable while at the same time enabling it to offer training to improve the skills of journalists and people working in public communications in Zambia and other countries of the region.

Meanwhile, the DFID capacity building programme funded a series of consultancies to help ZAMCOM staff develop their skills so that they could offer good quality and marketable training services to clients. DFID also funded the purchase of teaching aids which greatly improved the quality of training offered by ZAMCOM.

The British Council also organised a two-week study tour of Britain for me in preparation for implementing the programme. The British tour was similar to that which I had previously made to the USA, both in approach and purpose. Whilst in Britain I attended a media and governance seminar in London entitled 'How the media can promote democracy and explain economic change: exploring the impact of media training in transitional and developing countries'. I also visited and held meetings with representatives of media training institutions and allied NGOs. These were CBA, CMDF, CPU, CSD, Gemini, Panos Institute, Radio Guild, Thomson Foundation, University of Wales, Cardiff and Westminster Foundation for Democracy. My discussions with these organisations were based largely on curricula, marketing of courses, arrangements for recruiting associate trainers and costing of trainng. We also examined the type of cooperation that might be possible between these organisations and ZAMCOM.

Backed by this solid preparation, ZAMCOM was now holding three, four or more workshops and courses simultaneously. Sometimes the radio studio and the manicured lawns outside were turned into classrooms to accommodate the many course and workshop participants who were drawn not only from different media organizations, non-governmental organizations and government departments in Zambia, but also external participants coming to Zambia from Angola, Botswana, Lesotho, Malawi, Mozambique, Namibia, Rwanda, Somalia, South Africa, Swaziland, Tanzania, Zaire (now Democratic Republic of the Congo) and Zimbabwe.

The broadcasting department began to produce high quality audio and video products for various clients as well as fully-fledged programmes for broadcast on Television Zambia. Among the most important programmes was a business series called, "Can You Bite The Bullet?" produced and presented in the ZAMCOM television studio by Broadcasting Manager, Chibamba Kanyama, and recorded for broadcast on Television Zambia. The radio department also had its successes. The ZAMCOM Radio Studio recorded Zambia's first locally-produced commercial music compact disc, Pontiano Kaiche's 'Katyeye' album. It was becoming evident that the Institute's departments were ready to contribute to ZAMCOM's independence and sustainability.

Meanwhile, while all this was going on I was also busy networking at the national and regional levels. At home I was an examiner in the Journalism Diploma Programme at my Alma Mater, the Evelyn Home College, Vice Chairman of the MISA Zambia Chapter and a Board Member of the National AIDS Council (NAC), Global Fund for AIDS and the Zambia National Tourism Board (ZNTB). I was also among the business leaders that initiated the establishment of the Institute of Directors of Zambia.

At the regional level I was a Board Member of the NSJ Southern Africa Media Training Trust established in 1993 as part of a bilateral agreement between the Southern African Development Community (SADC) and the Nordic countries aimed at boosting professional journalism skills and knowledge in Southern Africa. I was also the founding Chairman of the communication for development organisation, Panos Institute for Southern Africa and assisted Ghanaian media personality, Aida Opuku-Mensah, the founding director with the formalities for registering the organisation in Zambia. I was also an active member of the African Council for Communication Education (ACCE) which was at the time the biggest association and forum for media professionals, educators in journalism and associated disciplines in Africa. So, I was busy and productively engaged.

16. *Complaints and accusations*

I was beginning to implement and follow up on the ideas and plans agreed during my visits abroad when I realised that the positive developments taking place at the old Broadcasting House, which had now been turned into the glittering new ZAMCOM campus had, in fact, begun to generate some serious negative backlash.

Admittedly, there were many people who were happy and pleased with the transformation that was taking place in the classrooms, studios and surroundings as well as the quality of services that were being provided by the Institute. However, there were also those who were not happy with what they felt was too much donor support being channelled to ZAMCOM. There were yet others who were also unhappy because they thought that the director was personally benefiting too much from the largesse that was accruing to ZAMCOM.

And, of course, there were those former employees who had been laid off or retrenched during the reorganisation process who thought that they had been treated unfairly and were entitled to the benefits of the new ZAMCOM. Then there were those officials at the ministry who were very unhappy that they were losing control over what they still regarded as their own institution. This combination of negative attitudes and feelings meant that what were being seen as good times at ZAMCOM could not last, especially for the person seen to be the one benefiting most or, indeed, responsible for denying others from enjoying the benefits. It was only a matter of time before accusations and complaints started flying about.

Initial efforts to destabilize my position, or remove me from my position, were made via an anonymous letter, ostensibly, written by members of staff of ZAMCOM and sent to the Ministry of Finance in August, 1996, alleging serious malpractices on my part. I can only surmise that the people involved were those who had lost their jobs in the reorganisation exercise or, possibly, those who had been fired on disciplinary grounds. But there could have also been some disgruntled employees who were simply unhappy with my leadership.

The Ministry of Finance sent a copy of the letter to the Ministry of Information and Broadcasting Services. The permanent secretary, Ms Laurah Harrison asked the ZAMCOM auditors, Thewo and Company, to undertake a special investigation at the Institute. The ministry did not send a copy of the anonymous letter to the Institute. However, I was later to find out that the broad terms of reference given to the auditors were to institute audit investigations into the financial conduct of ZAMCOM management, particularly the director and the management accountant.

The auditors were also asked, among other things, to determine to what extent the director had diverted ZAMCOM resources to his personal use in terms of vehicles, equipment and funds. Thewo and Company submitted their report to the permanent secretary. The report exonerated me of all the charges and operations at ZAMCOM continued as normally as they could under this new atmosphere of accusation and suspicion.

However, those who were baying for my head and blood were not giving up and eight months later, on the afternoon of 1st July, 1997, fresh indications that the fight was not yet over came by way of a telephone call. A colleague working for the Office of the President telephoned me and said that he needed to meet me urgently. The Office of the President or OP, as it is generally referred to, is the country's leading security agency. My friend was an assistant director and, although we called each other from time to time, he sounded as if this was not a courtesy call.

Like all government security agencies, OP operations generated a lot of fear and a serious phone call coming from the OP meant real trouble. I met with my friend at the Zamsure Club, east of Lusaka at 5.30 p.m. and the story he told me was that a minister (he did not say who) had lodged a report with OP suggesting that I was a UNIPist and was working too closely with donors. Both accusations were very serious. Being accused of being UNIPist during the early years of the MMD government was the same as being said to be anti-government. The new rulers had not quite settled down in office and were quite paranoid and were seeing enemies everywhere. Those they labelled as UNIPist were among those they regarded as some of their worst enemies. Similarly, being referred to as 'being too close to donors' was the same as being accused of working too closely with, or for, foreign governments.

I needed to clear my name – urgently. I explained to my friend that I was not UNIPist and that although in the past I, like every other government media head, had been coerced to buy a UNIP membership card, I had stopped doing so after the return of multipartyism to Zambia. I said that the OP had the means to establish whether or not I was a member of UNIP and whether or not I was in regular contact with its leaders.

On the allegation that I was too close to donors I informed him that this could not be so because the support that donors had provided was to ZAMCOM, as an institution, and not to me as an individual. I explained that I had not personally benefited from donor support although, through my efforts, ZAMCOM had become an internationally-recognised media training institution which all Zambians needed to be proud of. I asked what would happen to the report made by the minister – whoever he or she was – and he told me that investigations would be carried out and a report made to the president.

This was certainly not the sort of issue I thought I would be dealing with on this particular day. The first day of July, 1997, was a special day for me. It was my silver jubilee. I had clocked twenty-five years of continuous work in the public service. I had planned to leave early from work so that I could have a celebratory dinner with my family, but there was little celebration that night because I could not cheer up no matter how much my wife and kids tried to lighten my mood.

The days that followed were worrisome and I had every reason to be anxious because, although the OP matter quietly died down, I knew that my enemies would not relent. In fact, the worst was yet to come. And if anyone had told me then that I would be sent on forced leave and that I would be investigated by another auditing firm and five government agencies, I would have told him that he was insane.

17. Suspension from work

A month later three board members: Chairman, Mr. Sichula, and Members Mr. Chimuka and Mrs. Mwale came to my office and informed me that the minister, Mr. David Mpamba had summoned them to his office and that in the presence of the permanent secretary, Ms. Harrison, had briefed them on the contents of an anonymous letter which accused me of serious abuses. 'Is it the same anonymous letter or another one?' I wondered.

They told me that in view of the seriousness of the allegations I should be sent on leave to facilitate investigations. I explained to them that the minister had no jurisdiction over ZAMCOM and that the full Board of Trustees was the correct body to decide on the matter. I pointed out that a meeting held in the minister's office could not constitute a meeting of the ZAMCOM Board of Trustees. I also pointed out that I could not be sent on leave on the basis of accusations contained in an anonymous letter.

The three board members disregarded my plea and sanctioned my suspension from work. The chairman, Mr. Sichula, speaking on behalf of the other trustees said, 'There have been accusations made against the director. I feel the best thing to do is to have them investigated so that the matter can be finally resolved'. He did not concern himself with the need for the board to ask me to exculpate myself before asking outsiders to investigate. He and the other two board members did not even want to establish who originated the anonymous letter or the veracity of the allegations of malpractice made against me. They felt that they could not reverse a decision taken in the presence of the minister. The fact that the minister no longer had any jurisdiction or oversight responsibility over ZAMCOM did not seem to worry them.

A day later I received a letter containing my marching orders. The letter stated, 'The Board of Trustees has received allegations against you as Chief Executive of ZAMCOM some of which appear quite serious. At its meeting on the 6th of August, 1997, the Board decided that an independent firm of accountants be appointed to investigate such allegations. In order to facilitate the investigations the Board decided to request you to stay away from the office for the duration of this investigation with immediate effect. Please make yourself available as and when required. Your co-operation will be appreciated'.

I vacated my office and stayed at home. This was, and remained, the worst time of my life. I had worked hard, consistently and honestly to build a unique and modern Zambian institution and, instead of being congratulated, I was being persecuted. Ironically, this agonising experience is what propelled me towards gaining the real freedom that I had been seeking all along. I could not have known then that this would turn out to be what someone in similar circumstances described as 'the best worst time of my life'.

But that part of the story comes later. At that particular moment what seemed important was to find out what the anonymous letter was accusing me of and hoping that the investigation would absolve me from the accusations as quickly as possible. The anonymous letter had apparently been sent to the Minister of Labour and Social Security, Dr. Peter Machungwa, who, in turn, had sent it to his counterpart at the Ministry of Information and Broadcasting Services, David Mpamba.

In his covering letter Minister Machungwa said he was enclosing a letter from ZAMCOM employees containing allegations of very serious abuses, fraud and violations of the Act pertaining to ZAMCOM on the part of the director. He said it was his strong view that these allegations must be investigated and the situation rectified otherwise ZAMCOM would not serve the purpose it was designed to address.

As soon as I received my letter of suspension I decided to seek legal advice and met with my lawyer, Mr. Andrea Masiye who wrote a letter to the board chairman reacting to his letter requesting me to stay away from my office pending investigations. The letter registered the lawyer's protest and objection against the Board of Trustees' disregard for my legal interests by deciding to suspend me before giving me the letter of accusations and hearing my story. It was put to the chairman that the action was a gross breach of natural justice. To enable me to make a meaningful representation to the allegations levelled against me, the chairman was requested to send to the lawyers the name of the independent firm of accountants tasked to carry out the investigation, their terms of reference and all relevant documents.

'It is only fair that our client be afforded a chance to know the full extent of the allegations, the makers of the allegations and, indeed, he must be given a chance to fully exculpate himself,' my lawyer wrote.

I personally delivered the letter to the chairman on Wednesday, 20th August, 1997. He had little to say apart from telling me that I had support from many people who respected my professionalism. A few days later I received a call from Trustee Chimuka who told me that the auditors were ready to meet me and that I should go to the Institute. The two-man team of auditors from Deloitte and Touche Zambia comprised Chisanga Chungu, audit manager, and Humphrey Mulenga, accountant. They were courteous but professional. Our meeting took nearly two hours. But, as I was unable to find three documents which had information they needed, I advised that they meet with my secretary, Ms. Bridget Nkonde, who would be able to find the additional information that they required.

As soon as I became aware of the terms of reference for the Deloitte and Touche Zambia investigation, I realised that the strategy used by those who wrote the letter was to throw a lot of mud at me hoping that something would stick. There were nine allegations: excessive entertainment expenditure, irregular drawing of travel allowances, non-recovery of house loan, non-recovery of salary advances, non-retirement of imprest and unauthorised funding by the Institute of private motor vehicle's maintenance and running expenses, construction of a private house using the Institute's resources and dictatorial form of management. I felt relieved and confident because I knew that the allegations had no basis.

18. Audit findings and Board decision

Deloitte and Touche Zambia presented its report to the ministry (and not the Board of Trustees) on 27th August, 1997. Immediately upon receiving the report, the permanent secretary called for a meeting of the ZAMCOM Board of Trustees which had as its agenda one item only, 'To consider the draft report of the auditing team from Deloitte and Touche...'

The following day, Friday, 29th August, 1997, at 8.25 a.m. the ZAMCOM receptionist telephoned and informed me that the chairman wanted to see me at his office. I phoned him and he sounded cheery. 'Hello, Mike. How are you?' he said. Didn't he know how I was? Anyhow, I said I was fine! He said we should meet and I told him I would be at his office within two hours. There was no indication in his voice of the news he had for me. I strongly resisted the urge to ask him. At 10.10 a.m. I was parking outside his offices just as he was driving in. He shouted, 'Just on time!' as he got out of his vehicle and rushed upstairs. As I walked up behind him I wondered if there was a message for me in his conduct.

I walked into his office and found him standing at his desk. He greeted me again and put on a serious countenance. 'I received the draft report on Wednesday,' he said, adding, 'We had a board meeting on Thursday. The PS did not attend but sent in her reaction. Dr. Phiri was also not present because he is away in South Africa...' He paused and I waited, looking at him with a straight face. 'The auditors have found that the allegations were not true and the Board decided that you should return to work,' he said this as he signed a letter which he handed to me. The two paragraph letter read, 'Further to my letter dated 7th August, 1997, I am pleased to advise that the investigators have now completed their assignment at ZAMCOM. As the reasons for your continued stay away from the office are no longer there, it would be appropriate for you to resume your duties with immediate effect.' After I had read the letter he said the board would soon look at issues of my conditions of service. He then handed me a copy of a press release which he said he would issue to the media when they asked for it.

The press release generally repeated what the letter said, but it also included a paragraph about the need to clarify my conditions of service and to tighten financial systems. I did not comment but noted to myself that this was an attempt to justify my suspension. It had taken twenty-three days, including weekends, for my name and integrity to be, somewhat, restored. Mr Sichula told me that Minister Mpamba had been briefed about the findings of the audit and the decision of the board to reinstate me. He said the minister had no objection to the board decision.

I left his office that August morning with a deep sense of sadness. I was in no doubt that the Board of Trustees would not stand up to government or to any other real pressure that would threaten the independence of ZAMCOM. During the three-week period of my forced leave, and after I returned to work, my greatest regret was that the three board members who met with the minister had failed to defend me when it mattered most.

A meeting of an independent ZAMCOM should not have taken place in the minister's office and the board should have called for its own meeting to consider the allegations made against me. By not standing up for me or, indeed, giving me the benefit of the doubt, the trustees had put at risk my position and integrity as their director as well as the status and future of ZAMCOM.

It became clear to me that although I had been seeking strong independent people for the ZAMCOM board, there were very few such people who could be said to be truly independent, or strong enough to parry, or withstand government and political manipulation and pressure.

Also, the issue of my employment contract best illustrated the weakness of the ZAMCOM Board of Trustees. The new board took office in November, 1996, but it was not until January, 1998, that the Staff Committee met to begin to consider my contract. For more than one-and-half years I had worked without a contract. Meanwhile, my salary and conditions of service were *ad hoc* and loosely based on my previous contract which ended with the dissolution of the statutory board. When I raised the matter with the chairman, he had told me not to worry because my old contract was still in place until the new one became effective.

The first meeting to consider my new contract was held on 7th January, 1998. Four months later a special meeting was called to consider the contract and the appeal I had lodged against the decision to make me get a loan for settling my legal fees. The trustees finally resolved to allow ZAMCOM to settle my legal fees. The Service Agreement, as the contract was called, was finally given to me on Thursday, 16th July, 1998. It was nicely bound in a blue cover and the accompanying letter from the chairman said it was for my scrutiny. 'If you are agreeable with the provisions therein, please append your signature accordingly. On behalf of the Trust, I apologise for the delay in finalising this document and thank you for your understanding and patience,' the Chairman wrote.

I did not agree with seventeen of the clauses and said so in very specific terms. I said that my overall impression was that the document had the air of a disciplinary code. I went further to state that in my opinion the major thrust of a service agreement should be to convey a sense of goodwill and to engender confidence in the employee while at the same time encouraging and promoting good performance. My observations were circulated to all trustees for their reactions. The most significant comments came from Dr. Phiri who felt that the agreement should not be tailored for me alone but should aim at meeting the needs of future office holders.

The document was returned to me with hardly any changes. I realised that I was not getting anywhere and signed it on 15th October 1998. It was effective from 1st November, 1996, and valid until 30th October, 1999. Interestingly, the delay in finalising my contract had provided me with a small windfall in salary arrears.

19. Media and donor interest

The ZAMCOM case, my suspension and reinstatement attracted a lot of media attention. The first story carried by 'The Post' newspaper on 11th August, 1997, read, 'ZAMCOM Boss Sent on Forced Leave'. It quoted a ZAMCOM source as saying that I had been sent on forced leave for unexplained reasons. On Friday, 22nd August, 1997, the state-owned 'Times of Zambia' carried a front page story headlined 'USAID to Pull out of ZAMCOM'. The story said USAID was threatening to withdraw aid and equipment from ZAMCOM in what was perceived as a protest against my suspension. The newspaper quoted USAID as saying it would terminate its project with ZAMCOM at the end of September and would withdraw its equipment and give it to a US private volunteer organisation that would carry out non-governmental organisation strengthening activities.

The 'Times of Zambia' referred to unnamed sources as saying that the threat to grab equipment meant for the project and to withdraw aid amounted to blackmail. The paper followed up this story with another on Saturday, 23rd August, 1997, which was headlined 'Auditors Probe Zamcom Financial Position'. The story, which was attributed to the chairman, Mr. Sichula, said the board had appointed an independent auditing firm to investigate the financial position of the institution. The newspaper quoted Sichula as saying that suspended ZAMCOM Director, Mike Daka's fate would be decided after the auditing firm finished its investigations. Mr Sichula, who refused to specify why I was suspended, said the ZAMCOM Director was merely asked to stay away to facilitate investigations. He said all the programmes at the institution were on course and that there were no formal threats of withdrawal of aid by the major funders, the British and USAID.

Although this was reported on 23rd August, 1997 a letter had been written to him, signed by British Deputy High Commissioner, Barrie Jones and dated 8th August, 1997, which was copied to the permanent secretary in the Ministry of Information and Broadcasting Services. The letter read, 'This mission has been preparing with Mr. Mike Daka a project to improve the quality of training available to journalists at the Zambia Institute of Mass Communication. In view of Mr. Daka's absence it has been decided to put this project on hold until further notice.'

On Tuesday, 26th August, 1997, all the daily newspapers carried a story from a statement released by six media organisations expressing concern at the hounding out of office of media heads by government. The organisations were the Commonwealth Press Union, Zambia Chapter; the Media Resource Centre; the Press Association of Zambia; Zambia Media Women's Association; the Zambia Independent Media Association and the Zambia Union of Journalists. The 'Times of Zambia' carried the story on page 3 under the headline 'Media Groups to Shun ZAMCOM' and 'The Post' had it as its lead on its Media News page with the headline 'Hounding of Media Heads Worry Press'. The 'Zambia Daily Mail', which had not carried any stories on this issue ran a story on page 2 headlined 'State Actions Worry Media Bodies'.

The media organisations said they were particularly disturbed at the manner in which I had been sent on forced leave without following normal disciplinary procedures. They said they suspected political interference in the running of ZAMCOM, an institution that was legally established as an independent trust. They threatened to boycott all training programmes at the Institute should the independence of the Trust be undermined. They also noted that the managing editor of the government-owned 'Zambia Daily Mail', Patrick Fungamwango had also been relieved of his duties.

On Wednesday, 27th August, 1997, the 'Times of Zambia' carried a story which was a reaction from Minister of Information and Broadcasting Services, David Mpamba to the threat by the six media organisations. The story was headlined 'We've No Hand in ZAMCOM Issue, Says Mpamba'. It quoted Mpamba as saying, 'We as government have never interfered with the operations of ZAMCOM because it is an independent Trust. Government can only come in if ZAMCOM operations proceeded contrary to Government policy. Mr. Daka was sent on forced leave by the ZAMCOM Board. People saying that politicians have engineered the suspension of Mr. Daka do not know what they are talking about. How can politicians involve themselves in an independent institution?' he asked.

I did not know whether Mpamba was trying to distance himself from the problem or was, in fact, laughing at the whole question of ZAMCOM's independence! On 30th August, 1997, ZNBC radio and television carried the story of my reinstatement as a headline item in the afternoon and evening bulletins. The 'Times of Zambia' also frontpaged the story.

The media coverage, however, had an unfortunate result, the loss of my privacy. Although I was a media person and had worked in media for twenty-five years, I was very much a private person. The only media coverage that I had received over the years arose from my speaking at workshops at ZAMCOM, or contributing to debate and discussion at workshops, seminars and conferences. I had never deliberately sought media attention and had spurned approaches from journalists for interviews for newspaper articles and radio or television stories. This time I was a subject of media attention whether I liked it or not and whether I had any comment to make or not. In any case all the stories that were published were based on what other people said about my case. There were leaks to the media from some members of my staff and there were statements from members of the ZAMCOM board, statements from the Ministry of Information and Broadcasting Services as well as from those who came out to support me.

As a spectator of what was being said about me, it was all very weird, in fact, surreal and I was happy when it was all over and I will forever remain indebted to my colleagues in the media and the donor representatives who believed in my innocence and stood by me at this most trying of times.

20. Back at ZAMCOM

Suspension from a job under any circumstances is painful but when it is part of an orchestrated campaign against an innocent individual, the harm it can cause to that person could be irreparable. In my case I was disappointed but not embarrassed. I knew I was innocent and that I was being harassed and persecuted unfairly and that I would be vindicated by the investigation that was taking place. The most important thing that I did was to reassure my children of my innocence.

They were worried because they were being asked questions by their friends who were picking up bits of information from the media and, perhaps, from hearing the conversations of their parents. Despite the disappointment that I felt, I realised that the false accusations and forced leave offered me time for introspection. It provided me with time to focus on what I had done up to that stage and what my priorities ought to be going forward.

I returned to work after three weeks on Monday, 1st September, 1997. I had always been a morning person and I always arrived at work shortly after 7 a.m. every day. But that Monday morning I arrived at 7.50 a.m. That was going to be my new arrival time. I had resolved to keep standard hours of work from then on. As I parked my car in the slot reserved for the director, I realised that I was a free man. I felt neither anguish nor elation. No emotion; no feelings. The emotional attachment that had previously driven my work was gone. ZAMCOM had become an ordinary working place which I could now leave, for good, whenever I chose to do so.

I do not know how I came to the decision not to be resentful or vengeful. I did not go into the 'Why me?', 'What will happen to me?' or 'Who is behind this?' mode. I did not feel sorry for myself, nor seek to deal with the members of my staff whom I suspected to have conspired with former employees and others to have me removed. I remained calm and centred in what was an extremely provocative and stressful situation. I think that this is what saved me from sinking into negativity and endless conflict and what quickly transformed me from what appeared to be defeat and humiliation to quick recovery and, in fact, victory. The positive attitude is also what allowed me to carry on with my work and to be in a position to do, and achieve much more, at ZAMCOM and later in my other work and life.

At my 8.30 a.m. meeting with the managers that day I had no speech to make. Three sentences were enough. I was happy the month of August was over. We had lost some time and focus and all needed to work hard to accomplish our programme before the end of the year. I thanked them for keeping things running well in my absence.

That first day back at work was generally uneventful. I had telephone calls from two family members and a few friends in Zambia but, surprisingly, many email messages of support from professional colleagues in other African countries, Europe and America.

It was interesting that the number of people who contacted me from outside the country was far greater than those who contacted me from within Zambia, despite my extended family, my work within media and my position at the higher echelons of the industry which meant that I knew many people in Zambia, whom I was supposed to be close to, or who I regarded as friends. It dawned on me that people do not rejoice with others who are more successful than them and that such people relished what they thought was my downfall. I realised that the whole affair had provided me with an opportunity to review my relationships. It was as if I had died and temporarily gone to Heaven and the Good Lord had asked me to look down and see who was sad about what had happened to me and who was not. I began the process of cutting contact with unnecessary people.

That same day I left the office early. Usually I was in my office until after 6 p.m., sometimes later but this time I left at 5 p.m. sharp. I had made some useful resolutions. No more early or late hours. No more weekend work. My own time, from now onwards, was mine alone and for the family. And for that I thanked the people who had sought to have me removed from ZAMCOM for bringing sanity into my life. I used to spend an average of ten to twelve hours a day at work.

Most Saturdays and Sundays were used to tackle the most difficult tasks because the office was quiet with no visitors or telephone calls. Not anymore. Weekends were now for relaxation with the family. One of my priorities after returning to my office was to clear things out and to put myself in a permanent state of preparedness. I was never one for clutter but I decided to remove all personal items so that when the time came to leave the office I would have very little to remove.

The most satisfying development over that period came eight months after I resumed work. My family celebrated a momentous occasion. During the Easter weekend, on Thursday, 30th April, 1998, we vacated the Institute-rented house in the Northmead area of Lusaka and moved into our own house in the Bonaventure area of Makeni, on the southern outskirts of Lusaka.

The construction of the house had largely been carried out by my wife, Catherine, after obtaining a loan from her employers. (I had previously bought the plot with a foundation slab and had given it to her as a birthday present.) Our house was much smaller than the Northmead 'mansion' but as the kids commented when we arrived to take occupation, 'This house may be small, Dad, but at least it's ours.' Anyone who has built and occupied their own house, without resorting to stealing or corrupt practice, will understand the wonderful sense of security that one gets from sleeping in one's own home for the very first time. My joy was boundless because I was the only head of a government or quasi-government media institution who had not been offered a house to buy under the government's housing empowerment programme even though I had worked in the public service for twenty-five years. Anyhow, government house or no government house, I and my family now had a home of our own and I was confident of building or buying another house, or other houses and properties, in due course.

21. Efforts to undermine ZAMCOM's independence continue

21.1 MMD and Press Freedom

Although the MMD took over political power with the promise of reintroducing democracy and in the early years, in words and deeds, attempted to safeguard the freedom of the press, the attitude and behaviour of some of the party and government leaders after settling in office was undemocratic and showed a lack of respect for the media and its operatives.

While I cannot speak for other media leaders my own experience, as head of a media training school, was that most ministers, permanent secretaries and other senior officials at the Ministry of Information and Broadcasting Services did not attach much importance to the promotion or protection of freedom of the press. No real interest was shown in the high levels of professional media training that were going on at ZAMCOM apart from attempts to reign in ZAMCOM's director and the institution.

I have no doubt that the issue of the independent status of ZAMCOM and how it was subverted by government for simply and honestly carrying out its mandated work of improving the skills and professionalism of media practitioners and their institutions is a good example of how the MMD government dealt with media and the important issue of press freedom. Despite having been cleared of wrongdoing and returning to work, for a period of over three years I was required to explain one thing or another to various government institutions about the operations of my institution or the decisions that I was making as I carried out my work.

21.2 The Directorate of State Enterprises

Initial indications that government was not happy with the independent status of ZAMCOM emerged through various communications from the Directorate of State Enterprises, an agency established following the dissolution on 31st March 1995, of the country's parastatal holding company, ZIMCO. The Directorate of State Enterprises was established under the Ministry of Finance and Economic Development in its capacity as ultimate shareholder of state enterprises.

The mandate given to the directorate was to safeguard the interest of the state in its enterprises. The functions of the directorate included monitoring the performance of state-owned enterprises, forecasting, collecting and recording receipts of dividends, assisting in the privatisation of the state-owned enterprises and commercialisation of government departments. In order for the directorate to perform these and other duties, it demanded periodic financial information, minutes of board meetings, corporate plans, budgets and forecasts from state-owned enterprises.

The first contact I had with the directorate was a letter from the Ministry of Information and Broadcasting Services dated 21st April, 1997, which was also addressed to the director general of ZNBC and managing editors of the 'Times of Zambia' and 'Zambia Daily Mail'.

The letter, which was signed by Assistant Secretary for Administration, Mrs. E. I. Musonda, was drawing our attention to the contents of a circular letter issued by the Ministry of Finance and Economic Development on 5th February 1997. The letter explained the role of the Directorate in monitoring the operations and performance of companies and corporations in which government had investments either in form of share capital or loans and requested ministries to write to chief executives of their respective companies asking them to extend their 'fullest cooperation in providing any information the Directorate may deem necessary for the purpose of evaluating the performance and profitability of the companies'.

My first direct contact with the directorate was made through a letter dated 12th May, 1997, from Director, Stephen Mwamba. It was headed 'Monitoring of Operations and Performance of Companies and Corporations in which Government has Investments either in the form of share capital or loans'. In the letter, Stephen Mwamba requested me to submit to his office a copy of the audited accounts for the year ended 31st March, 1996, or 31st December, 1995, (whichever was applicable) as well as the current budget. He gave me a deadline of 31st March, 1997. The letter was copied to the permanent secretaries for the Ministry of Information and Broadcasting Services and the Ministry of Finance and Economic Development. I neither responded to the letter nor sent the documents.

Two days later, I received another letter addressed 'To all Chief Executives of State-owned enterprises' headed 'Flash Results for 1996/97 Financial Year'. It read 'In order to allow the Directorate to assess the likely performance for the year ended 31st March 1997 or 31st December 1996 as the case maybe, kindly furnish us with the following information'. The information sought was actual turnover for the period 1995/6 and preliminary turnover for the period 1996/7.

From then on until early 1999, a period of nearly two years, I received letters of a similar kind forcing me in February, 1999, to answer Mr. Mwamba. I told him that ZAMCOM was not a state enterprise and that he should, therefore, 'stop sending circulars and/or any other correspondence that had nothing to do with the Trust or its operations'. I enclosed copies of the various Statutory Instruments that wound up the parastatal ZAMCOM and the Certificate of Incorporation of the new ZAMCOM. His response was swift. 'Please be advised that your organisation is among the institutions which were submitted by the Ministry of Information and Broadcasting as part of their portfolio of state enterprises. If you have a different view from that of the ministry, please advise them as such so that they can communicate to us accordingly. In the meantime we will continue to send you circulars and other correspondence as per our mandate'. He copied the letter to the usual offices. Well, at least now I knew where the instructions for his ceaseless attempts to harass me had come from.

It was clear now that the Ministry of Information and Broadcasting Services had not accepted – and did not respect – the delinkage of ZAMCOM from the government. I wondered why a government ministry was not respecting the independence of an institution whose delinkage had been authorised by Parliament, the highest legal entity in the country. I also wondered what kind of individuals or institutions acted, not on the basis of legality or principle, but on political whim or expedience.

21.3 The Ministry of Information and Broadcasting Services

The position of the Ministry of Information and Broadcasting Services on the status of ZAMCOM came out in the open shortly after I returned to work after the three-week period of forced leave. The ministry did not allow me to enjoy the good 'come back kid' feeling for long. Early upon my return my secretary received a telephone call from a senior official at the ministry requesting a copy of the *curriculum vitae* for David Simpson, a trustee of the board. David Simpson was unpopular with government because of his repeated criticism in his position as chairman of the media advocacy organisation, MISA, Zambian Chapter.

I told my secretary to tell the mimistry that we were unable to find a copy of David's CV. Not long after, the official came in person to my office to ask for copies of the ZAMCOM Statutory Instruments and Trust Deed. She said that the ministry was in the process of reorganising the Boards of Directors of government media organisations. I asked why the ministry was including ZAMCOM in the reorganisation exercise when it was an independent trust but she could not give a clear answer.

Shortly after that, in June, 2000, the Ministry issued a press statement saying that it had dissolved the boards of all government media institutions – the list included ZAMCOM – as part of plans to reorganise them. I asked the ZAMCOM board chairman, Mr. Sichula to call for an urgent meeting to discuss the matter, whereat it was resolved that the board seek legal opinion from the Office of the Attorney General. The permanent secretary also proposed that legal opinion be sought on the provision on the appointment of trustees in the Institute Trust Deed, particularly the requirement that the responsibility for recommending members of the board to the trust be vested in the director.

The resulting Legal Opinion from the Office of the Attorney General squashed the schemes by the ministry to undermine ZAMCOM's independent status and, actually, asserted ZAMCOM's independent status, declaring that the ZAMCOM trust had been established under an Act of Parliament and that 'the principles of autonomy it enjoys shall continue to be upheld.'

Efforts to undermine ZAMCOM's independence continue

However, the Office of the Attorney General found fault with the issue of the director, who was appointed by the Board of Trustees, being the one to recommend members of the board to the Trust. 'There is a contradiction in terms of the Constitution where it provides for the Director to recommend the appointment of the Board of Trustees,' said the Office of the Attorney General. However, no advice was offered on how trustees would be appointed. I thought that this legal position weakened the Board of Trustees by taking away the main provision for ring fencing office bearers from political intrusion. Nonetheless, I was not too bothered since the independence of the trust had been protected by none other than the Office of the Attorney General.

The ministry may have been happy about lessening the powers of the director but could not have liked the fact that the independence of ZAMCOM had been protected. Their irritation was, in fact, aggravated further by a letter from the Royal Norwegian Embassy querying press reports about the dissolution of the ZAMCOM board. The letter, signed by Charge d'Affaires, Kikkan Haugen, explained that the embassy assumed that the press reports were based on a misunderstanding, or incorrect reporting, and requested 'more information about the issue'. Mr Haugen explained that the embassy had signed a three-year contract for institutional support to ZAMCOM and that the basis for the support was that the institution was an independent trust. 'Please note that any changes in the institutional set-up or institutional independence of ZAMCOM may force us to have to reconsider the support that is given to the institution,' Mr Haugen said.

Both the legal opinion and the concern from donors temporarily helped to rein in the ministry's attempts to undermine ZAMCOM's independence but, obviously, upset the government officials immensely.

Meanwhile, a newly designated Minister of Information and Broadcasting Services also tried to impose his authority on ZAMCOM very soon after taking office. On the afternoon of Friday, 22nd January, 1999, the minister telephoned me and complained that ZAMCOM had employed Chibamba Kanyama, a man who, he claimed, had been blacklisted. I suggested that instead of talking on the telephone it would be better to discuss the matter in his office and three days later in his office, the minister informed me that Chibamba, while working for ZNBC, had been too closely associated with Afronet, the human rights non-governmental organisation, which was very critical of the government. He pointed out that it was also known that Chibamba was sympathetic to Anderson Mazoka, the former Chief Executive for Anglo-American Zambia, who had just formed his own party, UPND. According to the minister, Chibamba could be used by Mazoka to carry out propaganda work while at ZAMCOM. He also said that such a man could not be entrusted with the training of young journalists.

I responded by confirming that Chibamba was employed as broadcasting manager in charge of radio and television training and production work. I said this position had been vacant for a long time because it was not easy to find a suitable candidate and explained that although Chibamba was responsible for radio and television operations, all work at ZAMCOM was carried out on a consultative basis and that no individual could commission any work without other senior members of staff knowing. I also informed him that management had signed an Employment Agreement with Chibamba which could not just be discarded and that, although Chibamba was new to his job, his performance was already very promising. I also told the minister that since the matter was serious I would include it on the agenda of the next board meeting.

The board meeting took place on Thursday, 4th February, 1999. The minister's concerns were raised and during the discussion, board members examined Chibamba's employment file, which had been obtained from ZNBC. The file did not appear to contain correspondence to suggest that Chibamba had committed any serious offence although there was mention that he had been running a private company while in employment. The board resolved that Chibamba's appointment would not be terminated unless his performance was not up to the required standard. The chairman and I were tasked to meet the minister and present the board's position. The minister was not happy but the board stood by its decision.

21.4 Enter Ministry of Labour and Social Services

More indications that my troubles were not over were soon to follow. While I was relishing the feeling of being back at work, I received a telephone call from the Ministry of Labour and Social Services. It was Assistant Labour Commissioner for Industrial Relations, Mr. Christopher Pasomba. He wanted to meet me to discuss complaints from employees.

'Here we go again,' I thought. I was, of course, aware that the two anonymous letters which had led to my suspension had been sent to the Ministry of Finance and the Ministry of Labour and Social Services before being forwarded to the Ministry of Information and Broadcasting Services. 'But why does a senior official in the Ministry of Labour and Social Services want to see me when everyone knows that I had returned to work after being cleared by an independent audit?', I wondered.

I decided to cooperate and cheerfully told Mr. Pasomba that he could see me any time. We agreed to meet the following day at 2.30 p.m. Our meeting was reasonably cordial. Mr. Pasomba explained that his ministry was trying to establish whether I had adhered to the provisions of the Employment Act when I dismissed and retrenched some workers from the Institute. I gave him a comprehensive rundown of the reorganisation exercise, as well as copies of the documents and letters relating to each case of retrenchment. Mr. Pasomba listened patiently and at the end of our discussion thanked me for agreeing to meet and for cooperating fully with him. He promised to let me know what decision the ministry would take over the matter. I had to wait about four months to be informed that the matter had been closed.

21.5 Office of the Auditor General

Government interference included using the office of the Auditor-General to intimidate me. On Monday, 16th February, 1998, on my return to work after a week's absence, I received a letter from the Office of the Auditor-General dated 26th January, 1998. I was surprised because I had never been in direct contact or communication with the Office of the Auditor-General in all my years of heading government or quasi-government institutions; not as acting editor-in-chief of ZANA, nor during the years that I headed ZAMCOM through its initial phases as a government department and then as a statutory board.

My channel of reporting to government was through the Ministry of Information and Broadcasting Services. The Ministry was supposed to pass my reports to all relevant institutions of government. So, how could it be that when I was running an independent educational trust I was being contacted directly by the Office of the Auditor-General? The letter was as intimidating as any such letter could be.

It read, 'I note from my records that you have not been sending Audited Accounts and Management Letters to this office for my review. Please make appropriate arrangements to have the above documents delivered at the office. Provide the Audited Accounts and Management Letters for the years 1993 to 1996 soonest.' It was signed by Acting Assistant Director of Audits, Mr. M.C. Hara. I was, of course, irritated but put together the statements requested and on Wednesday, 18th February, 1998 decided to deliver them personally.

The Office of the Auditor-General was located next to the old City Airport, on the eastern end of Lusaka. Despite its hallowed reputation, it was housed in an unimpressive two-storey building, which appeared to be poorly maintained. The driveway was unpaved and dusty. After a guard had opened the gate for me, I could see that most of the surroundings were overgrown with rainy season grass and weeds. The reception area was unmanned and so I decided to venture further. I found a lady who asked a messenger to take me upstairs to Mr. Hara's office. Mr. Hara was very pleasant. He had kept abreast of developments at ZAMCOM, particularly my tribulations and said he had read about it all in the press.

After several minutes spent on courtesies, I handed over the documents. He glanced through them quickly and immediately raised issues concerning the Institute's operations and performance. It was evident that he knew his job well. We talked a little more, exchanged telephone numbers and promised to meet under different circumstances. We shook hands and I left. After several weeks I was told that the matter had been closed.

21.6 Anti-Corruption Commission moves in

The most threatening and exacting inquiry was that carried out by the ACC, the Anti-Corruption Commission. Their first visit to ZAMCOM was while I was on forced leave. After I resumed work, on the morning of Friday, 12th September 1997, two officers, Mr. Humphrey Mwiinga and a Mr. Lusanje visited ZAMCOM, but I was out of the office. They saw the assistant accountant, Charles Chikoti, who passed on their message to me. I immediately telephoned Humphrey Mwiinga and he explained that the

ACC was carrying out an inquiry and wanted to talk to me. We agreed to meet at 9 a.m. the following Monday.

Mr. Mwiinga, a young man in his thirties, had a fairly pleasant personality. He confirmed that the ACC were making an inquiry and that they wanted to inform me about it before asking for access to documents. I asked who the complainant was and he said the inquiry was based on an anonymous letter. I thought that unusual, as the ACC was not supposed to commence investigations unless the complainant could be clearly identified. (I later learned that, unhappy with the outcome of the Deliotte and Touche Zambia audit, the Ministry of Information and Broadcasting Services had impressed on the ACC to go ahead with the investigation on the basis of the anonymous letter.) I assured the ACC officer of my full cooperation and took him to the accountant whom I instructed to provide any documents that the ACC officer requested.

On Tuesday, 30th September, 1977, "The Post" newspaper carried a story on the ACC investigation headlined 'ACC probes ZAMCOM Boss', the story was attributed to 'sources at ZAMCOM'. It quoted ACC acting Director of Operations, Bradford Malumbe, as confirming that investigations had been instituted. Mr. Malumbe declined to divulge the nature of the investigations.

Two weeks later an officer of the ACC requested the ZAMCOM driver, Clayson Mwanza, to report to their office. Mr. Mwanza was interviewed by Humphrey Mwiinga, the officer who had been to see me a month earlier. According to Mr. Mwanza, who reported back to me, two officers began the interview by demanding that he give them a statement about his trips to Chengelo Secondary School in Mkushi, Central Province, the boarding school where three of my children were studying. Mr. Mwanza said he had confirmed that he sometimes travelled to Chengelo, but only when I was busy and he always used my personal vehicle. He said the ACC officers were surprised when he told them that at that particular time I had no company car and was using my own car for both personal and official duties. After writing a statement from the answers that he had given them, the ACC officers asked Mr. Mwanza to read and sign it, which he did.

I was not very worried about the ACC investigation, especially since the Deloitte and Touche Zambia audit had already exonerated me. However, I was aware that, while Deloitte and Touche Zambia was part of an independent international auditing firm, ACC was a government agency which – possibly – could be manipulated by government officials bent on discrediting me. I seriously hoped that ACC did not operate in that way. On Wednesday, 19th November 1997, I received a telephone call from Humphrey Mwiinga asking me to see him at the ACC offices in Findeco House, in the Lusaka Central Business District, the following day at 2.30 p.m.

Findeco House was Lusaka's tallest building at that time. Situated on the southern end of the city, the building was notorious for having poorly maintained elevators. I arrived at the building fifteen minutes early but was held up for nearly twenty minutes in a queue for the elevators. The ACC offices occupied the entire 18th floor. The office in which my interview took place was, like most government offices for middle level and lower level staff, sparsely furnished with worn carpeting and files piled on the floor in one corner. My interrogator, Humphrey Mwiinga, was with another officer who did not give his name but who came up with questions from time to time.

Mwiinga opened by reading to me a warn-and-caution statement outlining the allegations drawn from the anonymous letter. He then asked me to sign it. I asked if I could consult with my lawyer and Mwiinga and the other officer did not object. I phoned and my lawyer confirmed that there was nothing wrong with signing as long as I understood the allegations. The interview took two hours and was conducted in a fairly professional manner. I answered all the questions as best as I could, whereafter Mwiinga read back the statement to me. I was surprised with the fluency and accuracy of the report. I was given an opportunity to ask questions and I inquired what the next step would be. Mwiinga said he would examine all the information he had gathered and decide what course of action to take. He said there were three options: recommend the case to be closed, measures to be taken by the Institute, or decide to prosecute.

At the end of the ACC interview, I asked if I could have a copy of the warn-and-caution statement as well as my own statement. Mwiinga promised to bring copies to my office the following Monday. He said he needed to look through some of the supporting documents. However, on Monday 24th November 1997, the day on which I was marking my forty-fifth birthday, Mwiinga did not come to my office. He instead telephoned my secretary, Ms. Bridget Nkonde, and asked to see her the following day. Ms Nkonde was clearly uneasy about the ACC interview. Before she knocked off she told me that she would that night pray for strength so that the interview could go well. The following day she went to the ACC office, carrying with her copies of documents Mwiinga had requested. Her interview took only thirty minutes and she told me that it centred on what she knew about the house that I was building and how my local and foreign trips were organised and by whom.

I heard nothing from the ACC about my request for a copy of the warn-and-caution statement or anything else. I was, therefore, shocked and surprised when on Tuesday, 23rd December, 1997, I received a Christmas card from the ACC proclaiming 'Best Wishes at Christmas and New Year' from the 'Chairman, Commissioners, Director General and Staff of the Commission'. I did not know what to think. Was this an assurance that all was well and I should, therefore, enjoy my Christmas holiday, or was it a reminder that the investigation was still continuing. As the days went by a reliable source told me that the Ministry of Information and Broadcasting Services had been trying to get the ACC to speed up its investigations into my case. I was told that the ministry contacted the ACC on two occasions, forcing the ACC to write back and advise that the organisation had its own way of carrying out its work and that it did not operate under pressure from whatever quarter. The ACC indicated that once the investigations were concluded normal reporting procedures would be followed.

I heard nothing from the ACC until 14th March, 1998, when Mwiinga called at my office. I was away and he met my secretary from whom he requested copies of documents concerning my retirement benefits. (I later discovered that he had been to ZAMCOM on several occasions and had met with Assistant Accountant, Charles Chikoti.) I telephoned Mwiinga later that day and our conversation went like this:

'Mr. Mwiinga, good afternoon. You behave like our seasonal mushroom. Today you are seen and tomorrow you are not.'

Some chuckling on the phone. 'Yes, Mr. Daka. You see with our work, you make your report and others tell you to get more information about certain things.'

Me: 'I am told you want some documents?'
Mwiinga: 'Yes, I need the documents on your benefits.'
Me: 'I will send copies to you this afternoon.'
Mwiinga: 'Thank you.'

I had no further contact with the ACC until towards the end of July, when I was proceeding on leave. Exactly one year to the time when I was hounded out of office I decided to take my full vacation. I needed the break because I had not taken any real vacation since joining ZAMCOM. Instead, each time I needed to rest I took a week or so and returned quickly to carry on with my work, or because something important had cropped up. This time I thought, 'To hell with what happens in my absence.' So before departing I called ACC Director of Operations, Mr. Malumbe and jokingly said that there was some uncompleted business between me and his office and that I wanted him to know that I would be out of the office and Lusaka for some time. He laughed and said the ACC had no problems with 'high-placed people like you. It is only when we deal with people of no fixed addresses that we worry,' he said, adding, 'We know where to find you when need arises.' I could not discern whether that statement carried a threat or not.

The investigation went on for a long time and ended quietly. On 10th July, 2000, three years after the investigations had been instituted, I wrote a letter to the ACC director general requesting for a copy of the report. The response was written on 8th August, 2000, and stated that investigations had established that the conditions of service for the position of ZAMCOM director at that time were vague and thus prone to abuse. The letter, signed by Director of Operations, Mr. Malumbe said, 'It has been felt that administrative remedies would be more appropriate than criminal proceedings. This recommendation was communicated to your Permanent Secretary at the Ministry of Information and Broadcasting Services and our docket was closed'. In this roundabout way the ACC's investigation ended. I never saw the report and the ministry never raised the matter with me directly.

I later became aware that the closure of this and other investigations did not mean the end of interest in me or my activities whilst I was at ZAMCOM and, subsequently, when I relocated to the provincial town of Chipata and set up and started operating my own radio station. I will not get into the details of the harassment that I continued to experience and suffer; suffice to say that my origins were thoroughly investigated. I was also put on continuous surveillance, my mail was intercepted, my telephones tapped and my movements closely monitored. At ZAMCOM in Lusaka and later at Breeeze FM radio station in Chipata some of my subordinates and employees were recruited to report to the authorities. Then, and later, only my honesty and positivity kept me focused on my work and, in the process, saved me from these ill-intentioned machinations.

22. Contract renewal

As the surveillance continued and one investigation after another floundered I became convinced that the campaign to get me removed from my position would definitely fail and that the investigations would only serve to exonerate me. It dawned on me, of course, that those working against me were hoping that if the campaign to remove me failed I would, in any case, be so intimidated that I would resign anyway, which would still serve their purpose.

But I was neither intimidated, nor ruffled. Instead I grew stronger in my position and my confidence soared. I decided to stay put and complete my assignment at ZAMCOM.

And so, in May, 1999, while the harassment was still ongoing, I decided to write to the board chairman giving notice of my desire to renew my Service Agreement. The term of office for the director should have been five years, but I asked for a reduction to three years, instead, explaining that this was going to be my last agreement.

I was already making arrangements to set up a media organisation in my home town of Chipata, the provincial capital of Eastern Province and after completing my contract I was going to leave Lusaka. I am not sure whether Mr. Sichula and other board members took what I was telling them seriously. It is obvious that most people in my position would have preferred a long contract with options for renewal. Maybe, like everyone else, they thought that I was upset about the investigations and would change my mind as time went by. This could not have been further from the truth. I had already made up my mind that it was time to move on and that I wanted not only to establish my own media company but to do so in person, 560 kilometres away from Lusaka.

I was psychologically ready to go. No hanging around Lusaka and running my company by remote control. I was going to retire from my job, relocate and, through my own media organisation contribute further to media work and media development.

Of course, the chairman and some of the board members might have, perhaps, been happy that the director, who was too assertive and, sometimes, even headstrong, would finally be leaving the Institute. It is a known fact that most board members generally prefer to work with a chief executive whom they can manipulate and coerce to do their bidding including facilitating business deals, and some of them attempted to do so, but I was definitely not that kind of chief executive. Whatever the case, two months after I applied to renew my agreement, I received a letter from the board chairman which stated that at its meeting of 29th June, 1999, the board had approved the renewal of my agreement for the three years requested.

Given the background of accusations, suspicion and lack of trust, the tone of the board chairman's letter was surprising to me. He wrote, 'I wish to take this opportunity to congratulate you in the manner you have ably conducted the affairs of the Trust as Chief Executive and for the commitment you have shown to the objectives of the institution. I can only hope that the same spirit will prevail during your renewed term of office'. The new agreement took effect on 1st November, 1999, giving me until 31st October, 2002, to complete my assignment at ZAMCOM.

I was confident that I was finally ready go it alone, to gain real control over my work and time. I was very happy with the prospect of being a 'free' man by the time I reached my fiftieth birthday, five years early, since the regular retirement age in Zambia at the time was fifty-five years. In truth, many people in the public service were not ready to retire at the age of fifty-five.

Some were known to go as far as to alter their birth dates on their National Registration Card in a desperate effort to extend their stay at work. Others struggled to arrange for post-retirement contracts in order to remain in gainful employment. Not me. The decision to quit my job and retire early was final and I was confident about the direction of my new purpose and goal and the successful outcome of my next venture.

23. Training at ZAMCOM thrives

With my contract in place, I immersed myself fully in my work. At this particular time training activities at the Institute were at their highest level. Several organisations began to use – and work with the Institute on regional training programmes. The most consistent was the NSJ Southern African Media Training Trust, which was based in Maputo, Mozambique. NSJ was a regional training facility supported by the Nordic governments with the Danish International Development Agency, Danida, as the lead coordinating organisation. Although well funded, NSJ had no permanent training facilities at its base in Mozambique, so it held its workshops and courses in different countries and locations. This entailed huge logistical challenges. As a way of minimizing these challenges, and in an effort to assist in building the capacity of media training institutions in the region, NSJ decided to locate some of their regular workshops and courses in three institutions. ZAMCOM was identified as the host institution for print media programmes, Rhodes University in Grahamstown, South Africa was assigned the responsibility of hosting management courses while Namibia Broadcasting Corporation, NBC, was given the task of hosting electronic media courses. During my tenure as director of ZAMCOM I also served as a board member of the NSJ, which strengthened contacts between the Institute and the Mozambican-based trust because I regulary visited their Mozambique headquarters.

Two other international organisations, the UK-based Thomson Foundation and the Economic Development Institute of the World Bank, EDI, began to hold their annual regional broadcasting and business courses at ZAMCOM, attended by journalists drawn from east, central and southern Africa. The regional training activities, as well as local courses and workshops created a serious problem of where to accommodate the high number of foreign participants.

Although the ZAMCOM hostel on Church Road, in the Rhodes Park

149

residential area, had been cleaned up by FNF, who also created additional room space, the number of rooms was still limited and the standards of the hostel were rather tacky. On many occasions, ZAMCOM was forced to book rooms in nearby lodges and hotels. This arrangement did not, of course, solve the accommodation problem. Lusaka, at this time, had two standards of hotel accommodation, up-market expensive and low-level cheap; both were unsuitable for housing foreign course participants. Participants from outside Lusaka and other countries were mostly booked into lower level hotels or lodges and as a result there were many complaints about overall poor standards.

We were also confronted with a bizarre situation. Almost always, a week into the training, the enthusiasm and excitement of the male participants seemed to suddenly drop. The situation got out of hand during a NSJ course facilitated by Zimbabwean veteran trainer, Farai Munyuki (a.k.a. Albert Mvula when he worked at the Zambia Daily Mail in Lusaka). The participants demanded that the course be cut from three weeks to two weeks.

I had noticed that the female participants were not as vocal as their male counterparts, so one evening I decided to take a couple of male participants out for a drink. After putting away a couple of beers, the guys blurted out that there was nothing wrong with the quality of training or calibre of trainers but that nearly all of the male participants had run out of money. They said that the lodge where they were staying was frequented by 'nice, good-time girls' whom they could not resist and that, before they knew it, all their money was gone.

After discussions with Farai Munyuki, it was agreed to change the arrangement for dinner. In order for the course to proceed without disruption it was agreed that in place of pre-paid meals, participants would be given money so that they could arrange for their own evening meals. With money in their pockets the participants quietened down and the course continued without further disruption. But the message was very clear. ZAMCOM needed to upgrade its hostel into a lodge, which could not only accommodate its participants comfortably, but also earn income for the Institute by taking in non-participants during periods when there were no courses or workshops. This idea fitted in well with my ongoing search for different ways of making ZAMCOM work as a self-financing educational institution.

24. NORAD Programme Support

The answer to how to upgrade the hostel came when the ambassador at the Royal Norwegian Embassy, Mr. Jon Lomoy, a real friend of journalists in Zambia, hosted a dinner for senior representatives of the media at his residence. Mr. Lomoy wanted to know the best way of supporting media development in Zambia. Several ideas were put forward, the most consistent being the need for effective pre-service and in-service training. True to his word, Mr. Lomoy set aside a large sum of money for pre-service and in-service media training.

The pre-service support in journalism training over many years was given to the Department of Journalism at the Evelyn Hone College, while in-service training support was based at ZAMCOM. On 25th May, 2000, the Royal Norwegian Embassy signed a contract with ZAMCOM entitled, 'Programme Support 2000-2001' which was worth 5 million Norwegian kroner, equivalent to US$540,000. The contract was a culmination of discussions with First Secretary for Development at the Norwegian Embassy, Kikkan Haugen, and the development of a project proposal covering various areas of training and the rehabilitation of the student hostel.

The main goal of the project was to contribute to a diversified, open and sustainable quality media sector in Zambia and to heighten the professional level of journalism in Zambia. Forty-eight per cent of the money was allocated for training over the three-year period, while 52 per cent of the budget (K2.6 million or US$280,777) was given for the rehabilitation of the student hostel. Under the agreement ZAMCOM was to do two things, increase the student user fees from 10 per cent to 20 per cent and use its own funds to complete the hostel if NORAD funding proved to be insufficient.

Training activities went on well and participants, media organisations and the Norwegian Embassy, were all happy with the regularity and quality of the courses. In January, 2001, Kikkan Haugen in a letter to ZAMCOM wrote, 'Please be informed that we have read your reports with great interest and are pleased to learn that the programmes are well on track. We have also assessed your expenditure reports, and found them to be in good order.'

Meanwhile, the job of planning for the construction of the student lodge was put to a public tender and Mutema Associates, Architects and Designers won the bid. Principal Architect, Lemmy Mutema, was professional and consistent with drawing up the diagrams, seeking planning and construction permission and overseeing the construction work.

Mutema Associates initially planned for the development of a two-storey facility with forty self-contained rooms, a spacious verandah and a dining area. Bids were invited for companies to carry out the construction work and the task was given to a Chinese company based in Zambia, Wong Kong Construction.

There was one snag. The project architects found that the old house at plot number 4614/2, Andrew Mwenya Road, built in the colonial times and renovated by FNF to serve as a hostel, had no foundation and, therefore, could not be rehabilitated. This meant that the old structure needed to be pulled down and a new building erected. This revelation was followed by renewed discussions with the Norwegian Embassy who were very understanding and approved my request to erect a new building. I was, of course, fully aware of the second condition of the 'Programme Support 2000-2001' project – that ZAMCOM was supposed 'to use its own funds to complete the hostel rehabilitation if NORAD funding is not sufficient.' The Embassy reminded me of this proviso but acknowledged that the increase in cost was largely due to unforeseen circumstances. Kikkan Haugen gave me three conditions under which the Embassy was willing to consider some additional funding. He stated that the embassy needed to know what resources ZAMCOM had on its own to put into the completion of the project, explore other possibilities of funding, for instance through a bank loan, get back to the contractor and renegotiate the price and the terms of payment.

ZAMCOM had no money of its own which could be put into the project. The Institute was, at this stage, also not in a position to get a loan from a commercial bank. We could, however, renegotiate the construction costs with the contractor and did so. This was only possible with adjustments to the building without compromising the basic facilities or quality. We sacrificed half the structure, the top floor and reduced the number of rooms to twenty. Within three weeks the new ambassador, Mr. Halvard Lesteberg, with whom I had already discussed ZAMCOM and its operations as well as progress on the project, and board chairman, Maxwell Sichula signed an addendum to the original contract for a grant of NOK1,070,000, approximately US$116,000.

A pertinent provision in the addendum stated that, 'by signing this addendum, ZAMCOM commits itself contractually to complete the hostel project and that no further funding from the Norwegian embassy will be given to this project.' Indeed, no further funding was sought from the Norwegian embassy or anywhere else.

The Chinese company, Wong Kong Construction, carried out the work expeditiously and satisfactorily and the new, glittering ZAMCOM Lodge was completed and commissioned for use by course participants and other clients on 15th March, 2002. The lodge was a progressive new landmark on Lusaka's Church Road and became an instant income generating facility for the Institute, as had been planned.

25. Winding down my work at ZAMCOM

With the commissioning of the lodge my work at ZAMCOM was, essentially, also complete and I was ready for the next and, definitely, final phase of my formal working life. The situation at the Institue had calmed down considerably and months were passing by slowly. Three months before the end of my contract I reminded the board chairman that I had completed my assignment and was ready to retire from my position of director. He asked me to assist in the recruitment of my successor. The position was advertised, interviews were carried out and someone who appeared to be a good candidate, Dr. Emmanuel Kasongo, a Zambian academician working in South Africa, was selected to succeed me. I spent the month of September, 2002 orienting him to the Institute and the office of director.

I took Dr. Kasongo around to our most valued client organisations: media institutions, government ministries, parastatal organisations, embassies and non-governmental organisations. I also managed to convince a Dutch media development organisation, Free Voice, to include Dr. Kasongo on their invitations to a meeting of partners which was to take place in

Windhoek, Namibia. At the meeting I was not only able to introduce my successor to Free Voice officials, but also to many representatives of media training institutions in Southern Africa.

Upon our return from Windhoek, although there was still one month to go before the end of my contract, I asked the Board of Trustees to allow me to leave early. I had been sharing the office with my successor for one full month and I was convinced that he was more than well briefed about the organisation and its operations. Looking back on my thirteen years at ZAMCOM, although I had, in so many words, been to hell and back, the Institute had also, undoubtedly, helped me to grow, both as a person and as a media leader. With my previous employer, ZANA, the management system had been authoritative and dictatorial, but at ZAMCOM my management and leadership style had definitely begun to change into a participatory one. The nature of the institution and the organisational development work that was carried out there demanded strategic thinking, planning, delegating, coordinating within ZAMCOM and consulting and negotiating with government and donors. ZAMCOM with the diversity of its partners, clients and range of activities as well as its challenges, had been the best training school that anyone in my position could have hoped for.

ZAMCOM taught me to think critically, to question everything and to be a good planner and manager. The Institute taught me everything from developing a successful business to managing people and resources. I also learnt how to deal with deception and duplicity and government manipulation. I was the better for it, in fact, because I had become a much better and stronger manager.

The experience was totally enriching. At the end of my service I had built ZAMCOM into an internationally-recognised media training school while ZAMCOM had also helped to establish my professional *bona fides*. There is no doubt that ZAMCOM, its good and bad experiences, marked the most important turning point in my life. More importantly, my trials and tribulations at ZAMCOM were a veritable case of good triumphing over bad and evil. And as can be expected it helped to reignite my spirituality. I realised that despite my honesty and sincerity I would not have survived the many spurious accusations levelled against me if a more powerful force had not interceded on my behalf.

My spirituality was expressed largely through eternal gratitude and thanksgiving for all the good in my life and by my doing whatever good I could for all who came into contact with me through my work, knowledge and ideas.

26. The idea of going it alone is born

The idea of reinventing myself, again, came when I was at home for three weeks in August, 1997, on suspension from work. Instead of moaning and whingeing about my predicament, I made up my mind to leave ZAMCOM but on my own terms. I was at the peak of my professional life, a time one is not expected to think about leaving. But I felt strongly that the challenges that I was facing were tests for preparing me for the next stage of my existence and a new life. There was no doubt that ZAMCOM had made me stronger and more determined to take on new challenges and attain even higher personal and professional goals, but I knew that getting a job was out of question even though two organisations had contacted me already.

OSISA, the Open Society Initiative for Southern Africa, funded by the international financier and philanthropist, George Soros, had just opened an office in Johannesburg, South Africa. The organisation was expanding its activities and needed a well qualified and experienced hand to manage its media programme. A teleconference interview was conducted between Cape Town, Johannesburg and Lusaka. All was going well until the issue of salary and conditions of service came up. I indicated that my job at ZAMCOM paid me a salary and perks equivalent to US$5,000. I could hear the gasps down the telephone lines as the people in Cape Town and Johannesburg reacted. They said that kind of salary would spark a revolution in the organisation because no one was being paid that much. I decided not to take the job on a lower salary because I knew that relocating to South Africa on a job contract would result in my losing my national status and, of course, the many fringe benefits, opportunities and support systems that go with working in one's own country.

The second job offer was from One World, a London-based non-governmental organisation which needed someone to open their regional operations at the British Council offices in Lusaka. I had interviews with officials of the organisation at Gatwick Airport in London while transiting to Lusaka from Geneva, Switzerland, where I had been to attend a meeting at the head office of UNAIDS, the UN agency dealing with HIV and AIDS. But again the issue of salary and conditions of service was the contention problem. While the organisation said that they wanted to engage an experienced African media expert, they were not prepared to pay a salary commensurate with the knowledge and experience of such a person. In the end, the interviewing team thought that I was over-qualified for the job and told me so.

During my flight back to Lusaka, it dawned on me that I was wasting my time considering the possibility of a job after my service at ZAMCOM and as days went by the idea of setting up a newspaper in my home town of Chipata occupied my mind. My plans were for Chipata and not my Lusaka childhood neighbourhood of Matero, where the idea of becoming a journalist first came to me. By this time I had realised that Matero was a complex multi-populated area with too many disparate interests and needs. There was no doubt in my mind that quitting my job and relocating to Chipata to start a newspaper from scratch needed serious planning and organisation to get everything in place.

I was not foolhardy and did not want to rush, preferring to prepare well before getting started. So I approached the office of USAID-funded International Executive Services Corps, IESC in Lusaka and sought the services of an experienced volunteer who could help me carry out a feasibility study on the establishment of a provincial newspaper in Chipata. I think that my reputation at ZAMCOM and my track record from working with USAID on the Good Governance Project helped IESC to support my idea. IESC engaged Charles 'Chuck' Treat of Scottsdale, Arizona, USA to come to Zambia to help me. Charles Treat was a retired newspaper man who had worked for various newspapers in editorial and management positions. He was ideally suited for the role. Although in his seventies, he was energetic and had a great sense of humour. He travelled with me on the potholed road to Chipata for Phase 1 of my project. In those days the Lusaka-Chipata stretch was really rough terrain and it took twelve hours to cover the distance of 560 kilometres.

The idea of going it alone is born

Official contacts in Chipata were made for me by my former school mate and close friend, Mambo Banda, who happened to be the vice chairman of EPCCI, the Eastern Province Chamber of Commerce and Industry. Mambo had bought a lodge near Chipata airport and was spending a lot of time there. He was fervently trying to convince other enterprising Easterners to join him in establishing businesses in Chipata and other districts and got EPCCI to help me set up meetings with business, civic and government officials. Chuck and I met with twenty-nine community leaders from different sectors and discussed with them the idea of starting a publication in the province.

The approach taken in gathering information for my project was to pose two main questions, 'Does the area want and need a newspaper in English and the local Chinyanja (Chewa) language, covering local events?' and 'Will you support a venture of this type?' We also requested the community leaders to underline their support by providing verbal intent for both advertising and circulation sales as well as editorial interests and distribution logistics. To find out about the availability and capacity of printing facilities in Chipata and its environs we visited Kolbe Printing Press run by the Catholic Church Diocese and the Weekly Chronicle newspaper in Lilongwe, Malawi. We also visited the Mozambique High Commission in Lilongwe to find out whether there would be any interest in the project and what assistance would be available to support the distribution of the newspaper in the Mozambican adjoining province of Tete, where the Chewa language, which is spoken in eastern Zambia and Malawi, is also in use.

By the end of the week our two questions were answered positively. We established that there was need for a newspaper in Eastern Province published in English and the Chewa language. The business community and other sectors were willing to support the project and suitable printing facilities would be available in Lilongwe, Malawi. The agreement with Robert Jamieson of the Weekly Chronicle was to deliver the newspaper to Mchinji/Mwami, the Malawi/Zambia border post.

Meanwhile Chuck and I used our time in Chipata to work out business details such as format and size, general content, policy and advertising potential in both languages. We also had time to examine issues related to staffing and use of correspondents and stringers, news sources and the use of the internet, frequency of publication, distribution, production process, pricing of advertisements and selling price. We also drew up the timetable for completion of the project.

We then returned to Lusaka, prepared our Phase 1 report and submitted it to IESC. The final report, which was to constitute Phase II of my project, was prepared by Chuck after he returned to the USA in October, 1998. The report included a list of equipment and supplies as well as estimated start up costs and a strategic operational budget and forecasts for the first five year period. I was thus armed with a project that I could start as soon as I was ready to do so but I dutifully continued with my work at ZAMCOM.

27. Radio, it is

It was not long before word reached me from Lilongwe that the Weekly Chronicle printing press had been moved from Lilongwe to the commercial city of Blantyre, nearly 500 kilometres from Chipata. The transportation costs of the newspaper from Blantyre in Malawi to Mchinji/Mwami on the Malawi/Zambia border would push up the cost of the newspaper to a level which people in Chipata would not afford. I needed to make a quick decision on whether to go ahead with my newspaper project or think of something else to do.

Fortunately, two years earlier, the Zambian government had liberalised the airwaves, effectively ending the monopoly of ZNBC, the state broadcaster. This landmark decision had precipitated the setting up of privately-owned and community radio stations in different parts of the country. My organisation, ZAMCOM, began providing training to communities planning to open community radio stations. The most intensive training programme was that supported by UNESCO for the establishment of Mazabuka Community Radio Station. My team and I took our field equipment and camped in Mazabuka for two weeks to provide orientation and practical training to board members, managers, reporters, producers and presenters.

The bad news from Lilongwe, about the relocation of the printing press, reached me when I returned to Lusaka from Mazabuka. And so, while I was considering whether to carry on with my newspaper project or to consider doing something else, I saw an advertisement in the daily newspapers from the Ministry of Information and Broadcasting Services entitled 'Invitation for Broadcasting Licence Applications'. Under the category of FM Radio, the advertisement stated, 'Applications are invited for the establishment of Radio (FM Stations) for all provincial centres throughout the Republic of Zambia in the frequency range of 87.5 to 108 MHz.' The advertisement provided the perfect answer to my asking myself a rhetorical question, 'If I can help others to set up radio stations, why can I not set up one for myself?'

I decided to switch from newspaper to radio and then moved really fast. I explained my predicament to IESC and Chuck and assured them that I had not abandoned my newspaper project but would revisit it when conditions were more favourable. Then I proceeded to incorporate Chipata Radio Services which was later to trade as Breeze FM. This was done on 16th February, 2000. The company had two shareholders, myself and Philip Haggar, a British colleague based in London, who had previously helped to set up and manage Radio Christian Voice in Lusaka. Our ideas gelled and we agreed to partner in setting up the radio station in Chipata with me holding 80 per cent of the shares in Chipata Radio Services while Phil Haggar held 20 per cent.

We worked together to develop a business plan to guide the implementation of the project, spelling out the vision and mission of the station, the various operational policies and the type of equipment and facilities that were required. The plan also reflected the economic, legal and social factors under which the radio station would operate and gave a prognosis of what was required for the station to be ready for start-up as well as objectives for the first year and prospects for the future.

Backed by solid preparation, I now needed to come up with an implementation plan. In order to do this properly, I decided to enrol in a goal setting training programme being run by an old friend, Patrick Chisanga. I had known Patrick since our Evelyn Hone College days. Since then, he had served in various senior public sector positions and was now running a company called Dynamic Concepts Limited which provided personal and corporate goal setting training programmes, and was a licencee in Zambia of SMI, Success Motivation International of the United States of America. Patrick and I and other colleagues had been among the people who had initiated the setting up of the Institute of Directors (IOD) in Zambia, and so I did not need much convincing in trusting him and the programme he was organising.

I started the one-on-one Dynamics of Personal Goal Setting programme on 21st February, 2000. Each week I prepared two seven-day goals, one personal and the other for business. The purpose of the exercise was to form the habit of setting and reaching goals every week. At the beginning of each session I reported on progress on the goals from the previous meeting. At this stage in my life I had already become accustomed to the idea and habit of setting goals but the programme helped me to focus more clearly on how to develop short term specific goals which needed to be accomplished in order for me to achieve my long term goals. I was required to write down the specific goals, follow them up and review them during my sessions with Patrick. Along with a project implementation plan for the radio station, the programme helped me to draw up an exit plan from ZAMCOM.

Three main activities required attention: finalising arrangements for training projects with various donors, finalising departmental development plans and completing the construction of the ZAMCOM Lodge. The implementation plan for the radio station involved six activities: locating premises and an antenna site within three months, applying for a licence, identifying and training on-air staff within six months, recruiting commercial sales agents within six months, constructing the radio station within eighteen months and starting test transmissions within eighteen months.

It was at this stage, when I was armed with both my plans that I declined the five-year contract offered to me by the Board of Trustees and instead opted for the three-year one. This was, undoubtedly, a huge risk for me and, particularly, for my family. I had a good job which provided for a decent lifestyle in Zambia. I also had young children whose private school education was being paid for by my employers. In rejecting the five-year contract I had burnt my bridges and made any retreat or failure impossible.

Radio, it is

As soon as word got around about my plans, professional colleagues, friends and some of my family members, including my wife, thought that I had gone crazy. How does someone give up a good, regular job in Lusaka, with a secure income in order to relocate to a place in the middle of nowhere in pursuit of what was thought to be a far-fetched dream? I could not blame anyone for thinking that I had gone out of my mind, because in pursuing my dream I was making the ultimate sacrifice.

I sold the family house that I had been building, quit my job and invested my benefits from ZAMCOM and all my savings in my project and had no salary for nearly two years after I moved to Chipata. Meanwhile I had school fees to pay for three children at an expensive boarding school.

At the time of writing this, in June, 2018, only the eldest guy Gerald had missed out on solid tertiary education although he settled down to a busy family life in Lusaka with his wife, Anita and their four children. His siblings did much better. Dalitso and Dabwitso underwent undergraduate studies at Notre Dame University and Mudorch University in Perth, Australia and stayed on to work and naturalise their status, while Chimfwembe got her first degree at Monash University in Johannesburg, South Africa and Masters degree at China's leading university, Tsinghua in Beijing.

Dalitso was working as acting Team Leader at the Ability Centre which specialises in helping patients suffering from celebral palsy in Perth, Australia. He was married to an Australian wife, Sineada, and they had a baby boy, Logan. Strangely, Dalitso was so much like his Uncle William for it took him twelve years to come back home after going to school in Australia and his visits were infrequent. Chimfwembe had worked as marketing manager of FranklinCovey Zambia, a performance improvement company and later was conflicted about taking up PhD studies and starting her own company. Our youngest son, Dabwitso, was a business banking manager with one of Australia's biggest banks, Westpac in Perth but had also set up his own company, Kuyasa Energy Solutions Limited, an alternative energy firm. Kuyasa means lighting up. Dabwitso was, predictably, most committed to Zambia and was a regular visitor to Zambia and Chipata. Unsurprising to me he was one of twenty-two Zambian and 1,000 African young entrepreneurs who participated in the 2018 Tony Elumelu ten year, US$100 million Entrepreneurship Programme created to identify, train, mentor and fund outstanding African entrepreneurs who have start-ups or business ideas with the potential to grow and provide jobs for the African continent.

The question many people were asking was why did I choose to establish a commercial radio station in a rural area at a time when the country's economy was not doing well? I had several reasons all of which I felt were sensible. To start with, I was fed up of my job and of living in Lusaka. I had been in the same position for thirteen years and had transformed ZAMCOM from a small government training department to a respected independent regional training centre. There was little else for me to do in my work. In addition, I had lived in Lusaka most of my life and was no longer in tune with the attitude and mood of the place. And lastly, I did not think that I could work well in a big organisation. I had been my own boss, more or less, for more than ten years and knew that it would be difficult to have to report to someone in a large hierarchical organisation.

By this time, the Zambian government had opened up the broadcasting sector to players other than the national broadcaster, ZNBC. I had no doubt in my mind that the 1994 liberalisation of the airwaves was one of the most important developments that had taken place in the media sector in Zambia in a very long time. I also believed that the new scenario presented a wonderful opportunity for any media person wishing to move on to a new professional challenge. Fortunately for me, I had had radio production and management training with the BBC in London and back home in Zambia had gained practical knowledge and experience in setting up a radio station. Also, I had been in charge of a training institute offering broadcasting training to working journalists.

So, in relocating to Chipata and setting up my own radio station, I had a great opportunity for practicing what I had been preaching at ZAMCOM and for showing that a commercial radio station could be successfully established and operated in a rural area. An amazing challenge and motivation.

At a personal level, I could not ask for a better way to give back to my community while at the same time establishing my traditional roots and reclaiming my heritage. So for very strong professional and sentimental reasons, I found the idea of relocating to the 'home town' that I had never known an exciting and truly worthwhile proposition.

28. Securing a building in Chipata

Luckily, I had a backlog of unutilised leave days amounting to six months, because the changes that had been taking place at ZAMCOM had made it difficult for me to go on vacation for long periods of time. Those leave days were now extremely important to me. I negotiated with the board to take my leave days as and when I needed to within the three year contract period. The board agreed and so I started visiting Chipata on a regular basis and was able to familiarise myself with the layout of the town, key institutions and leading personalities.

A senior engineer with ZNBC, Frank Mushota, helped me to draw up a floor plan for my radio station which I pasted on the wall alongside my desk at ZAMCOM. Each time I looked up from my desk I saw my new life. I also visualised the radio station each time I drove to Chipata and, with that sketch in mind, I began in earnest to look for a site for the radio station. Finding a secure and centrally located building for the radio station in Chipata was not easy. The search for a good location was made even more difficult because I was new to the town. Local businessmen, like most small town business people, were suspicious of this fellow from the capital city and unconvinced of my plans to set up a commercial radio station in what they felt was 'their' town.

I applied for a commercial plot from the Chipata Municipal Council and the council kept making promises to allocate land to the company but did not deliver. There were several offers of buildings from local businessmen, including a house on Lumumba Road owned by Ziah Construction Company and the site office for Crystal Springs Hotel, but all the buildings were unsuitable because they were either too small, or not centrally located, or the owners demanded too much money in rentals.

Eventually, I found an ideal location for the station when a local businessman, Idriss Ugrader, who was popularly known by his company name, 'Mosali', took me to the building that had housed Lima Bank, an agricultural bank for small scale farmers, which was then under liquidation. The former Lima Bank building was for sale but, apparently, local businessmen were trying to force the price down. The building was located at the heart of the Chipata Central Business District. The office block comprised six offices, a banking hall, strong room, registry room, storeroom, two toilets and an adjoining storage shed. Water, electricity, sewerage and telephone services were already available and it had a tarred frontage to the road. The building also had line-of-sight congruence with the telecommunications tower where the transmitter and antenna were to be sited. The tower was sixty metres high and was situated on Kanjala Hill I, one of the highest points in Chipata.

When I walked into the building that hot October afternoon, the place was crowded. There were several small companies and traders of all kinds operating from there. Every office and space, including the strong room, were taken up yet I instantly felt that it was the place for my radio station. I marvelled that the station would be plumb in the centre of town, next to a taxi rank, down the road from the town's main fresh produce market, close to the main banks and surrounded by restaurants and shops. The station would be fully accessible to the people. Interestingly, the final configuration of the radio station inside the building was not too far removed from that on the sketch of that original floor plan.

I spoke to the caretaker, Mr Geoffrey Sakala, who referred me to the liquidators, Grant Thornton Associates Limited, in Lusaka. Immediately I arrived back in Lusaka I had a meeting with the liquidation manager, Mr. Miza Phiri who told me that they had been experiencing problems in trying to sell the building because offers from all those who were expressing interest were low. He said the minimum sale price for the building was K80 million, just under US$20,000 and there were liabilities relating to outstanding payments to former employees which needed to be offset. I was given three months to make the payment or lose the offer. At that time I only had the US dollar equivalent of about K69 million. But what happened between October and December, 2000, was simply miraculous. Perhaps, it was the strong intention that I had to set up my own radio station. It could also have been my eagerness to leave ZAMCOM or, indeed, pure Divine intervention.

Whatever the case, the rate of the Zambian Kwacha against the US Dollar in October was around 3,450:1; in November 4,000:1; in December 4,157:1. This loss in value of the Zambian currency was a great fillip for me. And so, before the offer deadline was up, the US$20,000 that I had in the US dollar account converted to over K83 million. I had enough money to pay for the building and immediately wrote to Grant Thorton Associates Limited offering K80 million for the Lima Bank building in Chipata.

During the second week of April, 2001, I travelled to Chipata and met with the tenants in the building. Eight small companies were still operating businesses there and I had a letter for each of them. The caretaker, Mr. Sakala, had intimated to me that the tenants were seeking an extension of their stay whilst making arrangements to find alternative premises. My message to them was simple. I said that as their new landlord I would allow them to remain and conduct their businesses in the building for a period of three months, up to 30th June, 2001. When I informed them that I was not going to charge them any rent for the period, there were shouts of jubilation. (My lawyer, Alfred Lungu of Chilupe and Company had advised me against taking any money in rentals from the tenants because that would give them occupancy rights when I wanted them to vacate the premises.) I wished them and their businesses good fortune but hoped that they would cooperate by taking good care of the premises and vacating their offices/spaces on or before 30th June, 2001.

Unfortunately, the excitement about not paying rent did not translate into any serious attempt to vacate the building because three months later, when I returned to take possession of my building, all the tenants were still there. I met with them on a Monday morning and this time did not mince my words. I gave them up to the end of the week to move out, warning them that on Friday I would lock the building and anyone who wanted to collect their goods would have to travel to Lusaka to negotiate with me. That Friday I found that all but two tenants had gone. The two who remained tried to entice me into allowing them to stay on and in return provide services, such as food and photocopying, to the radio station. I was not listening. They left that afternoon and I finally took possession of my building.

I asked the Lima Bank Limited liquidation manager, Mr. Phiri, to write to the Chipata Municipal Council informing them that the building had been sold to me and that I was now the rightful owner. He indicated that the liquidators were in the process of obtaining title to the property as this had not been obtained by management of Lima Bank Limited prior to liquidation. According to Mr. Phiri the title, once obtained, would be transferred directly into my name. The liquidators did not vigorously pursue the matter of obtaining title to the property but my lawyer did – and doggedly, too. He wrote letters to the liquidators nearly every other week but in vain. Legal recourse through a 'Notice to Complete' also failed. An attempt was made to seek a court order to compel the liquidators, as the vendor, to complete the transaction but this was abandoned.

On advice from my lawyer and nearly five years after purchasing the building, I wrote a letter to the Chipata Municipal Council requesting for what was referred to as 'legalisation of existing property' so that the Commissioner of Lands could treat the matter as a fresh application. From then on things moved faster and on 6th February, 2007, exactly six years after buying the property, I received the Certificate of Title, the first one to be issued, for Plot Number 866, Parirenyatwa Road, Chipata.

The building was registered in my name and not that of the radio station. It was an important decision for safeguarding my personal interests from those of the radio station or my business partner.

29. A home at home

Efforts to secure residential accommodation in Chipata were equally cumbersome. My frequent trips from Lusaka were proving very costly, because I had to meet all the travel, accommodation and most other set-up and logistical costs. I was in desperate need of a place of my own if I was going to continue making regular visits to Chipata and to carry out the work required for the construction of my radio station.

Shortly after I had bought the former Lima Bank building, I found out that the liquidators also had some Lima Bank houses and flats for sale in various locations in Chipata, including two blocks of flats just two minutes drive from the CBD.

The two blocks comprised seven two-bedroom flats, five of which had already been sold, one was on the verge of being sold while the last one was still available because the sitting tenant was failing to pay the money for the sale of the flat. The tenant had been given the final extension to the offer of sale which was due to expire at the end of July, 2000.

In August, I expressed interest in purchasing the remaining flat, was given an offer which I paid and took possession in May, 2001, although the certificate of Title was only issued three years later in February, 2004. Upon taking possession, I refurbished it extensively, replacing and adding many fittings and getting a phone line installed. In the garden I planted guava, granadilla (passion fruit), orange, paw paw (papaya) trees and started a vegetable garden to ensure that I had my own fresh fruit and vegetables when I was settled in. I also found a housekeeper and, for the eighteen months that I was working at ZAMCOM in Lusaka and visiting Chipata regularly and staying in my own home, all I needed to do was to make a telephone call and I would find warm food ready whenever I arrived.

I regarded my flat as my 'chikonjo' or 'halfway home'. I knew that my permanent home would come at an appropriate time. However, even though it was a 'halfway' home, it was a really convenient place and helped to keep costs to the minimum while I was converting the building into radio studios and production areas. The technical team, the architect and I were all accommodated in the flat whenever we visited Chipata and were able to work long hours because of its proximity to the building. The flat's convenience was even greater when I relocated and started running the radio station. Imagine living two minutes drive and five minutes walk from your work place?

30. Permit to construct

With somewhere to stay in Chipata, the process of setting up the radio station was greatly speeded up. I applied to ZAMTEL for transmitter and antenna space at their mast site on Kanjala Hill I. This site was already hosting the transmitter shelter and antennæ for ZNBC radio and television services. ZAMTEL responded positively and I quickly made payment to secure the use of the mast and the area where I wanted to locate the radio station's antenna dipoles. Unfortunately, ZAMTEL only offered space for antenna dipoles on their mast, but made no room in their shelter for the transmitter, on the grounds that the remaining space was earmarked for their own future requirements. I wrote to ZNBC Director General, Duncan Mbazima requesting space in the ZNBC shelter, which thankfully, was given, albeit at a fee.

On 31st May, 2000, and now armed with the technical specifications for the location of the transmitter, I lodged an application to the Ministry of Information and Broadcasting Services for a Construction Permit and Broadcasting Licence. Zambian broadcasting regulations at the time required a person to get a broadcasting licence from the Ministry of Information and Broadcasting Services and a frequency permit from ZICTA, an organisation which fell under the Ministry of Transport and Communications. Both licences were renewable annually.

Applications for broadcasting licences to the Ministry of Information and Broadcasting Services were considered by the Technical Licencing Committee whose membership was dominated by engineering staff of the national broadcaster, ZNBC.

Being an interested party, ZNBC should not have been a member of a committee charged with the responsibility of determining who should – or should not – be granted a broadcasting licence, because all new stations, whether radio or television, would be in direct competition with the state broadcaster for listeners as well as advertising.

As required by the licencing regulations, my application was followed up with a broadcasting notice published in the daily newspapers informing the public of the application. The notice gave the transmitter output capacity and locations of the antenna. It also asked members of the public wishing to bring information to the attention of the minister regarding the legal, financial and technical or programming qualifications of the applicant, either positive or negative, to do so within thirty days.

Two months later I received a letter from Assistant Secretary, Mr. Stephen Kazeze, in his capacity as secretary of the Radio and Television Technical Licencing Committee, which said that the committee was happy that I and my business partner intended to set up a radio station in a rural area. However, the committee wanted to know the implication of my partner, Mr. Haggar's joint bank account with his wife on the project, noting also that the Statement of Accounts showed that I, the majority shareholder, had less money than Mr. Haggar.

The Committee also wanted to know how we intended to utilise the funds shown in the Statement of Accounts. I responded immediately, enclosing a letter from Mrs Samantha Haggar, explaining that she was committed to the project. I also enclosed a copy of my latest bank statement, which now held money from my gratuity from my last contract at ZAMCOM. I explained that between the two of us we had 76 per cent of the required funds for setting up the radio station and that we hoped to secure the remaining 24 per cent from the Media Trust Fund, MTF and the Southern African Media Development Fund, SAMDEF. I explained that on the basis of available funds Chipata Radio Services Limited had the capacity and would be in a position to complete the construction of the radio station facilities within the time allocated. 'We, therefore, hope that the Committee will at its next meeting grant us the Permit to Construct for the radio station,' I wrote.

The issuance of the Broadcasting Station Construction Permit was communicated to me in a letter signed by Minister of Information and Broadcasting Services, Mr. Newstead Zimba on 12th December 2000. The permit, for which I paid a fee of K750,000 (about US$180), was valid for a period of eighteen months, effective from the date of the letter. The minister went on to give the conditions of the permit which included inviting officials from the Radio and Television Technical Licencing Committee to inspect the radio station to determine whether it met the required standard for issuance of a Confirmed Broadcasting Licence.

The minister advised that once construction of the radio station was completed, the station was authorised to carry out test broadcasts. The permit gave us twenty-four hours of operation on the frequency of 99.6 FM with transmitter output power of one kilowatt. During the period of test broadcasts, the station was to be allowed to play music for four hours in the morning, from 6 a.m. to 10 a.m. and for four hours in the afternoon, from 4 p.m. to 8 p.m. The station was required to announce, during this time, that it was only test broadcasting and would only start full programming after being issued with a Confirmed Broadcasting Licence. The minister wished us success as we embarked on what he described as an important project which should benefit the people in its area of coverage.

Many people expressed surprise that the ministry had given me the permit because the uneasy relations that I had had previously with the ministry were common knowledge. Reflecting back later, I realised that the ministry may have used the radio permit and licence to remove me from ZAMCOM. It must have appeared to them that gaining back control of the Institute was much more important than giving me a licence to operate a radio station in a rural part of Zambia. Whatever the reason, I was overjoyed.

Although, when applying for the construction permit, I had told the Ministry of the Information and Broadcasting Services that we had nearly all the money we needed for constructing the station, in truth I faced many challenges in raising start-up capital as well as operational funding.

I used a large part of my resources and connections to secure a complete radio start-up equipment set comprising studio equipment and a one kilowatt transmitter. The equipment was sent to Lusaka while I was still working at ZAMCOM and I held it in storage while continuing to make arrangements to construct the radio station facilities.

31. Audience survey

While the radio station was about to commence operations, a colleague from the Danish School of Journalism, Professor Lisbet Ravn, was visiting Zambia. Her school had an assistance programme with the Department of Mass Communication at the University of Zambia and she always visited me at ZAMCOM whenever she came to Zambia on her UNZA assignments.

Lisbet asked to accompany me to Chipata to see for herself the progress that I was making in setting up my radio station. Two important developments came out of that visit. Her positive report helped to convince the Royal Danish Embassy that my project was worth supporting, also she linked me up with her colleague, Jens Troense of Horsens, Denmark, who fifteen years earlier had started his own radio station. She thought that Jens had the kind of experience needed to help me identify and train the people to launch the operations of my radio station.

Shortly after our visit to Chipata, I held a meeting with the counsellor at the Royal Danish Embassy, Mrs Sanne Olsen, whom I briefed about my plans for the radio station, progress already made and the type of support that would be useful. Mrs Olsen asked me to present my request in form of a proposal. I did so and two months later, on 2nd November, 2001, she and I signed a contract under the Embassy's Media Programme for support to the establishment of Chipata Radio Services.

This was really unusual because I was still an employee of ZAMCOM, which was receiving support for its training programme from DANIDA, but it reflected the trust that I had built up in the international development community. The initial support towards my private project had two fundamental activities. The first was to bring Jens Troense to Zambia; his air ticket cost to be covered by the embassy, while local costs for accommodation and meals would be covered by me.

The second focused on the proposed audience and included assessing audience needs and interests, ensuring that radio planning and programming would be responsive to those needs, researching the impact of community radio services in Chipata and, finally, developing a practical guide for carrying out audience surveys which could be used by other community radio stations. (Apparently, very few radio stations were carrying out such surveys either before or after start-up.)

My partner, Phil Haggar, assisted in identifying a well qualified consultant to lead the research team. John Coghill, a New Zealander, was a senior marketing executive of the Economist magazine in the United Kingdom and had wide experience as a researcher and market analyst. John assisted in designing the questionnaire, supervised the data collection, compilation, evaluation, interpretation and analysis.

The survey was carried out with fifteen to twenty-five minutes face-to-face interviews. The fieldwork was conducted in two phases: October, 2002, just before the launch of Breeze FM and June, 2003, eight months after the launch. In all 150 interviews were carried out in the first phase and one hundred in the second. The sample was collected randomly, by knocking on doors every five to ten houses in designated areas. A random sampling of households and respondents was employed in four areas covering low density and high density residential areas, squatter settlements and villages.

The survey established that the adult African population of Chipata was reasonably educated, religious, spoke English and was employed mainly in agriculture, government and retail. They tended to be married with children and to own their own homes. Nearly all had a radio in the home but less than half had a television. It was found out that radio was the dominant medium. Nearly all those who were interviewed said that they listened to radio daily and more than a third said they did so at home and at their workplace. Most interviewees indicated that they read very little - only 14 per cent of those who said they read "The Post" newpaper, the most popular newspaper at the time, said that they read daily. The national TVZ-dominated television viewing with 62 per cent of the sample watching but only around half said that they watched the national television channel daily. The initial survey showed that there was high radio listenership in Chipata and Eastern Province. Apparently due to poor Radio Zambia shortwave reception from Lusaka, MBC from Malawi was the most listened to station in Chipata and Eastern Province.

The results of the audience survey were very enriching. The survey helped to establish the demographics of Breeze FM's listeners, radio ownership and listening habits and even more importantly, whether or not the community needed a new radio station in their area. We also found out what type of programmes the listeners wanted the new radio station to broadcast which other radio stations were not providing.

The programmes which the people in the community wanted were those that could assist them in improving their farming activities, deal with their health problems and help them to improve their standards of living. A tall order indeed, but the survey helped Breeze FM to draw up a programme schedule that provided a balanced menu of the programmes listeners wanted but also needed. The survey also helped the station to determine when to broadcast which programmes and in which languages.

Eight months later, in 2003, during the second survey, 70 per cent of those surveyed gave Breeze FM as the most listened to radio station, followed by ZNBC Radio 2 with 12 per cent, Radio Maria with 11 per cent and ZNBC Radio1 with 4 per cent. At the time of the second survey Breeze FM was on air for eight hours from 1 p.m. to 9 p.m. and this was given as the peak listening time. The positive results of the audience survey had additional benefits for Breeze FM. The Royal Danish Embassy decided to give further support to the station to help with building redesign costs and furniture.

The results of the audience survey also helped Breeze FM to recognise that it had competition, locally, from Radio Maria of the Catholic Diocese in Chipata. Although Radio Maria's original mission was to evangelise through radio, the establishment of Breeze FM had pushed it to start producing development-oriented programmes, to begin playing secular music and to charge competitive market rates. With support from the Rome-headquartered Radio Maria family of radio stations, the station had embarked on a geographical expansion programme, clearly driven by the desire to reach out to a wider audience beyond the area covered by the Breeze FM signal.

Breeze FM closely monitored the operations of Radio Maria, as it did those of the other community and commercial radio stations in Chipata and the province. Radio 1 and Radio 2 of the state broadcaster, ZNBC and, much later, QFM of Lusaka, were competitors because their signals were received in the region, as was the signal of Channel Africa of SABC, South Africa. However, the major weakness of Radio 1 and Radio 2 of

ZNBC, QFM and Channel Africa in our market was that they were not local. I believed that Breeze FM's 'localness' made it distinctive in its core marketplace.

32. Feasibility study

The planning process for establishing Breeze FM included a simple feasibility study which I carried out on one of my visits to Chipata. We needed to work out the costs of operating the radio station against estimated income coming from an identifiable client base. The start-up costs were more or less the same as we had anticipated in our application for the Construction Permit and Licence. I just needed to add operational costs, taking into account fixed and other costs. The more demanding work was clearly how to convince potential clients not only to advertise on the radio station but also to sponsor some of the essential programming that was going to be broadcast.

Fortunately, Chipata was a vibrant little town seen by many as one of the fastest growing towns in Zambia. With a population of around 400,000 people, the town hosted district and provincial administration offices, two hospitals, clinics, schools, colleges, as well as NGOs and the offices of international agricultural marketing companies.

The town centre had a diverse business sector, several banks, supermarkets, shops, markets, restaurants, transport services and other service providers. In carrying out the feasibility study I used an approach similar to the one I had used a few years earlier when I was looking at newspaper viability.

I drew up a list of well established companies and organisations in Chipata and over a five-day period went around and talked to forty managers of banks, agricultural finance companies, NGOs, government departments, the chamber of commerce, the municipal council, hoteliers and recently privatised companies. I also visited utility companies, transport haulers, wholesalers and light industries.

Rumours had been doing the rounds about the opening of a new radio station in town and so I started by introducing myself as the person behind

Feasibility study

the project. I spent a few minutes explaining the idea behind the radio station and what its role would be in the community. In my meetings with managers of companies I asked two simple questions, whether or not the company was advertising its products in the national media and whether or not they would consider advertising on a local radio station. For heads of government departments and NGOs, I asked whether they would consider using radio to explain their work and to get their messages to a wider audience, at a cost, of course. The responses were generally positive although some of the banks talked about needing to consult with their bosses in Lusaka since they had no authority to spend money on advertising. With the help of the local chamber of commerce I was able to establish that Eastern Province had over one hundred well established private and other business enterprises that could advertise on the radio station.

This market research helped us to split the market into several segments: individuals and small local businesses, local companies, government departments and NGOs, national advertising agencies and international development agencies. I was being presumptuous, of course, because the inclusion of national companies and international organisations was based on observing the nature, type and frequency of advertising in the national media which could be extended to the Eastern Province. I was also certain that the radio station would later build the capacity to carry out information campaigns for national and international organisations seeking to reach out to people in the region.

At the time of our planning, I and my partner, Phil Haggar had been sure that the market size, defined as the total amount which could be spent on advertising in the radio station's broadcast area, would increase when the station was operational and able to reach a wider audience. Our optimism was buoyed by the fact that the economy of Eastern Province had been growing at 3.5-4.5 per cent per annum. Further growth was expected over time with the promised arrival of railway transportation, potential exploitation of gold and uranium and build-up of production capacity for cotton and tobacco.

The strategy was to initially target those who could become innovators – the advertisers and programme sponsors who would be the first to take the opportunities presented by radio to deliver their messages to many people.

175

That other businesses were already advertising in the national newspapers, on national radio and television was an indication that there was a market which was not being fully met. However, without extremely accurate market research detailing how frequently local businesses advertised on radio, it was not possible, at this stage, to quantify the size of the market.

I had high hopes that the market would develop substantially when the projects of the Zambia, Malawi and Mozambique 'Growth Triangle' which was being spearheaded by the business sectors of the three countries, started operating.

The 'Growth Triangle' concept had gained prominence in the late 1980s in Asia and was designed to yield integrated development on the common area utilizing proximity of areas, cultural and linguistic affinity and initiatives of business communities and governments. On this high note of expectation, we were ready to move ahead.

33. Rezoning the building

As developments in the planning of the establishment of the radio station progressed I began preparations for rezoning the building that I had bought from the liquidators of Lima Bank.

In July, 2001, I engaged planning and design consultants, Violet Enterprises Limited of Lusaka, to carry out modifications and the rezoning of the property from the business of financial services to communications. The modifications included a redesign of the entrance area, general operational area, kitchen and toilets and addition of a 25-metre communication tower and on-site parking area.

Fortunately, there was not much delay with our application for rezoning of the building and within four months, Town Clerk, Bernard Siwakwi confirmed that the Council had approved the application. The Town Clerk advised that we proceed with the developments based on the approved drawings.

As a no-nonsense administrator, Siwakwi was credited as being the most effective Town Clerk to have worked in Chipata. He intimated to me that a group of Chipata businessmen of Indian origin, who had been unhappy about the former Lima Bank building being bought by someone they regarded as an 'outsider from Lusaka', had gone to see him to request that the council deny me the licence to operate a radio station from that location. They told him that the local authority should not allow me to use the building for a radio station because the noise from the radio station would disturb business activities in the Chipata CBD.

Either they were joking, or had no idea how a radio station operated and were assuming that there would be loudspeakers placed outside the building which would be blaring out music.

If anyone would later make noise in the town centre it was some of the Zambian businessmen of Indian origin from whose shops blasted loud, recorded messages to attract customers, not to mention the daily 'call to prayer' from the two mosques. Other regular loud noise in and around Chipata, was generated by the government information department, ZANIS, with its public address system which, apparently, was for hire to anyone who had an announcement to make and some money to pay. There was also noise from loud music played at the Wildlife & Environmental Conservation Society Club during music performances and from the beating of drums by youth groups at churches, such as the Anglican Church on Church Road and the party music at the children's playpark in the Moth residential area.

The issue, therefore, was not about the radio station making noise, but that an indigenous Zambian had, for the very first time, bought a building at the centre of the Chipata CBD, where all other buildings were owned by local businessmen of Indian origin who controlled the mercantile business in the province.

After approval was secured I engaged a Lusaka-based company, Mangrova Engineering Systems Limited, to carry out a technical assessment of the building and to design and construct studios and production facilities.

During this period large amounts of building materals were trucked from Lusaka to Chipata including a mast for the STL, Studio-to-Transmitter Link. However, by June, 2002, when the eighteen months period of the construction permit was coming to an end, we were nowhere near completing the renovations or preparations for start-up, so I requested and was granted an extension to the construction permit for an additional six months.

Fortunately, within the extension period, a ZNBC installation team travelled to Chipata to install a new television transmitter. I asked if I could synchronise my programme with theirs so that their team could, upon the completion of their work, assist in installing our studio equipment and transmitter. ZNBC accepted my request at a fairly reasonable cost and their technical team did a splendid job. The soundproofing, supported by the solid walls of the former bank building, was well done and completely eliminated the noise from the busy road in front of the building.

PHASE 3

1. Goodbye Lusaka and ZAMCOM

My last day of work at ZAMCOM was supposed to have been 31st October, 2002, but I requested to wind up a month early. I left Lusaka without any fanfare. ZAMCOM, unlike ZANA, organized a farewell party for me at which I was given a desktop computer as a parting gift which came in handy when starting up the operations of the new radio station. I chose not to bid farewell to anybody else and had a simple, quiet dinner with the family and we all went to bed early that night. The next day, a hot Tuesday morning, seven weeks short of my fiftieth birthday, at 5 a.m., I set off from Lusaka on the long road to Chipata.

They say that a person truly becomes himself or herself at the age of fifty and I did it in style. I was aware that each thing I had done and would be doing, quitting my job, selling my family house, relocating to a new place and starting a new company from nothing constituted some of the most stressful experiences in life. Despite all the accusations and investigations that I had endured I had no fear or concern about looking back over what I had done in Lusaka. I also had no fear or worry about what lay ahead. I was happily confident about one thing – I believed in myself. I knew that I could meet any challenge and that my plans to start and manage my own radio station would succeed. I had the confidence of a proven, competent man.

Lusaka, the place I had for so long regarded as my home and my town and all that it represented, would remain behind for good. It is said that you never forget your hometown the way you never forget your mother. Well, while I was never going to forget my wonderful and indefatigable mother, I had no good reason for not forgetting Lusaka. I was also aware that most people thought that a commercial radio station could not succeed in a rural town such as Chipata. Some predicted that I would return to Lusaka – and within a short time.

An old member of the media profession, Faxon Nkandu, while on a visit to Chipata, revealed to me that he had once criticised me on a live phone-in discussion programme on Radio Phoenix for 'abandoning

ZAMCOM in order to operate a radio station in a rural area'. Upon seeing and listening to Breeze FM he said he hoped he would have a chance to appear on another programme to 'put the record straight'.

And one of my subordinates at ZAMCOM, Jacqueline Kabeta, Broadcasting Coordinator, passed a remark I am sure she regretted for a long time. I was packing my gymnasium equipment, which I had stored up at the Institute, in readiness to take it to Chipata when she came around. 'Where are you taking that equipment, sir'?' she asked me. 'To Chipata,' I answered. 'You don't need to. You will lose weight without the need to exercise,' she commented, obviously hinting that I was going to have a difficult time in Chipata. How wrong, she was.

As could have been expected, people in Chipata were also sceptical about the prospects of the new radio station. The local businessmen of Indian origin always asked, 'How are going to make your money?' when I visited their shops to buy various items needed by the engineers working on the building. I always pointed a finger at my head to imply that the ideas for the business were in there.

The head of a leading NGO, CLUSA, Tim Henman, said to me a year after meeting him and his staff to introduce myself as the person behind the new radio station initiative, that when I left them they had all broken into laughter with one commenting that I was 'another crook from Lusaka'.

Interestingly, many of the people I had talked to in the government departments, banks, parastatal companies, agricultural finance companies and NGOs, and who regarded me suspiciously or as an outsider from Lusaka, were no longer in town by the time we celebrated Breeze FM's tenth anniversary in 2012. Many had been transferred or had relocated to other towns, while others had lost their jobs, or died. It is no exaggeration to say that very little evidence remained of the work of those NGOs, which had appeared to have been very active. Meanwhile, only the local businessmen of Indian origin remained, many of them less active than they had been when I moved into town, and no longer questioning my authenticity because they realized that I had come to stay and that Breeze FM was a serious proposition.

What all the doubting Thomases did not realize was that I was very well prepared for my new assignment. I had survived the inadequacies of

Magodi Village as a baby, the decadence of Matero Township as a child and youth and the ruthlessness of the Copperbelt as a young reporter. I had survived hostility, jealousy and pettiness at ZANA and ZAMCOM and had under my belt all manner of visits and experiences in many countries. Chipata, by comparison, was not going to be a walk in the park, but would be much more welcoming and accommodating. More importantly, the doubting Thomases were ignorant, while I was confident that someone who is committed and passionate about using his or her knowledge and skills to provide a unique and impactful service cannot fail.

2. Staff recruitment

The task of identifying the right staff for the station was quite challenging. Although I had worked for thirteen years as director and chief executive officer of a media training institution, I had no intention of recruiting any of those I had helped to train. I made a conscious decision to employ individuals who lived in the community and who understood and empathized with local issues and the people. This decision was also necessitated by the fact that people recruited from Lusaka would most likely have unrealistic salary expectations which the radio station could not afford, particularly during the start-up phase.

I arranged to have a poster put up at a local supermarket inviting applications from people with backgrounds in journalism and media, education and social work. The poster attracted up to a hundred applications. I reviewed them all and selected thirty-one whom I invited for interviews. Over two days in March, 2002, Jens Troense and I interviewed them and selected fifteen who became the first members of staff of the yet-to-be-named radio station. None of them had previous media, broadcasting or radio experience and only a couple of them had journalism training; only one had computer skills.

There was yet another major shortfall. The group included only three women, two of whom were best suited for sales and marketing work. While Jens was carrying out voice tests to help us identify those who could be fitted into presentation and programming roles, I kept wondering how we could start a radio station without women's voices, or first-hand appreciation and experience of women's issues? As part of the orientation exercise, I had asked the group to help identify the station's average potential listener. The consensus, after a lot of explanation and discussion, was that the average listener would be a woman of about twenty-seven years with several children and an irresponsible husband. How then, with that kind of listener in mind could test transmissions for such a radio station commence without women presenters and programme producers?

The solution was provided by a chance meeting with Antosh Skudlarek, the regional head of the World Food Programme, WFP, who had, apparently, just completed a staff recruitment exercise in Chipata. In our conversation, over an evening drink, I explained the difficulties I was having. Antosh offered to let me look at the applications of those his organisation had not selected. I picked up the files the following morning and in going through them was able to identify some women who appeared to be reasonably suited for radio presentation and programming work.

I proceeded to write to them explaining that, although they had applied for employment at WFP, I was inviting them for interviews for work at a radio station which would start operating shortly. They all responded positively and turned up for the interviews and from them we were able to recruit our first three women presenters. One of them, Memory Dulani, who had a diploma in Personnel Management, did not only become a good presenter and producer but ended up becoming the station's first station manager. Memory had such an assertive character that most of the male employees openly asked me to protect them from her. Memory made such an impact on the radio station and its operations that when she died eight years later, none of the men showed any eagerness to succeed her.

After completing our staff recruitment exercise we were ready to prepare our new employees for work in a radio station. The first training activity was a month-long orientation programme facilitated by Jens. This was followed by computer training in August, 2002, shortly before the commencement of test transmissions. My parting words to the newly recruited staff in April had been for each of them to obtain some computer training and skills. When I returned to Chipata in August, I found that none of them had sought or obtained any computer training at all, leading me to bring a trainer to Chipata from Lusaka for two weeks to introduce the staff to basic computer operational skills.

At this stage I was confident that the staff were in a position to receive additional advanced training and formally wrote to the ZAMCOM board chairman informing him that my radio station had been granted its provisional licence and that it had recruited its initial group of employees who needed some professional orientation and training. ZAMCOM offered placements in some of its reporting and programming courses and workshops scheduled for the remaining period of 2002. But since ZAMCOM was not offering any sales or marketing courses, I negotiated for an attachment programme for two of my sales staff with Radio Phoenix, the first commercial radio station to open in Zambia.

The final preparation for the staff came as a bonus from the Thomson Foundation which had for some time been running a two-week regional Television Production Course at ZAMCOM for journalists from East and Southern Africa. During 2002, the course was scheduled for October, the same month that I would be leaving my position at the Institute to open my radio station in Chipata. The course was run by Ian Masters, Controller, Broadcasting Division, who over the years had become a good friend of mine. When Ian found out about my plans to quit ZAMCOM and open my own radio station, he decided not to hold the television course at the Institute that year. But, since his arrangements for travelling to Zambia were already at an advanced stage he decided instead to run a news operations course for my staff in Chipata.

This is how, less than two months after commencing test transmissions, Ian Masters and Derek Woodcock (a broadcasting lecturer), arrived in Chipata to help kick-start the station's news operations.

Ian and Derek perfectly fitted the 'good cop, bad cop' approach to work. Ian was a tall, forceful character who pushed – and sometimes threatened – to get my guys to understand the concepts of news and news operations. Derek was of average height, caring and engaging. They were a superb team and complemented each other very well. Ian would demand while Derek would encourage and by the time they left for the United Kingdom, the Breeze FM newsroom was alive and buzzing. (My guys could not only write good stories with decent sound bites but present the news reasonably well.) Ian and Derek also assisted in crafting the station's news policy which championed accuracy, accountability, balance, fairness and truthfulness and sought to minimise harm and to promote gender sensitivity.

The follow up to the training was another great opportunity. As soon as he returned to UK, Ian, in his position as Controller, Broadcasting Division, Thomson Foundation offered a place to our news editor, Tobias Phiri, on the International Broadcast Journalism Course scheduled for June-September, 2003. The Thomson Foundation International Broadcast Journalism Course was one of the most sought after courses for radio and television journalists in the Commonwealth and Breeze FM, as a start-up operation, fresh from completing its test transmissions, was more than lucky to get a placement on the course. Most participants to the course had more than three years working experience.

Ian had secured the sponsorship for Tobias from The Grace Wyndam Goldie Trust. The sponsorship covered Tobias' tuition and accommodation and a weekly subsistence allowance of GBP120. Breeze FM was expected to find, or meet, his airfare to and from Cardiff. In April, 2003, I asked Samantha Chuula, Governance Programme Manager at the British Council in Lusaka, for assistance in getting Breeze FM an airticket. Samantha and I had jointly organised several programmes at ZAMCOM in the past, supported by the British Council. Samantha talked to First Secretary, Ian Mason, at the British High Commission, who agreed to find the resources for buying the ticket. And so, within the first eight months of operation, our news editor, Tobias, was in the United Kingdom attending a prestigious international broadcasting journalism course.

Meanwhile, I was in regular communication with Ian and also with Jackie Chambers at the BBC World Service, whom I had met on her visits to Zambia. In one of my emails I raised with Jackie the possibility of Tobias staying on for an attachment with the BBC World Service after the completion of his Thomson Foundation programme. Both Jackie and Ian supported the idea and arrangements were made which enabled Tobias to spend a month with the BBC World Service.

On his return, Tobias prepared an excellent newsroom training programme through which he shared ideas and skills with his colleagues. The objective of the training programme was to improve the skills of our reporters to write, report, edit news copy and audio and prepare the news bulletin for broadcast. Together with the Thomson Foundation two-week training, this in-house transfer of skills laid a solid base for the station's news operations and Breeze FM was soon to become one of the few new radio stations in the country that provided up-to-date and reliable news bulletins on time, every day.

3. Breeze FM, "Kamphepo Ka Yazi Yazi"

In February, 2000, when I incorporated Chipata Radio Services Limited, I knew we needed to come up with a fitting and catchy name for the radio station. My first attempt to do so was during the selection of the first group of employees in Chipata. Each of the fifteen people who were initially recruited was asked to suggest a name and logo for the new radio station. The Danish trainer, Jens Troense, was the first one to come up with a name. He suggested Radio Chipata. The logo that he designed to go with the name was not too bad. Others suggested Radio Searchlight, Radio Active, Eastern Radio Station and Radio Alpha. Most of the logo suggestions were completely ridiculous and I rejected them all. I carried the list of names with me to Lusaka and when I went over them again, I was certain that none provided an apt description of what I wanted the radio station to represent in the community.

And so, for a while we carried on making arrangements for establishing the station under the umbrella title of Chipata Radio Services. It was not until July, 2002, three months before Breeze FM started its test transmissions that the name for the radio station just popped into my head. I was at work at ZAMCOM, with everything that I needed to do both at the Institute and in Chipata almost completed and wondering when it would be all over when suddenly it occurred to me that I was missing Chipata. This was the first time I had ever felt that way. I realized that what I was missing most was the cool breeze I always enjoyed when having my meals under the big flamboyant tree in the gardens of Mambo Banda's Katuta Lodge, or when I was jogging early in the morning. 'Breeze, that could be a good name,' I thought.

I telephoned Chipata and asked Kephas Mvula of the Chamber of Commerce Eastern Voice newspaper, what the translation of breeze was in the Chinyanja or Chichewa language. Kephas was looking after some of my interests in Chipata while I was still in Lusaka. His comprehension of the language of eastern Zambia was as bad as mine and he asked that I give him time to find out from people who would know. Later that day he telephoned back and told me that breeze translated into Chinyanja or Chichewa as 'kamphepo ka yazi yazi' (the cool wind). I instantly liked the Chinyanja translation because it sounded melodious. I shouted to Kephas, 'Yes, *breeze* is the name of our radio station.'

Breeze FM, as the name for the radio station, aptly represented the cool air that blew constantly over Chipata from the surrounding hills, especially at dawn and dusk. (Although many of the listeners could not initially get the pronunciation or spelling right, they quickly identified with the name because even the English version sounded good.) I proceeded to register the name Breeze 99.6 FM as the trading name of Chipata Radio Services. I included the frequency because I wanted people to quickly internalize and tune in.

Unfortunately, the 99.6 MHz frequency is on what, in the broadcasting business, is referred to as the 'wrong end' of the frequency spectrum. Generally, lower frequencies are preferred. In fact I had initially hoped that the station would be allocated a lower frequency since at that time there were only two radio stations operating in the province: Radio Maria in Chipata on 90.00 MHz and Radio Chikaya in Lundazi on 98.1 MHz. It took seven years for me to get the opportunity to change the frequency to 89.3 MHz. The frequency change was made possible when ZICTA re-planned the national FM sound broadcasting band.

The new frequency helped the station to reach many more people, particularly those with Japanese second-hand cars, or South African-made cars which have short frequency bands ending at 90.0 MHz. As soon as the station started broadcasting, I and the staff came up with the motto 'Breeze FM, Lifting the Spirit of the People'. This was appropriate because the radio station truly did lift the spirit of the people of Eastern Province.

4. Test transmissions begin

My six months leave days had worked marvellously to help get the radio station ready for start-up operations and exactly five days after I arrived in Chipata, on 5th October, 2002, Breeze FM radio station commenced its test transmission. Most of the people who turned on their radio sets that Saturday morning were surprised to get a new channel that was broadcasting a wide range of music. The play-list had been very carefully put together. My colleague, Phil Haggar, had compiled the most popular British and international songs which were well mixed with a good choice of African popular hits from my extensive personal collection. The Breeze FM signal was strong and so it had temporarily submerged weaker frequencies as the new radio station played non-stop music for a full five days.

It was only early in the morning on Thursday, 10th October, 2002, that the first voice was heard saying, 'Good morning good people of Chipata. Good morning good people of Eastern Province. This is your new radio station, Breeze FM, Kamphepo ka yazi yazi, broadcasting from Chipata, the provincial capital of Eastern Province'. With those words Breeze FM announced its arrival, not only clearly, but very loudly. The station format was friendly and mature and different from those that the community had been used to. The people were instantly hooked to the radio station and many remained so from then onwards.

The start-up phase of any organisation is very exciting. For a radio station it is even more so. The initial members of staff are enthusiastic because they are speaking on radio for the first time. The listeners are overjoyed because they are listening to their own radio station, also for the first time. At the community level, such as ours, the listeners were even more excited because some of them knew, and others could easily associate with, the people speaking on radio because they were local people.

Listeners, who previously waited for days for programmes in the local Chewa language on the national radio airwaves, which were available for a very limited time, were now able to listen to the radio, in their own language, all day, every day. What made Breeze FM even more exciting was the fact that most of the issues covered on the news, or discussed in programmes were local and, therefore, relevant to the listeners.

187

Breeze FM was also unique because of its manner of interacting with its listeners. By opening up the station and the studios, bringing listeners in close contact with the presenters and producers, Breeze FM completely changed the way the people of Eastern Province viewed and interacted with radio. Previously when they listened to (national) Radio Zambia, radio content was distant. They heard the voices, yes, and got the information, yes, – but it all came from so far away. With Breeze FM *in* Chipata, radio had been brought to the doorstep of the listeners in the townships and villages.

Breeze FM had very promising prospects from the start of its operations because its establishment was carried out carefully. The private and community radio sector had just been launched in Zambia and promised to become the most effective means of providing information to previously marginalised communities. Breeze FM sought to pioneer the commercialisation of this sector in Eastern Province and, therefore, wanted to maximise its audience share. It sought to achieve this through promoting its 'localness', through quality programming and by effective sales and marketing. I and my staff recognised the fact that the development of the radio station's service was going to involve the day-to-day management of the output, active encouragement of feedback and using the feedback from the audience to improve presentation and programming.

Our intention, Phil and I, had been to set up the most versatile and effective radio operation outside the urban centres of Zambia. A lot of time had been spent in planning and putting together a configuration that would be both technically robust and productively efficient.

We were committed to turning Breeze FM into the premier local commercial radio station in the coverage area and one of the best in the country. We were also committed to providing the best possible service to our listeners and advertisers.

The commencement of operations of Breeze FM gave me a lot of pleasure. Most people who run their own business talk about how good it is to own and work in your own company. I doubt that it can compare to working in your own radio station, located in your own building, but I could be biased about that. The sense of independence and satisfaction that I felt, especially in the early years, made it all worthwhile.

What makes radio unique as a business is the amazing way in which it impacts on people the owner will never meet or know. People the world over enjoy listening to their local or favoured radio stations and feel close and connected to the presenters and producers.

The feeling one gets when listening to one's *own* radio station is also completely unusual and only those who are lucky enough can experience this inexplicable feeling. In my case the confusion extended to my dear old mother. She did not understand what it meant for her son to 'own a radio station'. Whilst on her way to Malawi for a church excursion their bus developed a fault in Chipata and had to be repaired. My mother took advantage of this time to look me up. Unclear about where to find me she went to Chipata's 'Saturday Market' to look for me among the people repairing radio receivers.

Fortunately, she found people who knew me and, realising that she was my mother, led her to the Breeze FM building. Whenever I visited my mother afterwards, we always laughed about that incident, but it explained the special nature of the undertaking that I had got myself into.

5. Confirmed broadcasting licence

Although we had planned well and gone to a lot of trouble to put systems in place, we still had many operational teething problems and, during those early days I spent a lot of time driving up to the Transmission Site at Kanjala Hill I with the technicians to sort out glitches affecting the transmitter. What helped the staff to gain confidence was that we increased the hours of broadcasting gradually to give them time to settle in. We started as directed by the Ministry of Information and Broadcasting Services with four hours of broadcasting and after three months increased this to six hours. Six months into broadcasting, with demands for more time from listeners, we increased the broadcasting time to eight hours before finally jumping up to eighteen hours of local programming.

On weekdays we opened at 6 a.m. and ended at midnight while over weekends we started our local broadcasts at 7 a.m. and wound up at midnight. The eighteen hour schedule was divided into four segments:

6 a.m. to 11 a.m. in English, 11 a.m. to 3 p.m. in Chewa/Chinyanja, 3 p.m. to 7 p.m. in English and 7 p.m. to midnight in Chewa/Chinyanja. In discussion with Jackie Chambers of the BBC, we signed a partnership agreement with the BBC and reserved the night drive, midnight to 6 a.m. on weekdays and midnight to 7 a.m. on weekends and holidays, to live BBC broadcasts. Soon we had all the 24 hours provided by our licence fully utilised and everyone settled down into their work, the 'problems' minimised and operations normalised.

Two weeks after commencing test transmissions I wrote to the Ministry of Information and Broadcasting Services requesting that they send members of the Radio and Television Technical Licencing Committee to come and carry out an inspection of Breeze FM. The Technical Licencing team visited three months later and was with us for only one day but carried out their work professionally. They inspected our facilities, asked our technicians some questions and visited our transmission site at Kanjala Hill I where they inspected our facilities and tested our frequency signal before returning to Lusaka.

Three weeks later, on 31st January, 2003, I received a letter from Minister of Information and Broadcasting Services, Mr. Newstead Zimba, confirming that the ministry had issued a Confirmed Broadcasting Licence to Breeze FM. Breeze FM was, in fact, one of the few stations to have been granted a Confirmed Broadcasting Licence in such a short period of time – within four months of test transmission. The licence was valid for seven years from the date of issue but renewable every year upon payment of the renewal fee and after satisfying the minister with the station's performance in the preceding year.

The minister stated that at least 80 per cent of our programming should be commercial and of local content 'for the interest of the community we served'. Mr. Zimba wished us well as we started our full broadcasting to our listeners and clientele in Chipata.

The licencing arrangements in Zambia forbid radio stations from earning income through advertising or programme sponsorship during the test transmission period. But while our test transmission was going on, the station began to incur running costs including rentals, salaries and wages, a burden unappreciated by many.

The location of the station, in a rural part of Zambia, created the impression that Breeze FM was a *community* radio station and, despite my explanation during meetings with members of the community, government departments, private companies and civil society organisations many people expected either free services, or very low charges. The idea of *paying* for radio was completely new in our coverage area, because everyone had been used to receiving free broadcasts from the national broadcaster, or from the local catholic station. Breeze FM, therefore, had a lot of work to do to change the thinking and attitude of people towards commercial radio.

The early years were not easy but things picked up and the staff and radio station quickly gained confidence. Later, new challenges arose when local competition increased with the establishment of a new radio station, Free Free, and a new television station, Chipata TV, each seeking a share of the limited advertising budget. Financial challenges, notwithstanding, Breeze FM grew in popularity, providing regular news and an increased range of programmes, as well as a diversified compilation of music.

6. Breeze FM - Three types of radio

Many people did not know or understand what kind of radio station Breeze FM was – was it commercial or community? In fact, Breeze FM encompassed three kinds of radio: it was incorporated as a private company limited by shares; it was editorially independent (I made sure of that); and it was community-based with a public contribution ethos. A Danish media consultant, Peter Erichs, who visited the station in 2011, wrote a detailed article, 'Radio Breeze FM – Local, Public Interest and Commercial with a Community Focus' that aptly reviewed the radio station and its operations.

Peter Erichs agreed that Chipata, the vibrant capital of Eastern Province, was a good location for a radio station such as Breeze FM because it was situated close to the main road between Lusaka in Zambia and Lilongwe in Malawi. From its base in Chipata, Breeze FM reached a minimum audience of about 800,000 people, of which 76 per cent were small-scale farmers living in scattered villages. The station's target audience was multigenerational, from the age of ten years to seventy years or older. These included peasant farmers and villagers, small-scale traders, workers, businessmen and businesswomen and members of the general public.

Audience surveys carried out by various organisations in the province, including Synovate Limited, an international media research organisation, confirmed our earlier survey results that Breeze FM was the most listened to station in Zambia's Eastern Province. Breeze FM had a broad multidimensional policy approach, including strong editorial and financial goals as well as a strong community commitment. The station's business model embraced elements of both its community location and commercial orientation and was inspired by the motto 'development at heart and business in mind'. This motto was intended to guide the station not only towards viability and sustainability, but to achieve its vision of pioneering the establishment of profitable people-centred and development-focused local/regional commercial radio station initiatives.

In Breeze FM's development and business sense, the two aspects are interconnected because the radio station could and would only be able to provide diverse and meaningful news and programmes if it was grounded upon the principles and practices of a profitable business.

Breeze FM's over-riding motto, 'Lifting the Spirit of the People', embraced the broader policy-aim of the station. Meawhile Breeze FM also had a broad development mission – to stimulate prosperity in its coverage area by providing useful, relevant and up to date information that gives growth at personal, family and community levels.

The radio station has three main goals/roles for the community it serves. It provides a channel to communicate information on development issues to the community, a voice to the community to communicate their perspectives in the public domain and a space for the community to engage in public dialogue and debate on the issues that affect them.

Breeze FM's daily work and its staff were divided into five departments: programmes, newsroom, technical services, sales and marketing and accounts and administration. At its peak, the station had thirty employees, including myself as exective director. Breeze FM, as a limited company, adhered to good corporate practice. It had a board of directors comprising five members. The founding directors comprised a qualified accountant, a Catholic priest specialising in land issues, a traditional leader who had trained and worked as an electrical technologist, a human resource specialist and myself as a media specialist. The board of directors, which I chaired, met four times a year and provided oversight by guiding and reviewing the operations of the station, approving the station's budget, quarterly performance reports, reviewing and approving annual audited accounts and appointing the station's auditors. As executive director, I oversaw decisions in the day-to-day running of the radio station. My management style was rooted not only in the conviction that Breeze FM could contribute to positive change in Eastern Province, but also in the culture that focuses on encouraging individual hard work and responsibility.

Looking back at my years in senior editorial positions, I later realised that, although I was a journalist by profession, I was actually a teacher by disposition, outlook and approach to my work. Danish media consultant, Peter Erichs, who observed me at work, thought that my management style seemed to be 'rather walking than sitting' and that I seemed to be a demanding manager because I insisted that plans agreed upon must be implemented and that decisions must be carried out in full.

I know for certain that I preferred to handle the high priority and the highest income impact-producing activities personally, while delegating all other activities to those whom I supported mainly through ongoing interaction. At the centre of this way of doing things was emphasis on departmental planning, coordination and review which were carried out in daily, weekly, monthly, quarterly and annual meetings. The most important and decisive daily staff meeting was the 'Log Review Meeting' which reviewed the station's broadcasting schedule of programmes, announcements, news bulletins and advertisements.

This meeting ensured that all material was broadcast on schedule. The most important weekly meeting took place on Monday morning when all staff members met to review the past week's broadcasting operations and planned for the coming week's activities and broadcasting schedule.

Although it appeared to be a situation of 'meetings, meetings, meetings', the station could not operate effectively without planning or reviewing what was being broadcast and how to operate effectively financially.

The meetings had the added benefit of developing management skills at departmental level and were strongly supported by my coaching, guiding and counselling. The totality of all this contributed to the stability of Breeze FM as an independent and effective information and communication institution for the local public in eastern Zambia.

I was proud that through its work, Breeze FM had contributed to making the people of Eastern Province among the most well informed villagers in Zambia and Africa. They received local, national, African and international news and information and voiced their ideas and concerns every day. Breeze FM also shared its unique approach to broadcasting with many other radio stations in Zambia, Malawi and Mozambique, making it a genuine regional station within Zambia and the sub-region.

By utilizing a business model that had four tiers of clients: local individuals and small local businesses; local medium scale businesses; local big business, government departments and NGOs; national business and international business, Breeze FM was able to break even by its fifth year of operation. This was possible because Breeze FM positioned itself as the communication channel of choice for everyone who wanted to reach out to the people of Eastern Province.

Interestingly, the first paid announcements that the radio station broadcast were for missing goats. The announcements gave clear descriptions of the animals and, to Breeze FM's credit, some were found and returned to their owners. On the other hand what made Breeze FM really unique was the radio station's 'Agony Uncle', Greyson Peter Nyozani Mwale, fondly known as 'Gogo Breeze' by the listeners. A retired teacher-turned-broadcaster, Gogo (grandfather) Breeze pioneered a new type of journalism which addressed the needs of the downtrodden in a practical way. In the early days he travelled on his bicycle from township to township meeting and talking to ordinary people, from office to office following up on people's complaints and grievances, from village to village interviewing the real people about their real issues and problems and, along the way, recording their long-ignored folklore and music.

He covered distances of up to 70 kilometres responding to the requests from villagers to visit their areas. When at the station, he spent a lot of time receiving ordinary folk who came into Chipata town for other business but would not return to their villages until they had visited the radio station and 'seen him with their eyes'. He featured all those who visited the radio station, and had the chance to find him, on a programme ably titled, 'Landilani Alendo' (Welcome to Our Visitors). His other programmes included the most popular 'Makalata ao Mvela' (Letters from Our Listeners) in which people, young and old, ask for his assistance in resolving a very wide range of issues ranging from family and community conflicts to poor governance and poor service delivery at central and provincial government, local and traditional levels. He travelled to find and interview the local or provincial government official, traditional leader, civil society representative and anyone involved or able to shed some light on the issues raised.

Gogo Breeze also helped to revive the use of the African idiom and traditional storytelling through his programmes 'Miyambi Mu Umoyo Wathu' (Metaphors), 'Mau Okuluwika' (Proverbs), and 'Zotigwera' (Fireside stories). All his programmes, of course, are in the Chinyanja/Chewa language which is spoken in eastern Zambia, most parts of Malawi and the Tete Province of Mozambique. As Breeze FM signal spills over into Malawi and Mozambique, Gogo Breeze has a following in these countries too.

I have no doubt that good planning, relevant programming, the personality of Gogo Breeze and the support of listeners, local, national and international advertisers and programme sponsors all contributed to making Breeze FM the most effective channel of communication and the most popular radio station in Eastern Province

7. Geographical expansion

After two years of operation, it was becoming evident that there was need to extend the station's radius. Many people in areas in which the station's signal was not accessible were demanding the Breeze FM service. Some government departments and private companies were also recognizing that extension of the coverage area would be cost-effective and valuable to them in reaching out to more people. Many organisations and private agricultural finance companies were completely overstretched in their efforts to serve people living in scattered villages outside of the station's coverage area. Some of them were already using Breeze FM for short advertisements, information to farmers and educational programmes. However, up to 40 per cent of the farmers and people required to be reached were outside the existing coverage area.

The 1 Kilowatt output transmitting power allowed under the station's licence had given Breeze FM an average radius of 120 kilometres. The station signal was very good in three districts, Chipata, Katete (80km) and Mambwe (130km), reasonably good in two or three others, Chadiza (120km) and parts of Lundazi (175km) and Petauke (165km), and poor or non-existent in at least two districts, Nyimba (255km) and Chama (365km). So three years after gaining the Confirmed Broadcasting Licence, I wrote to the permanent secretary in the Ministry of Information and Broadcasting Services requesting permission to extend the coverage area to Petauke in the west and Lundazi in the north. Our plans were to carry out the expansion programme in two phases starting with the extension westwards and then moving up north.

The response from the ministry was received a month later and was signed by the permanent secretary, Emmanual Nyirenda. It stated that our application was not acceptable as 'your licence restricts you to Chipata. The Radio and Television Technical Committee no longer grants permits for Repeater or Relay Stations'. Mr. Nyirenda explained that frequencies, which previously were being given for the erection of repeater stations, should now be reserved for applicants wishing to establish new broadcasting stations.

I appealed against the decision on the basis that our station was a commercial and not a community radio station. I explained that our licence had given Breeze FM output power of 1 Kilowatt which meant that the licence did not restrict the radio station to Chipata only but to a much wider radius. I reminded the permanent secretary that three commercial radio stations: Radio Phoenix and Radio QFM of Lusaka and Sky FM of Monze in Southern Province, which were initially granted licences similar to that of Breeze FM, were later allowed to extend their services to other urban areas. I queried why government could grant additional licences to three radio stations, whose coverage was mostly in urban areas, but deny this facility to Breeze FM, whose service was to marginalised areas, which were poorly served by national media and, therefore, needed the service most.

The response was written the very next day. The permanent secretary maintained that government policy was no longer to consider any applications for repeater stations. He added that government was re-planning the spectrum and wanted to move cautiously, especially in the wake of increased interest in the electronic media industry. I realized then that I would not make headway with the ministry and decided to lodge a complaint with the Zambia Competition Commission and on a visit to Lusaka I met with the executive director of the commission, Mr George Lipimile and his senior officials. The basis of the Breeze FM complaint was to establish why the ministry denied the station authority to expand its geographical coverage area within Eastern Province when three other stations had been authorized to do so – and beyond their original provinces into other regions. I put it to the commission that the decision by the ministry was both discriminatory and intended to stifle entrepreneurship.

A month later I received a letter from Mr. Lipimile stating that the commission had written to the Ministry of Information and Broadcasting Services over the Breeze FM complaint. To my surprise, the executive director stated that the commission 'does not have the mandate to proceed or intervene regarding your complaint'. I later found out that the ministry had written to the commission over my complaint, closing any further discussion on the matter. In the letter the pemanent secretary, Emmanual Nyirenda, declared that it was government policy to suspend the issuance of repeater station licences while the reorganisation and reclassification of licences was ongoing. The letter addressed to the Zambia Competition Commission Director of Consumer Welfare and Education, Dr. Muyenga Atanga, was copied to the permanent secretary, Ministry of Commerce and Industry, Special Assistant to the President, State House and to EPCCI, the Eastern Province Chamber of Commerce and Industry.

I do not know whether it was by commission or omission but the letter was not copied to me, the person who had lodged the complaint. I managed to get a copy because I had assumed the vice chairmanship of the local chamber of commerce, EPCCI. Meanwhile, despite the declaration by permanent secretary Nyirenda that government had suspended the issuance of repeater station licences, Radio Maria, our 'competitor' in Chipata and Eastern Province, was granted permits to establish relay stations in the years 2007, 2008 and 2009. I wondered how it came to be that Radio Maria was allowed to extend its coverage area into Katete and Petauke and later Lundazi at more or less the same time that the Breeze FM application was being vigorously denied.

The rejection of the Breeze FM application for expansion aside, I always considered the initial transmission facilities on Kanjala Hill I as only to launch the operations of the radio station. The facilities at the transmission site did not offer adequate space, nor ideal conditions, for such delicate equipment or good operational arrangements.

Although the agreement with ZNBC Head Office in Lusaka had given Breeze FM unlimited access, local technicians refused to give Breeze FM access to the ZNBC transmitter shelter and wanted to be present whenever our technical staff were carrying out their routine maintenance work, forcing Breeze FM to operate from the ZNBC shelter for a very short time only. To circumvent this situation I arranged for our transmitter to be housed in a waterproof metal box measuring 80 x 80 x 60cm which I placed close to the antenna tower. Unfortunately, although air-conditioned, the container got very hot during the summer months, causing serious harm to the equipment.

This awkward arrangement led to my engaging Mangrova Engineering Systems Limited, who had been the main technical subcontractor to Breeze FM since the establishment of the station in 2002, to carry out a feasibility study and propose the best way to create independent transmission facilities for Breeze FM and enhance the station's radius. The outcome was a proposal to upgrade the existing transmission system by moving it to a more suitable location and doubling the capacity of transmission equipment from 1,000 to 2,000 Watts. The proposal indicated that the project could be implemented within a period of three months.

Encouraged by these findings, I applied to the Chipata Municipal Council for a piece of land on the adjacent Kanjala Hill II. My application was made in October, 2007, but it was not until almost two years later, in July, 2009, that I received a response from the council confirming that Breeze FM had been allocated a site on Kanjala Hill II next to a new Zamtel cell phone mast. The decision by the council to offer the station a piece of land on which to establish independent transmission facilities made me again seek government authority to expand the Breeze FM broadcasting radius. The new application was made at the beginning of April, 2010, four years after the previous one had been rejected. My persistence was finally rewarded for, in April, 2010, I received a letter from Minister of Information and Broadcasting Services, Lieutenant General Ronnie Shikapwasha, stating that his ministry had no objection to 'your radio station expanding broadcast radio coverage to the entire Eastern Province under your current broadcasting licence'. The minister advised Breeze FM to apply to ZICTA for additional broadcasting frequencies.

At long last the station had the authority to expand its radius but where was the money going to come from? I sought a grant from OSISA to establish independent transmission facilities for Breeze FM, as well as to boost the station's transmitting capacity. OSISA was part of a network of autonomous Open Society Foundations located in many regions of the world. In Africa, OSISA worked in ten countries: Angola, Botswana, Democratic Republic of the Congo, Lesotho, Malawi, Mozambique, Namibia, Swaziland, Zambia and Zimbabwe and was committed to deepening democracy, protecting human rights and enhancing good governance in the region. The Breeze FM application to OSISA was made in May, 2010, and the grant approval for the sum of US$83,000 was given two months later.

The contract to carry out the initial geographical expansion work was given to Mangrova Engineering Systems Limited who moved on site in June, 2011, and successfully completed the project within a month. Mangrova procured and supplied the equipment, constructed a transmitter shelter and engine room, decommissioned the old transmission system at Kanjala Hill I, installed and commissioned the new 2,000 Watts transmission system at Kanjala Hill II and constructed a perimeter fence at the new site.

Breeze FM now had its own independent transmission facility and its radius had been extended but, to my disappointment, not to the entire Eastern Province. We were later to find out that there were technical shortcomings arising from the work carried out by Mangrova – such as a faulty transmitter which had to be sent to South Africa for repair at great cost. Even so, there were still some far-flung areas which were out of reach and people asking when they would have access to the Breeze FM signal.

The second and final stage of the geographical expansion process happened by sheer chance.

One morning in April, 2010, a colleague in Johannesburg, South Africa, sent me an email indicating that MDLF, one of the world's leading media development financing organisations was inquiring about expanding its investments in media in Southern Africa. When I contacted them I got an immediate response. MDLF turned out to be a serious and committed organisation. The chief operating officer, Marie Nemcova gave me a brief summary of MDLF's approval procedure. It comprised two phases: firstly the Board of Directors had to determine whether an organisation applying for a loan met the qualification criteria to become a candidate for funding and secondly, the board had to confirm MDLF's readiness to accept a loan application from a particular country. Only after there was a green light from the board would MDLF look into the financial, legal, management and other aspects of the project. During the second stage MDLF would help the applicant develop a detailed business plan and complete a legal due diligence process. Marie added, 'Knowing now that you have an interest in being considered as a loan applicant, we will propose Radio Breeze FM to be discussed at the next board meeting to be held in early December, 2010'.

I was asked to update the information that I had submitted about Breeze FM and to provide information about the station's programme structure as well as a breakdown of revenues and recent financial statements. I was told that while the board would not be making any decision about the funding at their December meeting, they would need to get a sense of the approximate amount of the loan Breeze FM wanted MDLF to consider. 'Please confirm and provide a brief outline of the investment you have in mind', she asked. I confirmed that Breeze FM had two areas of need. The establishment of relay stations to expand the station's radius and a marketing component comprising the establishment of station billboards in all the districts of Eastern Province. True to their word, the board meeting did take place in December, 2010, in Johannesburg, South Africa.

Coincidentally, MDLF decided to invite a number of people to make presentations to the board on the media situation in Southern Africa and I was asked to talk about the prospects for radio in the region.

On the sidelines of the meeting I was asked to provide documents such as Articles of Association, broadcasting licence and property registration to support the Breeze FM loan application. MDLF was a no time waster. Communication was regular and consistent and over the next three months I was asked to provide more documents and information in preparation for a meeting of the MDLF Investment Committee which was the body that made decisions about MDL funding and terms and conditions.

Just after Christmas, MDLF Financial Analyst, Hana Markova, worked with our accountant, Dailes Mwanza, who was assisted by a member of our Board of Directors, James Phiri, a qualified accountant, to complete our financial model. It was really demanding work. Meanwhile, MDLF assisted in drawing up the financial business plan. They also engaged a local law firm, Musa Dudhia and Company of Lusaka, to arrange for a Third Party Mortgage for the building which I had given as collateral for the loan. Marie then told me that MDLF wanted to organize a meeting of the Investment Committee with myself, to discuss and decide about the Breeze FM project. The meeting was to be held in Prague, Czech Republic.

The Investment Committee comprised Chief Operating Officer, Marie Nemcova, Secretary and General Counsel, Elena Popovic, Director of Finance, Anna Krynska, MDLF Adviser, Jaroslaw Gora and Financial Analyst, Hana Markova and the meeting took place on 31st March, 2011. It started at 9 a.m. and went on for many hours. During most of the time we were looking at the Breeze FM financial statements which were displayed on one wall of the room. I answered questions based on the financial statements, especially the five year projections and many more questions about the station, its operations and future plans. After a gruelling four hours, Jaroslaw, who chaired the meeting, brought the meeting and my stress to a temporary halt. He thanked me for being candid and open and said that I could take a walk around the town centre or go back to my hotel and rest for an hour whilst members of the committee made a decision. When I rejoined the group at 2 p.m. I could not guess what the decision was by looking at their faces. They all appeared friendly enough but gave no hint of what was to come. Then Jaroslaw gave me the good news. With a smile he announced that the MDLF Investment Committee had approved the Breeze FM loan application. He said that details of the loan would be communicated to me officially within the next few days. Everyone in the room shook my hand and we exchanged hugs before I left.

Exactly four days later, I received formal confirmation of the MDLF Investment Committee decision stating that the MDLF Investment Committee had approved a loan in the amount of up to US$200,000. The larger portion of the money, 70 per cent, was for the purchase and installation of transmission equipment, while 30 per cent, was for the marketing campaign. From then on things moved fast. Three different MDLF officials were in regular contact with me and I soon received the draft Credit Agreement and was asked to review, comment or give our company's acceptance to the terms and conditions.

On 10th May, 2011, the Credit Agreement for the loan was signed by Harlan Mandel, Chief Executive Officer for MDLF in New York and a copy was couriered to me to sign on behalf of Breeze FM. The loan had very good conditions. It attracted an interest rate of 5.5 per cent and a grace period for the principal amount of six months. The loan was payable in five years up to 31st December, 2016. There was, of course, a default interest rate of 11 per cent. To understand how good the conditions were one needed to remember that interest rates for loans in Zambia were at this time around 30 per cent. Within three weeks of signing the Credit Agreement, the MDLF lawyers in Zambia, Musa Dudhia and Company, executed and lodged for registration the Third Party Mortgage for the building in Chipata. Emails continued to fly between New York, Prague and Chipata and soon I was looking for engineering companies to tender for the expansion project. The Credit Agreement specified that the selection should be made from at least two tenders so I asked for offers from two companies which Breeze FM had worked with in the past and, therefore, knew well, Mangrova Engineering Systems Limited of Lusaka and Buck Broadcast of Cape Town, South Africa. The Zambian company had a good record in carrying out transmission installation work all over Zambia although it had, somewhat, let us down with its last project with us. Buck Broadcast, on the other hand, had wider experience across the African continent.

Mangrova Engineering Systems suggested the establishment of two receiver/relay stations without indicating how they had arrived at this solution. Meanwhile, their equipment bill was higher than the approved loan amount. The offer from Buck Broadcast was well thought out and more attractive. It suggested carrying out a study to establish how the expansion programme should be rolled out while promising to work within the budget. Breeze FM and MDLF were, therefore, unanimous with the choice of Buck Broadcast to carry out the expansion project.

If MDLF had been fast in arranging for the approval of the loan, it was even more efficient and persistent in finalizing the arrangements for disbursing the money. With only one month delay for finalizing the contractual arrangements, the first disbursement, totaling US$170,000, was made on 19th May, 2011. This was extremely fast considering that the offices involved in the arrangements operated from three continents, Africa, Europe and America. The money was divided into two amounts. The first amount of US$120,309.95 was transferred directly to Buck Broadcast and went towards the study, as well as part payment for the equipment. The second amount of US$49,692.05 was sent to Breeze FM as part payment for the creation and erection of billboards.

Buck Broadcast established strategically positioned FM rebroadcasting and link relay systems at Katete, Petauke and Lundazi and a UHF relay at Mponda to link Chipata to Lundazi. In the end the actual coverage attained was wider than had been planned, with many callers from far off places such as Mpika in Muchinga Province and Chongwe in Lusaka Rural as well as across borders in Malawi and Mozambique who reported clear reception. This new situation necessitated Breeze FM to slightly alter its logo to include the additional frequencies.

The financial reporting demands were rigorous. Breeze FM was required to provide detailed monthly and annual reports. The station also provided Profit and Loss statements and Balance Sheet statements from its audited financial statements. Each year MDLF, which had by now changed its name to the Media Development Investment Fund, MDIF, evaluated Breeze FM financial results. Thanks to the consistency of the station accountant, Dailes Mwanza, all this was achievable despite the fact that the station had to look for additional money to cover payments following the loss of value of the Zambian currency against the US dollar. The value of the Zambian Kwacha to the US dollar at the beginning of the project in 2011 was 4.8:1. It dropped to 6.5:1 at the beginning of 2015, a depreciation of about 36 per cent and dropped further to 10.1:1 by September, 2015, a fall of 110 per cent. During 2016, the Kwacha further lost value and was around 11:1, a loss of over 129 per cent. This continued depreciation of the Kwacha impacted negatively on the liquidity of the company since most of its income was now being used to service the MDIF loan and unfortunately for Breeze FM, there wasn't enough money for any effective hedging arrangement with the bank.

My greatest disappointment, though, was that the districts which benefited directly from the loan for extending the service contributed little towards paying it back. Most people in the districts talked about how happy they were to receive the Breeze FM signal and programming and went so far as to state categorically that they expected the service to continue – but they did not think about the cost of taking the service to them or how they could support the radio station financially. Even so, the loan repayments were completed in October, 2016, three months before the end of the repayment period. I was determined to clear the loan on 5th October, 2016, at a time when we were marking the radio station's fourteenth anniversary. What still amazes me is that a small radio station, located in a rural African town, managed to pay off, three months ahead of time, a US$200,000 loan, with interest, to a US-based organisation.

8. Challenges

Breeze FM and I experienced many challenges in the early days, starting with the exploratory and setting-up stages because of the huge distance between Lusaka, where I was based, and Chipata, 560km due east, on a road that challenged the very best; and where the journey time could be anything up to 12 hours. The poor telephone communication between Lusaka and Chipata was not a lot of help because it depended on an analogue telephone exchange system; this was, of course, the time before cell phones.

This resulted in serious delays in following up actions that needed to be taken. At the commencement of the radio station's operations there were also many teething problems because no member of staff yet knew what to do when confronted with the slightest of difficulties. I remember that I banned the word 'problem' at the radio station because every time someone failed to do something they would come to my office and say, 'Sir, we have a problem.'

Feeling somewhat exasperated with the frequency of 'problems' during the start-up phase, I told everyone at a Monday morning planning/review meeting that no one was to use the word 'problem' any more within the premises of the radio station. They could use any other word: situation, challenge, circumstance, whichever was appropriate as long as I was able to understand what had happened so that we could together think about what needed to be done. What began to be heard were statements such as, 'Sir, we have a situation,' or, 'Sir, there is a difficulty,' or 'Sir, there is an issue that needs your attention,' all in an effort to avoid using the banned word. This generated a lot of laughter and helped to lighten the mood as we grappled with whatever new situation confronted us.

Among the most serious problems – and they were indeed 'problems' and serious, too – were irregular supply of electrical power and power outages, poor internet connectivity, insufficient local business support and delays by clients to settle their bills. The irregular supply of power and power outages were horrible because the new radio station had generated a lot of excitement and high expectations in the community and broadcast interruptions were upsetting not only to me and my staff but the listeners too. Worse still irregular power supply and power outages caused a lot of damage to both studio equipment and transmitters. Early in our operations, we had to secure two generator sets, one which we placed at the station building and the other at the transmitter site on Kanjala Hill II which required us traversing a bad, rugged road climbing to an altitude of 300 metres.

Meanwhile, the poor quality of internet service in Chipata was also a source of major concern. During the first eleven years, Breeze FM worked – without much satisfaction – with four different ISPs, two of them on two separate occasions. The third challenge of insufficient local business support was a source of worry to me because it meant that Eastern Province was unable to sustain the operations of its own most effective channel of communication. The saving grace was the availability of advertising from national advertising companies and other organisations wishing to reach out to the people of the region.

The poor local sales were attributable to two reasons. The first was the failure by Breeze FM staff to carry out effective sales campaigns in Chipata and the districts. None of the full time staff, commission sales representatives or district correspondents seemed to know or understand the sales function. This was despite the company providing sales training to staff and an attractive sales commission scheme for those who brought business into the station. This sales commission was intended to encourage every member of staff to get involved in soliciting for business on behalf of the company, to broaden the revenue base and to provide a means for everyone to earn extra income.

The second reason for poor local sales was the tendency by government officials, staff of NGOs and company executives in Chipata and other parts of the country to take advantage of lazy and unwary reporters who unwittingly provided free publicity by substituting announcements and advertising material for the news. Over the years I tried hard to stop reporters from covering workshops and meaningless speeches and statements from all sorts of publicity seekers but did not succeed.

The situation of poor local sales was compounded by the large number of defaulting clients. Too many clients either took too long to pay for services or did not pay at all. It didn't help that most of our regular clients were based in far away Lusaka. The depreciating value of the local currency, even when a debt was cleared, eroded further the value of the money paid.

9. Political cadres attack Breeze FM

Perhaps, the most disappointing incident involving Breeze FM Radio Station was an attack by political 'cadres' from the ruling Patriotic Front Party. On Sunday, 29th November, 2016, Breeze FM was broadcasting a live phone-in discussion programme, "Political Hour", featuring Rainbow

Party President, Wynter Kabimba, who had previously held some of the highest positions in the ruling party, the Patriotic Front, as Secretary General and Minister of Justice. In fact, at one time he was believed to have been the most powerful man in the PF after its president, Michael Sata.

Usually, I was at the radio station to welcome leaders of political parties as a matter of courtesy. On that fateful Sunday, I did not manage to get to the radio station because confirmation of Kabimba's programme was given to me only twenty-five minutes before the programme was to start. Sunday is the one day on which I stayed late in bed and twenty minutes was not enough time to take a bath, dress and drive to the radio station. I told News Editor, Samuel Ndhlovu, who was to interview Kabimba, to apologise on my behalf for my absence. Probably, the Good Lord did not want me to be witness to, or get caught up in, the skirmish that was to take place.

The "Political Hour" programme that Sunday was scheduled to run from 10.15 to 11 a.m. However, about ten minutes into the programme Patriotic Front PF 'cadres' attacked the radio station. They threw stones which landed on the roof and hit some vehicles parked outside. The radio station senior staff acted quickly. They stopped the programme and assisted the Rainbow Party leader to leave the building through the back entrance. The 'cadres', who converged on the radio station from three directions, forced their way in and stormed all three studios in search of Kabimba while threatening members of staff. In the process they partly damaged the security gate at the front of the building and one station vehicle. Rainbow Party members, who had accompanied their leader to the radio station, and junior members of my staff had to hide for safety from the 'cadres' who only left after they realized that the man they were looking for was not in the building.

After Kabimba left the radio station News Editor, Samuel Ndhlovu and Head of Programmes, Peter Banda rushed to the police station to report the incident. But, by the time some police officers arrived, a distance of under 400 metres, all the troublemakers had left. The radio station later arranged a telephone interview with the Rainbow Party leader who was at an unknown location.

On the Monday, I went with the news editor, Samuel Ndhlovu, to the police station and lodged a formal complaint. Five members of my staff who were at the radio station on the Sunday gave statements about what had transpired during the incident. However, although the cadres, who attacked the Breeze FM building, were well known, none were arrested. When the matter was raised in Parliament by Chipata Member of Parliament, Reuben Mtolo Phiri, the Minister of Home Affairs, Davis Mwila told the House that police were late to get to the radio station because the distance between the radio station and the police station was two kilometres. The Minister also told Parliament that the incident had not been reported to the police. Eastern Province had nineteen members of parliament belonging to various political parties all of whom heard what the minister told parliament, but none of them challenged or corrected the minister's statement, especially about the distance between the radio station and the police station.

That attack on Breeze FM was the first of its kind in thirteen years of operations and came as a big shock and great disappointment to me, not least because, at 10 a.m. the area around the radio station was busy with passersby and onlookers. No one attempted to stop the attack or to assist the members of staff. The government media: Radio Zambia, Television Zambia, "Times of Zambia" and "Zambia Daily Mail" all ignored the incident. I felt let down by the acquiescence of the government media, the aloofness of the police and, perhaps, even more seriously, the indifference and lack of consciousness of the community.

How could such an incident have happened when Breeze FM radio station and all its staff had served everyone so loyally for so long? The new broadcasting regulatory agency, the Independent Broadcasting Authority, issued a statement saying that Breeze FM radio station would not have been attacked if it had police officers guarding the premises. This statement was issued without any understanding of the poor performance of police officers from the Protective Unit who guard strategic institutions such as banks and radio stations. Breeze FM had, from the start of its operations, utilised the Police Protective Service at a fee of K70 (US$7) per day. We discontinued this service after seven years because, despite the high cost, officers reported for work late, left early and generally did not provide any useful security.

There was no guarantee that a police officer would have been at the radio station during the time of the attack. In any case, even the police officer guarding the bank across the road was not in evidence during the incident. The only conciliatory gesture came from the provincial chairman of the ruling party, Andrew Lubusha, and his officials. Three weeks after the incident they visited the radio station to apologise. I did not think that they were sincere because they tried to disown the 'cadres' as being 'former members of the party'.

No one else, not the provincial minister, the provincial permanent secretary, nor the district commissioner, nor any other prominent person made any effort to talk in support of the radio station over the incident yet many of them were regular newsmakers on the station's news bulletins. Of the fifty chiefs in the province only one, Chief Mnukwa of the Ngoni sent a letter of encouragement. The only other traditional leader to speak on the matter was a Chewa chief of Katete district who did not mention the radio station or the safety of its staff but merely wondered why Winter Kabimba was not being allowed to speak on radio.

Either people did not empathise or care about the safety and welfare of the radio station and its staff or were too afraid to be seen to be supporting the radio station or criticizing the ruling party and government. Disappointingly, although my staff went out of their way to save the leader of the Rainbow Party from being lynched or severely beaten up, he, too, never thanked those who rescued him, nor the radio station for acting expeditiously to save him from the mob.

I was disappointed by the attack on my building and the radio station and the acquiescence of everyone. Having lived in the Eastern Province for more than fifteen years I was, of course, aware that the problem with the region was that, although it did not appear so on the surface, Eastern Province was a divided area. The major factors contributing to this division emanated from tribal disunity, especially between the two dominant tribes, the Chewa and the Ngoni. There was also the destabilising influence of Easterners of Malawian heritage and Easterners of Indian origin. Then there are those Easterners based in the capital city, Lusaka, who tend to be vocal when it suits them but whose commitment and visibility at home is only associated with annual tribal ceremonies. The result of all this was the failure to have a common purpose and vision and the absence of good and strong leadership. Against this divisive background it is impossible to engender the sense or spirit of community consciousness that is needed to protect and stand up for essential social institutions or causes.

The radio station had been doing a really good job for the community and I had provided the building to the radio station rent-free for ten years and at a rate lower than the market level for another four years. I realized then that it was possible to lose my investment in the building if there was another more serious attack, which could not be ruled out under the circumstances. I made up my mind to sell the building and use the money to complete the preparations for my farm and construction of my house. This I did and I secured a rented building for the radio station within the CBD. The other important decision that I made was to buy new digital equipment and software and set up a modern studio for the radio station.

At the very same time, Madison Insurance Company approved the radio station's claim for damaged transmitters and Breeze FM replaced three of them ensuring continued wide coverage and a clear signal to its listeners.

10. *Paving the way for the future*

The attack on Breeze FM radio station that Sunday morning helped me make up my mind to move into my next life. Breeze FM, by the year 2016, was at a stage of completing its growth phase. Whether the station would successfully move on to maturation depended on how continuity would be ensured beyond my direct participation. Now in my sixties, I was beginning to ask myself whether it was advisable to continue with my punishing work routine. Although I had previously retired from work on two occasions, from ZANA and the civil service at the age of forty-one and from ZAMCOM, at the age of fifty, I had never taken time off to rest in between. The transitions from ZANA to ZAMCOM and ZAMCOM to Breeze FM were all very tight, even overlapping. I would leave one office on one day and be in the other office the next.

That I was still energetic and in good health was credit to my discipline and commitment to regular exercise, good diet, not smoking and being mostly teetotal in my later years.

In spite of the advancing years I did not feel old and, in fact, looked and felt much younger than my age. But, I was now beginning to feel lethargic, particularly at the end of the day and when waking up in the morning. It was a clear indication that I needed the seven hours of sleep which I had not given myself during most of my life. I was now tired of waking up early each morning to go to work, tired of shaving every morning, tired of preparing to-do lists for each day and tired of checking emails when I got to the office in the morning. I was also very tired of being the chief marketing officer and chief reminder as well as chief solver of the challenges of running a radio station.

I was suddenly aware that I was one of only two people still active in media out of all those who were there when I joined the journalism profession. The other person was Richard Sakala, proprietor of "The Nation" newspaper and Millennium Radio. But Richard had left to join the government for ten years before coming back, while I had remained loyal to the profession and had stuck it out. Come to think of it, most politicians, civil servants and officials of non-governmental organisations were younger than me, while many journalists were even younger than my children. I was, of course, also aware that a company that one sets up and manages becomes like a baby or one of the children. But my thinking now was that, just as my biological children had outgrown their family home and parental attention, Breeze FM, if it was the last born child of my family, needed to become independent, too.

There were three options for me to consider. The first was to let the staff run the radio station, the second was to entice one of my children to take charge of the operations of the radio station, the third option was to find good partners with whom we could carry on the work of Breeze FM while I gradually played a reduced role. The first option was the most appropriate although none of the senior members of staff appeared to be ready to succeed me.

The second option fell away, too, because none of my children were interested in coming to work or live in Chipata and it would have been unfair for me to coerce any of them to move to Chipata. I had relocated to Chipata and set up Breeze FM because I had no doubt that it was fulfilling my purpose. I was aware that each of my children had their own purpose and that this could not necessarily be fulfilled by succeeding me at Breeze FM. The most important thing that I did for my children was to give at least three of them a good solid education which had helped them to continue with the transformation of the family and, hopefully, its posterity.

The third option was, therefore, the one that I considered the most appropriate and so I began to make arrangements to find suitable candidates. I received many offers, mainly from Lusaka. There were also offers from Tanzania and Zimbabwe. I received only two inquiries from Chipata and the Eastern Province which were both from religious organisations. I turned down most of the offers because I did not get a good explanation about plans for the future of the radio station. The most promising offer was from a company set up by a Zambian and Zimbabwean who both worked for the BBC. Unfortunately, this deal fell through just before the contract was finalised.

My hope, always, was that the most appropriate individual or company would come in due course. I had no doubt that the right partners to take Breeze FM into the future and a new period of maturity and sustainability would be found in the same way that I had been able to set up the radio station in the first instance.

While waiting for good players to come on board I continued to encourage and support the radio station and its staff in the the quest to serve the community better and efforts to attain viability. And in my spare time, I continued to do what I loved doing - talking to pupils and students about how to select and build the right career and speaking to widows, retirees and people with disabilities on how to make the most of their natural skills, talents, ideas, experience and knowledge. I also served for some time as the chairperson of Total Land Care Zambia, a progressive organisation supporting conservation farming in Malawi, Mozambique, Tanzania and Zambia. For a while I was also an examiner in the Mass Communication programme at the Saint Augustine University in Tanzania and a board member of the Catholic Church run DMI St Eugene University, Chipata Campus.

At the continental level I was an active member of the Africa Media Initiative which hosted the annual Africa Media Leadership Forum, a premier media gathering event on the African continent. Interestingly, I declined overtures from government to serve on government media boards and government provincial committees and also spurned offers of senior government positions from two presidents.

While all this was going on, however, it was also obvious that my relocation to Chipata was impacting very negatively on our family. My wife, Catherine, had not liked the idea of leaving Lusaka and moving to a rural town and, therefore, remained behind while I went alone to my new working place. For several years we maintained two homes, 560 kilometres apart. However, after ten years this arrangement became unmanageable and our marriage ended.

Although my first marriage ended in an amicable divorce, sadly, not all the children, although grown up, took the family break up well. What disturbed them further was the passing away of their mother, from brain cancer, in 2016. Although now married to my second wife, Baanga, I assisted in sending Catherine to India for an operation and treatment but the cancer had been detected when too advanced and could not be contained. As we put her to rest on that day, 22nd March, 2016, the children and I knew that, she had played an important role in all our lives.

What remained for the children and me were pleasant memories of our time together. My entire working life had been hectic because it comprised long hours, little time off and too much travel within and outside the country.

Although it was difficult to balance work and family life, I tried very had to make up whenever I was home, or had some free time, with some quality family engagements and excursions and in later years when I was able to afford it and through ZAMCOM's annual holiday package we took holidays in some of Zambia's wonderful national parks. On many occasions we drove across the border into Zimbabwe for extended holidays with family friends. In the 1980s, roads in Zimbabwe were better maintained than those in Zambia. When driving back the children were jolted awake by the first pothole that the car hit. 'Are we back in Zambia, Dad?' one of the children would ask. We also visited the lake in Malawi whenever we travelled to Chipata.

Two incidents always came up when we reminisced about our holidays in the national parks. The first one was at Lochinvar National Park on the Kafue Flats where I had gone with our daughter, Chimfwembe, and youngest son, Dabwitso, in 1990. Catherine, and our elder son, Dalitso, had remained behind and were going to join us later because Dalitso was sitting his Grade 7 examinations.

One afternoon the kids were in the swimming pool. Chimfwembe was a good and competitive swimmer and had won many awards at school competitions but Dabwitso was only then learning how to swim. I was reading a book on a sun lounger when suddenly there were sounds of screaming and water splashing. When I looked up I saw Chimfwembe in the middle of the pool, calmly holding her brother from behind and swimming slowly to the edge, where I was able to get hold of him and pull him out. Apparently Dabwitso's swim flippers had come off. Just as well Chimfwembe was a good swimmer because I was not and getting into the water for me would have been even more dangerous.

The other incident happened in the South Luangwa National Park, in Eastern Province, whilst on a visit to Chipata in 2001 to introduce the family to the place where I was about to move to. One afternoon we had a viewing vehicle to ourselves. The afternoon/night drive took four hours and at about 7 p.m. in the middle of nowhere, the engine stalled. The driver radioed 'base' at the lodge but there was no response. He then got down and started tinkering with the engine. After about fifteen minutes, which seemed much longer, the engine started and we were able to continue with the drive. When we returned to our rooms the children burst out laughing. I asked what was so funny and they said, 'Dad, we've never seen you so scared.' Scared? Who would not be scared when his entire family is in danger of being eaten by a hungry hyena or leopard?

11. Awards

Despite its numerous challenges, Breeze FM won several top broadcasting prizes for its efforts and outstanding work.

In its second year of operation, 2004, the station won the Best Electronic Media Award in recognition of its contribution to the development of the electronic media in Zambia. In 2005 the station's producer/presenter, Greyson Mwale, aka Gogo Breeze, won the Most Outstanding Broadcaster Award. In 2009 the station was granted two awards by the Department of

Culture for its contribution to the promotion of tradition and culture in the province, in recognition of the station's work in recording the history of the tribes of Eastern Province and its coverage of traditional ceremonies in the region. This outstanding work was carried out with the support of OSISA.

In 2010 and again in 2013 the station received awards for outstanding coverage of HIV/AIDS issues from the MISA Zambia: the Mildred Mpundu Prize and the Best HIV/AIDS Reporting Award. MISA Zambia also bestowed on Breeze FM the Best Children Participation Reporting Award for 2013. Also in 2013 and again in 2015 Breeze FM's producer of 'Our Environment' programmes, Peter Frank Banda won the Electronic Media Award in recognition of his contribution to environment and development journalism.

I, too, was the recipient of Zambian media and national awards. In 2012 I received the prestigeous Lucy Sichone/Bright Mwape Award from the Press Freedom Committee of The Post newspaper. This Award was presented every two years to deserving individuals for their accomplishment in outstanding service to the cause of media freedom and freedom of expression and other human rights. The Post Newspaper is no longer there and the award is not being given anymore.

The most significant award I received was Zambia's highest honour, the 50th Independence Anniversary, First Ever Special Single Class Golden Jubilee Medal for distinguished service.

I was among 1,356 people from across the country who received this award from the Zambian government in 2014. Prominent people on whom President Michael Sata conferred this special medal, many of them posthumously, included First President Kenneth Kaunda, members of Zambia's first Cabinet, out of which only two, Mr. Grey Zulu, Transport and Works and Mr. Sikota Wina, Local Government, were still living. Other recipients were former speakers of parliament, former defence chiefs and freedom fighters.

The recommendation for me to receive this award had not been made by any media association, but the Eastern Province Chamber of Commerce and Industry, EPCCI. The selection process, as confirmed by Acting President, Dr. Guy Scott, was intense and thorough and maybe even complicated in my case because of the love-hate relationship that I had had with various governments and their agencies. The citation for the award traced the beginning and development of my journalistic career in ZANA, the contribution I made to media training at ZAMCOM, the contribution I made to the development of the broadcasting sector and the service I gave to the community in Eastern Province through Breeze FM radio station.

The 50th Independence Anniversary Medal was, undoubtedly, a lifetime achievement. When the medal was pinned on my left lapel by Eastern Province Permanent Secretary, Dr. Chileshe Mulenga, on behalf of President Michael Sata that morning on 22nd November, 2014, I knew that I had not only lived to the fullest but had fulfilled my purpose which, essentially, had been to use journalism and media to help others help themselves. Although the news of this award was ignored by media colleagues in Zambia, a professional colleague based in New York, USA, best summed up my achievement in his message of congratulations.

Peter Whitehead of MDIF wrote, 'Mike, this is tremendous news! What a huge honour - and one that is totally deserved. You are and always have been a freedom fighter: freedom of the press, freedom of expression and freedom of thought - some of the most important freedoms that exist.'

Formal awards apart (and there were several others for the radio station, my members of staff and me), I believe that the greatest award that the radio station ever received was the acceptance and support of the community that it served.

Although a privately-owned commercial radio station, Breeze FM operated as a genuine community institution and was accepted as such by the listenership. This message was conveyed to us by a listener in a letter to the station very soon after we began broadcasting. He wrote, 'Mr. Daka, thank you for bringing the radio station to Eastern Province. Now it is ours'. I could not agree more.

12. New emerging media sect

Broadcasting in Zambia started in 1941, when the then Northern Rhodesia Government established a small radio station in Lusaka using what were called the 'saucepan' special sets to communally broadcast in six 'vernacular' languages. This station catered mainly for the African audience, while white settlers tuned in to the British Broadcasting Corporation (BBC) and the South African Broadcasting Corporation (SABC). When Zambia became independent in 1964 the broadcasting station was nationalised as Zambia Broadcasting Services (ZBS) and it became a department of the Ministry of Information and Broadcasting Services.

In 1987, through an Act of Parliament, ZBS was turned into the current Zambia National Broadcasting Corporation (ZNBC). Broadcasting remained state controlled until the liberalisation of the airwaves in 1994. Community, religious and commercial radio stations opened up in various parts of the country and ended the monopoly of the state-run national television and radio broadcasting organisation, ZNBC.

By 2018, Zambia had over 100 new radio stations. They included fifty-one commercial radio stations, forty-eight community radio stations and ten religious stations. With around 100 radio stations independent of government operating in many parts of the country, radio quickly became the most powerful mass medium in Zambia, reaching rural areas in provinces and districts and giving voice to previously marginalised communities which were not well served by television or newspapers. Radio became effective and popular because it has no language or literacy barriers and is able to localise its programming, thereby reaching and influencing hundreds of thousands of people.

Overall, the quality of Zambian journalism is very varied and, in spite of improvements, there is little emphasis given to upholding fundamental journalistic standards in relation to political and economic analysis and, not least, media ethics. The situation is even worse in the community radio sector where most of the staff, at all levels, have no formal media training and have little or no reporting, programming or management knowledge or experience. The only training or orientation that most of those working in community radio stations in Zambia get is the occasional thematic workshop held by organisations seeking to work with the media.These workshops regularly follow the old-fashioned approach to journalism training and practice which emphasises basic editorial work, placing little attention on how to make radio more effective in providing relevant and meaningful content and giving real voice to the majority of the people. As a result, despite the growth of the radio sector in Zambia, most community radio stations are underutilised or misused as most of their broadcast time is filled with music or meaningless chatter.

This is very sad because 100 radio stations constitute a communication infrastructure that can be put to much better use in a country where the majority of people need basic information just to survive and make ends meet. The government, through its ministries and departments and NGOs, can do a lot to work with the radio stations to provide information on policies and programmes that affect or require the people's involvement. The new licensing body, IBA, can also do a lot to strengthen and help professionalise this important emerging sector, instead of which the organization appears to enjoy constant whiplashing and threatening to withdraw licences from erring operators. And, of the various media associations, MISA Zambia and Panos Southern Africa have been the most effective for a long time. However, they operate like most NGOs.

They provide jobs for a few individuals who come up with ideas for projects that keep them engaged without consulting or fully addressing the real needs of media organisations or their membership and/or ordinary people. Over the years MISA Zambia, Panos Southern Africa and later the BBC Media Action received a lot of money from donors for projects whose value would have been greatly enhanced had they been conceived with the involvement of media organisations and addressed the real needs of this emerging radio sector. BBC Media Action worked more closely with a selected number of radio stations and later went as far as to seek and address their training needs.

I have no doubt that the liberalisation of the broadcasting sector is one of the most important decisions made by a government in Zambia for strengthening freedom of thought, freedom of expression and freedom of the press and promoting real development in the country. I am glad that I ended my long service in media by playing a part in this important effort, and in the process was able to fulfil my purpose and life as much as I could.

SELECTED BIBLIOGRAPHY

ZAMCOM

Agreement between the Ministry of National Guidance, Information and Broadcasting Services and the Friedrich Naumann Foundation of the Federal Republic of Germany, March 1980.

Project Evaluation Report on the Zambia Institute of Mass Communication (ZAMCOM) by Management Services Board (MSB), February 1988.

ZAMCOM Project Evaluation Report by Dr. Rainer Oppelt, March 1989.

The Zambia Institute of Mass Communication Act, 1991.

Zambia Privatisation Agency (ZPA) Study on the Privatisation and Commercialisation of State-Owned Media and Printing Companies, March 1992.

Memorandum of Understanding on the Democratic Governance Project Between the United States Agency for International Development and the Ministry of Information and Broadcasting Services of the Government of the Republic Zambia, May 1993.

Zambia Institute of Mass Communication, a Study in Financial Management, Fidelity Consultancy Services, December 1993.

ZAMCOM Potential for Profitability Report, Price Waterhouse, February 1995.

ZAMCOM Total Quality Management Report by Dr. Alex Moore, June 1995.

Democratic Governance Media Independence Consultancy Report, Southern University, June 1995.

Zambia Democratic Governance Project Mid-Term Review, July 1995.

Management Services Board Report on Organisational Analysis, Performance Appraisal System and Incentive Scheme, 1996.

ZAMCOM as a Business Project Report, January 1996.

Independent Media as a Demand Variable in the US/Zambia Democractic Governance Project by Folu Ogundimu, March 1996.

Zambia Institute of Mass Communication Report on Special Investigations, Thewo and Company, September 1996.

The Zambia Institute of Mass Communication (Repeal) Act, 1996.

The Zambia Institute of Mass Communication (Dissolution) Order, 1996

The Zambia Institute of Mass Communication (Vesting of Assets and Transfer of Staff) Order, 1996.

Zambia Institute of Mass Communication Educational Trust Constitution, 1996.

ZAMCOM Trust Deed, November 1996.

The Zambia Institute of Mass Communication (ZAMCOM) incorporated as an Educational Trust under the Land (Perpetual Succession) Act Cap 288, January 1997.

Zambia Institute of Mass Communication Summary of Findings, Deloitte and Touche, August 1997. Investigation

Financing Agreement Relating to Human Rights and Democratisation in Developing Countries, Commission of the European Communities Directorate-General VIII for Development, September 1997.

Zambia Democratic Governance Project Final Report, Southern University, September 1997.

Briefing for UK Consultants on ZAMCOM-DFID Project by ZAMCOM and British Council Zambia, March 1998.

Parliamentary Debates concerning ZAMCOM
Parliamentary Debates, 15th May 1996.
Parliamentary Debates, 16th May 1996.
Parliamentary Debates, 17th May 1996.

Radio Breeze FM

Business Plan for Chipata 99.6 FM Radio Station, Eastern Province, Zambia by Michael Daka and Phil Haggar, May 2001.

Breeze FM Audience Survey Report by John Coghill, July 2003.

Situational Analysis on the Radio Landscape in Malawi by Michael Daka, October 2004.

Breeze FM – Commercial Radio with a Community Focus by Peter Erichs, August 2011.

Acknowledgements

It is said that at least five people contribute to the growth and development of one's life. In my case many more people, individuals, groups and organisations contributed positively to my life, my media work and my experience.

Like most people who grow up within their own nuclear families, the two people who played the most critical role in my initial development were my parents: my father, Saulo Daka who, by migrating from the village to the capital city, gave me the opportunity to grow up in a multitribal, multilingual, competitive environment whilst my mother, Nelly Tikambenji Mwale shared with me the spirit of her strength, commitment and determination.

I am grateful to the young boys and girls with whom I grew up in the Lusaka township of Matero for challenging me relentlessly; my workmates at my first working place, ZANA, where I spent my formative professional years and my workmates at the Zambia Institute of Mass Communication, ZAMCOM, where I matured as a journalist. I am also indebted to the staff of Breeze FM, many of whom were new to radio and media, for sharing my vision of making the radio station the most effective channel of communication in eastern Zambia.

I am also grateful to my colleague, Dr. Sam Phiri of the University of Zambia and Dr. Harri Englund, Professor of Social Anthropology, Director, Centre of African Studies and Fellow, Churchill College at Cambridge University for going through the initial draft of this book and Nikki Ashley, a long-time friend and professional colleague, who completed the work of editing this book.

My final thanks go to Fay Gadsden and Gadsden Publishers for publishing this book.

www.ingramcontent.com/pod-product-compliance
Lightning Source LLC
Chambersburg PA
CBHW071407300426
44114CB00016B/2220